Intellectual Property Rights in a Networked World:
Theory and Practice

Richard A. Spinello
Boston College, USA

Herman T. Tavani
Rivier College, USA

 Information Science Publishing

Hershey • London • Melbourne • Singapore

Acquisition Editor:	Mehdi Khosrow-Pour
Senior Managing Editor:	Jan Travers
Managing Editor:	Amanda Appicello
Development Editor:	Michele Rossi
Copy Editor:	Jane Conley
Typesetter:	Jennifer Wetzel
Cover Design:	Lisa Tosheff
Printed at:	Yurchak Printing Inc.

Published in the United States of America by
    Information Science Publishing (an imprint of Idea Group Inc.)
    701 E. Chocolate Avenue, Suite 200
    Hershey PA 17033
    Tel: 717-533-8845
    Fax: 717-533-8661
    E-mail: cust@idea-group.com
    Web site: http://www.idea-group.com

and in the United Kingdom by
    Information Science Publishing (an imprint of Idea Group Inc.)
    3 Henrietta Street
    Covent Garden
    London WC2E 8LU
    Tel: 44 20 7240 0856
    Fax: 44 20 7379 3313
    Web site: http://www.eurospan.co.uk

Library of Congress Cataloging-in-Publication Data

Intellectual property rights in a networked world : theory and practice / Richard A. Spinello, Herman T. Tavani, editor[s].
    p. cm.
    Includes bibliographical references and index.
    ISBN 1-59140-576-9 (hardcover) -- ISBN 1-59140-577-7 (pbk.) -- ISBN 1-59140-578-5 (ebook)
  1. Intellectual property. 2. Right of property. 3. Copyright and electronic data processing. 4. Locke, John, 1632-1704--Views on property. I. Spinello, Richard A. II. Tavani, Herman T.
    K1401.I566 2005
    346.04'8--dc22

                             2004003761

British Cataloguing in Publication Data
A Cataloguing in Publication record for this book is available from the British Library.

All work contributed to this book is new, previously-unpublished material. The view expressed in this book are those of the authors, but not necessarily of the publisher.

For our spouses, Susan Brinton and Joanne Tavani

Intellectual Property Rights in a Networked World:
Theory and Practice

Table of Contents

Foreword

The rapid development of the "knowledge economy" has temporarily stalled, but few doubt that it will soon be getting a second wind. This new economy, in which a company's major resources are its intellectual assets, has undoubtedly moved the topic of intellectual property into sharp focus for decades to come. The notion of intellectual property rights, opposed by many cyberspace libertarians, triggers many elusive questions about the extent and precise nature of those rights. For example, the digital music and movie revolution has swept across the Web, and yet many of the vexing issues raised in the Napster case remain unresolved.

Network and digital technologies also have the potential to usher in a new era of decentralized creativity and public discourse. These technologies have made it so much easier to accomplish the distribution of creative material. So why shouldn't we celebrate this new found freedom?

Some critics maintain that the traditional property rights system, which tends to "propertize" all forms of information, will interfere with the realization of this ideal. On the other hand, how can we protect the rights of artists and content providers to distribute their creations and receive appropriate payment without preserving traditional copyright law?

Of course, intellectual property issues are not confined to the sharing of digital music files. It is not surprising that access to digital information is becoming a matter of great social and economic import. Poorer countries accuse wealthy nations of "information imperialism," contending that they cannot overcome the digital divide unless intellectual property rights are loosened considerably. As a result, the battle rages over whether intellectual property should be given strong or weak protection or perhaps no protection at all in the digital realm of cyberspace.

Intellectual Property Rights in a Networked World seeks to provide some fresh perspectives on this theme by presenting diverse papers that cover both theoretical and practical concerns. This book is based primarily on papers that were delivered at the Sixth Annual Ethics and Technology Conference that was held at Boston College in late June, 2003. These conferences, sponsored by a group of American Jesuit universities, date back to 1996 when the Internet's social challenges were just becoming apparent. At the 2003 conference, a joint effort organized by the Carroll School of Management and the Boston College Law School, information technology professionals, ethicists, and legal scholars from all over the world came together in order to grapple with some of the more thorny ethical problems that have great salience for the knowledge economy.

There were sessions devoted to the seemingly esoteric theories of philosophers such as John Locke and G.W.F. Hegel. These theories have shaped the debate about the moral primacy of property rights, and the writings of these thinkers can still be mined for valuable insights. Thus, included in Section II of this volume are papers that consider the relevance of Locke's philosophy as a grounding for intellectual property rights. Also included is a theoretical discussion of the problems inherent in distinguishing an idea from its expression, which relies on the ontological distinction between universals and particulars. That dichotomy is a crucial but unsettled element in modern copyright law, and the confusion is reflected in the philosophical debate over this matter that dates back to Plato.

In addition, more pragmatic issues were hotly debated at the conference. These issues included the scope of trademark rights over domain names used in cyberspace, the development and control of digital media, trespass in cyberspace, the ethical acceptability of copying software for one's friends, appropriate policies for webcasting technology, and the role of policy makers in promoting the use of open source software. Many of these topics are discussed in the papers included in Section III.

Finally, to round out the collection, this book opens with a comprehensive introduction that enunciates the fundamental issues underlying the evolution of intellectual property protection in cyberspace. This essay has been written by the two editors, Richard A. Spinello and Herman T. Tavani, and it will be an invaluable resource for every reader. It carefully considers the traditions supporting intellectual property rights along with the perspectives of those who contest those rights. Postmodernist scholarship, for example, questions concepts of authorship and originality, while some legal scholars point to the indeterminacy of traditional property theories. But Spinello and Tavani conclude that there is a case to be made for a regime of moderate intellectual property protection that spurs creativity and innovation without disrupting the integrity of the public domain.

If this is the reader's first plunge into these complex issues he or she may find that the waters are difficult to navigate. The introduction, however, should make the task of navigation much easier. Of course, all of the questions raised in the introduction and in the succeeding chapters deserve more debate and discussion. But the insights offered by each one of these authors are sure to be of great assistance to anyone daring enough to explore these uncharted waters.

John J. Neuhauser
Academic Vice President & Dean of Faculties
Boston College

Preface

In his Foreword, Dr. Neuhauser explained the origin of the essays in this book along with the book's general structure. Nonetheless, a few prefatory remarks are in order. Despite the centrality of intellectual property issues in our networked society, ethicists and other scholars outside the legal community have not sufficiently given this topic the attention that it truly deserves. With that in mind, we have collected in this volume some recent essays that attempt to fill this void by offering some insights and perspectives on these controversial issues.

The tripartite division of the book is designed to make this material more accessible and intelligible to readers of diverse backgrounds. Section I consists of a single essay that provides a broad overview of the main themes in intellectual property scholarship, such as normative intellectual property theory and the legal infrastructure for property protection. This essay also includes a cursory review of the main legal disputes that have shaped the current debate about property in cyberspace. For the uninitiated, this chapter will be an indispensable guide for what is to follow.

Section II presents several essays that are intended to deepen the reader's understanding of intellectual property theory and show how it can help us to grapple with the proper allocation of property rights in cyberspace. Particular attention is paid to Locke's seminal theory of property, including the question of whether a property right can be construed as a natural right.

Section III further develops the themes in Section II but in greater detail and with a more practical orientation. For the most part, the essays in this section illustrate the costs and benefits of applying property rights to cyberspace. While intellectual property rights create dynamic incentive effects, they also entail social costs, and they are sometimes in tension with the development of a robust public domain. The reader may find some redundancy between the introductory section and the subsequent chapters on Locke, copyright protection, or the information commons in Section II and Section III. Repetition of key arguments, however, will allow the reader to keep clearly in view some important and basic perspectives about intellectual property theory and law.

Each of these chapters presents critical issues that jurists and business people must face in the New Economy. While there is no uniformity among the viewpoints expressed, each essay contributes a complementary perspective on the intellectual property topics that have recently begun to dominate contemporary discussion of cyberethics and cyberlaw.

Chapter I, written by the book's two editors, comprises Section I of *Intellectual Property Rights in a Networked World*. It presents some foundational concepts and issues in intellectual property, and it reviews some of the normative justifications that have been advanced to defend the granting of property rights for intellectual objects. This sets the stage for some consideration of the philosophical case opposing intellectual property rights. That case is rejected in favor of a position for balanced property-rights frameworks that avoid the polar extremes of *over-* and *under*-protection. The chapter then reviews the four different kinds of protection schemes for intellectual property that have been provided by our legal system: copyright laws, patents, trademarks, and trade secrets. Finally, recent litigation, including the Napster, Grokster, Microsoft, and DeCSS cases, are critically examined. Many of the issues and controversies introduced in this chapter are explored and analyzed in greater detail in the subsequent chapters of this book.

The three chapters that comprise Section II of the book — Chapters II through IV — examine philosophical theories that undergird the rationale for many of our current intellectual property laws. Chapters II and III examine aspects of John Locke's theory of property as a backdrop for analyzing contemporary disputes involving ownership claims pertaining to intellectual objects. In Chapter II, Kai Kimppa shows how a "liberalist view" of intellectual property rights involving software can be justified using arguments found in Locke's *Second Treatise on Civil Government*. Kimppa notes that Chapter V of Locke's *Second Treatise*, titled "Of Property," has traditionally been seen as the starting point of the liberalist argument for property, in both its material or immaterial forms. Kimppa argues that even though Locke promotes the need for ownership of property, Locke does so from the viewpoint of necessity. (Because of the nature of material or tangible objects, Locke realized that one cannot have something that already is possessed by another.) But Kimppa claims that Locke's thinking about property in this respect should not be taken for granted as we move to the world of immaterial or intellectual objects. Kimppa believes that at this level, other values, such as cooperation, should be promoted, and he seeks to demonstrate that Locke would agree with this position through a careful exegesis of key passages in Chapter V of the *Second Treatise*. Kimppa points out, for example, that Locke "wants for a world in which there would be as much justice and good as possible" for everyone. Thus, Kimppa sees some of the goals espoused in the classic writings of John Locke to be compatible with those advocated by Richard Stallman, founder of the Free Software Foundation and powerful advocate of open source software. Kimppa concludes that Locke's and Stallman's goals of greater cooperation regarding the development of intellectual objects (such as software) are goals worth pursuing.

In Chapter III, Michael Scanlan examines another aspect of Locke's theory of property. Like Kimppa, Scanlan focuses his attention on the provocative fifth chapter of Locke's *Second Treatise*, and is especially concerned with the question: How can a right of ownership arise in previously unowned goods? He notes that many take Locke's theory, introduced in the 17th Century, to be applicable today in situations involving the original acquisition and ownership of intellectual property. Scanlan explains how a "quasi-Lockean theory" could support a "very limited natural right to a species of intellectual property." He also notes, however, that this theory by itself would not be strong enough to support a *natural right* in an intellectual property of the sort given by current copyright law. Scanlan concludes that such property rights must be provided as a result of *positive law*.

In Chapter IV, Thomas Powers analyzes the notion of intellectual property in general, and software copyright law in particular, via the classic philosophical debate known as the "problem of universals." At the heart of this problem is the ontological question: Are there universals, or classes of particular objects, that exist in addition to the particular objects themselves? And if universals do exist, in what (ontological) sense can they be said to exist? Powers notes that a distinction in US copyright law, which is of particular importance to protecting software, is made between ideas (themselves) and their expressions. He also notes that the "idea vs. expression" distinction has been the focus of many copyright cases in the courts. This distinction has been especially apparent, Powers points out, in cases where there is an alleged infringement of non-literal parts of a computer program, such as "structure, sequence, organization, and look and feel." Powers argues that this legal distinction ultimately relies on the ontological distinction between universals and particulars. Because copyright law relies on this distinction — one that has proved to be problematic for philosophers for more than two millennia — Powers argues that the legal doctrine of copyright has inherited many of the conceptual confusions and "philosophical troubles" underlying the problem of universals. He also argues that there are at least three plausible ways in which to construe the differences between universals and particulars, which in turn requires a closer examination of some arguments put forth on this topic by thinkers such as Plato, Aristotle, Locke, and (the later) Wittgenstein. Powers concludes that the unsettled nature of the philosophical debate about universals serves as a good explanation of the "meandering of case law" in the area of copyright law.

Section III of *Intellectual Property Rights in a Networked World* begins with Chapter V by Ann Bartow, who explains how the "likelihood of confusion" criterion is the basis of successful trademark infringement actions in the US. She argues that determinations of this "likelihood" are much too subjective, and that they are also too often premised on a very low estimation of the intelligence of the typical consumer. Nevertheless, in the US, "likelihood of confusion" jurisprudence has gained a strong foothold in cyberspace. Consequently, trademark holders win in most cases, and the result has sometimes been an especially broad set of property rights that prevail throughout the world.

Chapter VI, by Dan Burk, also focuses on cutting-edge legal issues. Professor Burk examines the relationship between hypermedia and feminist discourse. The essay takes a critical stance toward the role of copyright in suppressing such discourses. Given the salience of "non-hierarchical, associative webs to feminist discourse," digital media may be ideally suited to feminist modes of thinking. However, current copyright doctrine assumes that works should be more linear and more tightly controlled. According to Burk, copyright law is inimical to these nontraditional, collaborative works and to "relational user engagement." In the long run, this hostility will not further the promotion of creative discourse as the copyright law intends.

In Chapter VII, Herman Tavani critically examines current copyright protection schemes that apply to digital information. Beginning with a brief account of the way in which copyright law has evolved in the US, from its Anglo-American origins to the present, Tavani examines three traditional philosophical theories of property that have been used to justify the granting of copyright protection. Arguing that each property theory is, in itself, inadequate, he next considers and rejects the view that intellectual property should not be protected at all (and thus should be completely free). Tavani then critically analyzes the notion of *information*, arguing that it should not be viewed as a commodity that deserves exclusive protection but rather as something that should be communicated and shared. Building on this view, he argues for a new presumptive principle for approaching the copyright debate — namely, the principle that *information wants to be shared*. Finally, Tavani argues that presuming in favor of this principle would enable us to formulate a copyright policy that can avoid the extremes found in the two main competing contemporary positions, both of which are morally unacceptable: (1) access to all digitized information should be totally free; and (2) overreaching, and arguably oppressive, copyright laws, such as the Digital Millennium Copyright Act and the Copyright Term Extension Act, are needed to protect digital information.

In Chapter VIII, Richard Spinello focuses on the theme of trespass in cyberspace. In order to prevent unauthorized use of their data, several US companies have hastily filed lawsuits alleging "trespass to chattels." eBay, for example, has accused metasites of trespass for sending "softbots" that roam the eBay website in order to aggregate auction data. In the author's view, legal scholars have rightly criticized this trend because it creates a novel property right in factual data, which is not eligible for copyright protection. Aside from reviewing the legal issues in this case, the author argues that Internet companies like eBay should be less preoccupied with property rights and more concerned with the Internet's common good. Both Eastern and Western philosophies enunciate the need to recognize and respect the common good of a community or common venture. This awareness should temper a company's narrow focus on proprietary property rights. Corporations like eBay should seek a prudent balance between their property entitlements and their duty to support the Internet's common good, which is manifest in the sharing and communication of information.

Chapter IX, by Elizabeth Buchanan and James Campbell, examines the growing threats to the "information commons" that result from strong property rights that have excessive longevity or too broad a scope. This discussion follows up on and expands upon critical issues that were introduced in Chapter I of this book. The authors discuss the importance of the commons or public domain for future creative efforts. They advocate looser protection schemes that will make for a more robust commons.

Chapter X, the final selection in this book, is by Melanie Mortensen. This chapter examines the ethical and legal issues that are triggered by shifts in communications technologies such as webcasting. Her presentation is an example of how traditional laws are misapplied to new technologies with "troubling" ethical results. She argues persuasively that in this new milieu, we must consider carefully what constitutes piracy, and she offers some ethical guidelines for doing so. Those guidelines are grounded in principles that are based upon "the essential nature of communications technologies."

Acknowledgments

We wish to thank the contributors who so graciously agreed to have their work included in this modest volume. Their enthusiasm, cooperation, and strong support for this project have inspired our efforts.

As noted in Dr. Neuhauser's Foreword, most of these papers were originally presented at the Sixth Annual Ethics and Technology Conference held at Boston College during the summer of 2003. This conference is an annual event, and it is a joint effort of Boston College, Holy Cross College, Loyola University/Chicago, St. Louis University, University of Detroit/Mercy, and Regis College in Denver. We are grateful to the organizers from all of these schools for their support of this conference and for helping to stimulate dialogue in the nascent field of Information Technology Ethics. We also wish to thank both Boston College and the International Society for Ethics and Information Technology (INSEIT) for their modest financial support that made the 2003 conference possible. We encourage those with an interest in this field to see what INSEIT has to offer its members (www.csethics.uis.edu/inseit).

Finally, special thanks to Jan Travers, Amanda Appicello, Michele Rossi, and many others at Idea Group Inc. for their interest in this project and for their invaluable efforts in resolving the miscellaneous but sometimes complicated issues involved in coordinating the scholarly contributions offered in this book.

Richard A. Spinello, Boston College, USA
Herman T. Tavani, Rivier College, USA
January 2004

Section I

Overview

Chapter I

Intellectual Property Rights:
From Theory to
Practical Implementation

Richard A. Spinello
Boston College, USA

Herman T. Tavani
Rivier College, USA

ABSTRACT

*This chapter presents some foundational concepts and issues in intellectual property. We begin by defining **intellectual objects**, which we contrast with physical objects or tangible goods. We then turn to some of the normative justifications that have been advanced to defend the granting of property rights in general, and we ask whether those rationales can be extended to the realm of intellectual objects. Theories of property introduced by Locke and Hegel, as well as utilitarian philosophers, are summarized and critiqued. This sets the stage for reviewing the case against intellectual property. We reject that case and claim instead that policy makers should aim for balanced property rights that avoid the extremes of overprotection and underprotection. Next we examine four different kinds of protection schemes for intellectual property that have been provided by our legal system: copyright laws, patents, trademarks, and trade secrets. This discussion is supplemented with a concise review* *of recent U.S. legislation involving copyright and digital media and an analysis of technological schemes of property protection known as digital rights management. Finally, we consider a number of recent controversial court cases, including the Napster case and the Microsoft antitrust suit. Many of the issues and controversies introduced in this chapter are explored and analyzed in greater detail in the subsequent chapters of this book.*

INTRODUCTION

It is now a common refrain that the ubiquity of the Internet and the digitization of information will soon mean the demise of copyright and other intellectual property laws. After all, "information wants to be free," especially in the open terrain of cyberspace. John Perry Barlow and other information libertarians have argued this case for years, and there may be some validity to their point of view. Perhaps Negroponte (1995) is right when he describes copyright law as a vestige of another era, a mere "Gutenberg artifact" (p. 58). Even many of those who concede that this vision of cyberspace as a copyright free zone is too utopian argue for a system of intellectual property protection that is as "thin" as possible, just enough to encourage creativity (Vaidhyanathan, 2001).

The digital revolution has already thrown the music industry into chaos and the movie industry will probably be next. Both of these industries have been struggling with piracy, and peer-to-peer (P2P) networks, such as Gnutella, KaZaA, and Morpheus, are the primary obstacle in their efforts to thwart the illicit sharing of files. These P2P networks continue to proliferate, and users continue to download copyrighted music and movie files with relative impunity. Everyone knows, however, that the content industry will not sit idly by and lose its main source of revenues. It will fight back with legal weapons such as the Digital Millennium Copyright Act and technological weapons such as trusted systems.

Of course, debates about intellectual property rights are not confined to digital music and movies. There is apprehension that the Internet itself will be swallowed up by proprietary technologies. Currently, developing countries argue that they can never surmount the digital divide if intellectual property rights remain so entrenched. Governments debate the pros and cons of endorsing open source software as a means of overcoming the hegemony of Microsoft's control of certain technologies. And some claim that the impending "enclosure movement" of intellectual objects will stifle creativity and even threaten free speech rights. Hence, they argue, we must abandon our commitment to private ownership in the digital realm.

The result of these public and controversial squabbles is that the once esoteric issue of intellectual property rights has now taken center stage in courses and books on cyberlaw and cyberethics. The economic and social stakes are quite high in these disputes, so they should not be regarded in a cavalier manner or dismissed as inconsequential. The centrality of the property issue becomes especially apparent when one realizes that other social issues in cyberspace (such as speech and privacy) are often closely connected to the proper scope of intellectual property rights. For example, Diebold Election Systems, a manufacturer of voting machines, has pursued college students for posting on the Internet copies of internal communications, including 15,000 e-mail messages and other memoranda, discussing flaws in Diebold's software. The company claims that this information is proprietary and that these students are violating its intellectual property rights, while the students say that their free speech rights are being unjustly circumscribed. They contend that copyright law is being abused to stifle free speech.

This tension between intellectual property rights and the First Amendment has been addressed by many commentators on the law. As Volokh (1998) has pointed out, "Copyright law restricts speech: it restricts you from writing, painting, publicly performing, or otherwise communicating what you please."

One could easily use the intellectual property issue as a lens to examine the expanding field of cyberethics since the most salient issues seem to have a property dimension. In addition to speech, personal privacy is another issue closely connected with intellectual property. Employers, for example, often invoke property rights to justify monitoring the e-mail communications of their employees. Since the IT systems and e-mail software are the property of employers, they assume the prerogative to ensure that their property is being used in accordance with company rules and regulations.

Given the breadth of the intellectual property field, it is impossible to review all of the current topics and controversies. Our purpose in this introductory essay is merely to provide a comprehensive overview of the nature and scope of intellectual property rights. This overview will include a discussion of intellectual objects, the normative justification of these rights, the philosophical and ethical case made against property rights, the legal infrastructure, and some enumeration of the major cases that are reshaping the legal and social landscape of cyberspace. Our objective is twofold: to provide some important background that will make the remaining in-depth essays in this book more intelligible, especially to the novice reader, and to defend the need for a moderate and balanced regime of intellectual property protection. An ancillary purpose is to shed some light on several hotly debated issues from a moral as well as a legal perspective.

We contend that *information socialism*, where all intellectual objects are "unowned," is an impractical and unworkable alternative to the current system. But we also argue that *information capitalism*, which promotes strong rights and thick protection that can impair the intellectual commons, is also misguided. Policy and law should neither overprotect rights nor underprotect them, but instead should seek the Aristotelian mean or intermediate position between these two deficient policy options. It is difficult, of course, to determine the "right" amount of protection that rewards creators for their efforts and stimulates creativity while not impairing the intellectual commons, but in the course of this analysis we offer some suggestions.

Along the way, we hope to offer reasoned answers to some important questions. For example, how do we assess the validity of the normative justifications for intellectual property rights? Can a case be made for a "natural" intellectual property right, or can this right be grounded only on a more pragmatic, utilitarian foundation? Can cyberspace accommodate intellectual property rights (and the laws that protect those rights) without losing its most attractive features? What are the costs and benefits of relying on technology to protect digital content? Under what circumstances should secondary liability for copyright infringement be invoked? And finally what can moralists bring to this debate that so far has been dominated by legal scholars? We begin with a conceptual background on the nature of intellectual objects.

INTELLECTUAL OBJECTS

Property is a dynamic concept, which has evolved dramatically since the 18th Century. Originally, it referred exclusively to land but eventually it was extended to include things or physical "objects" such as farms, factories, and furniture (Hughes, 1989). The kinds of objects that count as property now include entities that reside in the non-tangible or intellectual realm as well. Different expressions have been used to refer to the kinds of objects or entities at stake in the intellectual property debate. Sometimes these objects are referred to as *ideal objects* or *non-tangible goods* (Palmer, 1997). Following Hettinger (1997), however, we use the expression *intellectual objects* to refer to various forms of intellectual property. Unlike physical property, intellectual property consists of "objects" that are not tangible. These objects are creative works and inventions, which are the manifestations or expressions of ideas.

Unlike tangible objects, intellectual objects (such as software programs or books) are public goods. Public goods are both non-rivalrous and nonexclusive. An object is non-rivalous if consumption by one person does not diminish what can be consumed by others. So if A owns a desktop computer, which is a physical object, then B cannot own that computer, and vice versa. However, consider the status of a word-processing program that resides in A's computer. If B makes a copy of that program, then both A and B possess copies of the same word-processing program. B's use of this non-rivalrous intellectual object does not take away from A's use.

A good is nonexclusive if it is impossible to exclude people from consuming it. For example, the national defense and protection of the United States is a public good that covers all citizens regardless of whether or not they pay taxes. Since public goods are non-exclusive as well as non-rivalrous, there is a tendency that they will be underproduced without some type of protection or government intervention that will provide some measure of exclusivity. This has critical implications for intellectual objects. As Gordon (1992) explains, important intellectual property markets will remain uncultivated where the up-front investment cost is high, copying is simple, and free riders threaten to undercut the innovator's prices and thereby appropriate that innovator's created value.

The characteristic of *scarcity* that applies to many physical objects — which often has caused competition and rivalry with respect to those entities — need not exist in the case of intellectual objects. Consider that there are practical limitations to the number of physical objects one can own, and there are natural and political limitations to the amount of land that can be owned. However, most kinds of intellectual objects are easily reproducible and shareable. For example, countless digital copies of a Microsoft Word program can be reproduced and distributed at a marginal cost of zero.

Intellectual objects are also distinguishable from physical objects by virtue of what exactly it is that one can legally claim to own. It is impossible to "own" an abstract idea or concept, at least in the same (legal) sense that one can own a physical object. One cannot exclude others from using that idea once it is revealed, as one can exclude people from using land or some other physical object.

As a result, abstract ideas and algorithms are not the kinds of things for which governments have been willing to grant ownership rights to individuals. Instead, legal protection is given only to the tangible *expression* of an idea that is creative or original. If the idea is literary or artistic in nature, it must be expressed (or "fixed") in some tangible medium in order to be protected. Such a medium could be a physical book or a sheet of paper containing a musical score. And if the idea is functional in nature, such as an invention, it must be expressed in terms of a machine or a process. Whereas authors are granted copyright protections for expressions of their literary ideas, inventors are given an incentive in the form of a patent for their inventions. Both copyright law and patent law, along with other legal schemes for protecting intellectual property, are discussed in detail in later sections of this chapter.

Finally, even if an intellectual object, such as a novel or musical composition, "belongs" to its author in some way, should it be described as that author's "property?" Are other characterizations more suitable? While references to "intellectual property" have become commonplace, many scholars regret the ill-effects of the ascendancy of this form of "property rhetoric." One such effect is the tendency to regard the unauthorized use of intellectual objects as "piracy" or "theft," with all of the negative connotations of those words. The popularity of the term "intellectual property" can be traced back to the foundation of the World Intellectual Property Organization (WIPO) by the United Nations in 1967. To be sure, this term appeared prior to the founding of WIPO, but according to Lemley (1997), these previous uses "do not seem to have reflected a unified property-based approach to the separate doctrines of patent, trademark, and copyright … "

NORMATIVE JUSTIFICATIONS FOR INTELLECTUAL PROPERTY RIGHTS

What is the basis for the claim that intellectual property (or, for that matter, any kind of property) ought to be protected? The current legal system offers such protection in a web of complex statutes. But we must inquire on what philosophical grounds are these laws based?

From a legal standpoint, intellectual property rights specify the ownership privileges for intellectual objects. Normative approaches to intellectual property (IP) are focused on the justification of intellectual property rights. What is the moral ground for giving an author or publisher a "right" to possess and control an intellectual object? Is the genesis of intellectual property rights to be found in instrumentalist theories or in a natural rights perspective? Normative theory also encompasses the perspective of distributive justice, which compels us to ponder the scope of these rights. In this section, we sketch out some primary justifications for intellectual property rights, drawing heavily upon the resources of philosophers such as Locke and Hegel, who attempt to set forth some defensible rationales for determining the boundaries of those rights.

It must be said at the outset that no single theory presented here is comprehensive enough to withstand critical scrutiny. Each is subject to interpretation and each has certain flaws and shortcomings. Nonetheless, the ultimate indeterminacy of these theories should not discourage this endeavor. At a minimum, these theories are useful as avenues of reflection that can provide a more orderly method of thinking through the moral implications of intellectual property policy decisions. They can also help to resolve specific disputes when the law is unclear or ambiguous. According to Fisher (1998), while these theories may not always persuade us with inexorable logic, they can be used to "strike a cord of sympathy" and evoke a response, such as "that rings true to me."

Locke and the Labor Desert Theory

John Locke, in *The Second Treatise of Government*, was one of the first philosophers to thematize the issue of property in a comprehensive manner. Locke's theory of property has undoubtedly been one of the most influential in the entire philosophical tradition. Locke's main thesis is simple enough: people have a natural right or entitlement to the fruits of their labor. In general terms, labor establishes the boundaries of one's property before civil society even exists. Thus, property is a natural right because it precedes civil society, which comes into being in part in order to protect property. But how do the specific elements of Locke's argument unfold?

Labor belongs to the laborer and when that laborer takes an object from the bountiful commons and mixes that object with her labor, it can be said that she has appropriated that object. Thus, if someone takes common, unusable land and through the sweat of the brow transforms it into valuable farm land that person deserves to own this land, which has been "mixed" with her hard work. According to Locke (1952), "As much land as a man tills, plants, improves, cultivates, and can use the product of, so much is his property. He, by his labor does, as it were, *enclose it from the common*" (p. 20; emphasis added).

As the preceding citation implies, if labor is to engender a property right, it must be useful and purposeful. Moreover, such labor often involves infusing one's very being or personality into the object in question. According to Olivecrona (1974), one's labor is an extension of one's personality and "when the object appropriated has been included within [an individual's] sphere [of personality], it will be an injury to the possessor to deprive him of it."

Locke's argument for a property right is partly based on the premise that labor is an unpleasant and onerous activity. Hence, people engage in labor not for its own sake but to reap its benefits; as a result, it would be unjust not to let people have these benefits they take such pains to procure. In short, property rights are required as a return for the laborers' painful and strenuous work. As Locke (1952) maintains, one who takes the laborer's property "desire[s] the benefit of another's pains, which he has no right to" (p. 20). Appropriation of this property against the laborer's will inflicts an unjustifiable harm on this laborer. If someone comes along and takes from you what you have worked for, that person has done something immoral. For example, if someone takes wood from a common forest in order to build a useful object such as a chair, that person would be harmed by the theft of that chair. As Gordon (1993) argues, Locke espouses a nonconsequentialist natural right to property based on this simple "no-harm principle."

In summary, then, Locke provides two reasons for his normative claim that a person's labor entitles that person to the thing constructed by means of that labor: (1) the right is derived from a prior property right in one's body and the labor that emanates from that body; (2) a property right is deserved as a just return for the laborer's pains (Becker, 1977). Hence, for Locke, an unowned item appropriated through the activity of labor is "just property" (p. 28).

Locke insists on an important condition limiting the acquisition of property that has come to be known as the Lockean proviso. According to this moral principle, one can only appropriate an object from the commons through labor when "there is enough, and as good left for others" (Locke, 1952). Thus, individuals should not be greedy or wasteful and take from the commons more than they can use "to any advantage of life before it spoils" (p. 17). One must have a need and a use for what one appropriates from the commons.

Although Locke had in mind physical property such as land, it would seem logical that this theory is applicable to intellectual property as well. An author or creator owns her labor and therefore must own the creative product of that labor. After all, should not those who expend intellectual labor be rewarded by ownership in the fruits of their labor and be allowed to "enclose it from the common"? In this case, the relevant common resource is not land or unowned physical objects but common knowledge or the "intellectual commons" (that is, unowned facts and other raw material such as ideas, algorithms, musical scores, or general plot lines). And the Lockean inspired argument is that one's intellectual labor should entitle one to have a natural property right in the finished product of that work, such as a novel, a computer program, or a musical composition.

This application of Locke's theory to intellectual property seems plausible enough. As Easterbrook (1990) remarks, "Intellectual property is no less the fruit of one's labor than is physical property." Thus, a person has a legitimate claim to ownership in works to the extent that they have been created by that person's labor. If it is the case that people deserve a property right in tangible objects through their labor, why shouldn't they deserve a property right in the intellectual objects which they have created?

Of course, the Lockean proviso must also be applied to the appropriation of intellectual property. If that appropriation impairs the commons and interferes with the public good, there is a conflict. This proviso would seem to preclude the propertization of abstract ideas such as laws of physics that may be discovered by ingenious individuals. If those ideas became enclosed and off limits to others, the public good would undoubtedly suffer. As Nimmer (2001) observes, "To grant property status to a mere idea would permit withdrawing the ideas from the stock of materials that would otherwise be open to other authors, thereby narrowing the field of thought open for development and exploitation" (pp. 13-60). Although there are different interpretations of this proviso, many scholars tend to favor ones that are more protective of the public domain (Gordon, 1993; Yen, 1990).

How might the Lockean theory with its proviso be applied to cases where there is a potential threat to the integrity of the public domain? Gordon (1993) cites the example of the U.S. Olympic Committee's (USOC) successful efforts to trademark the word "Olympic." The USOC took legal action against another group seeking to use the term "Gay Olympic Games." She describes this as a conflict between a prima facie right to an "unimpaired commons" and the USOC's prima facie right to be "free of interference" in its use of the term "Olympics" to describe its games. Gordon (1993) contends that the right of the public to an unimpaired commons must take priority, and she criticizes the Supreme Court's judgment, arguing that this word cannot be "owned" without "violating both concerns — equality and harm — found in the proviso."

At the same time, if I write a novel about star-crossed lovers and a tragic interracial marriage set in 21st Century Alabama, a copyright for this novel will not hurt the commons. Since U.S. copyright protects expression and not ideas, others can still make use of the general plot line, the setting, and the themes of this novel as long as they do not copy the "web of the authors' dramatic expression" (Hand, 1936). If the law is applied correctly, my limited property right in this novel should not impair the intellectual commons or prevent others from writing similar stories or from being inspired by this story to develop works with related themes.

Critics of Locke's thesis contend that his emphasis on labor as a grounding for property rights is misplaced. According to Drahos (1996), "labor is either too indeterminate or too incomplete a basis on which to base a justification of property." Labor works in some cases (e.g., writing a long novel) but not in others (e.g., discovery of a creative idea that can be put into concrete terms and yet consumes little time). The primary problem seems to revolve around determining an appropriate criterion for intellectual labor. Does it depend simply on time and energy expended, or is it any activity that results in social benefits? What do we do about intellectual objects that can be created with little or no labor? And does this labor have to be some sort of creative activity that yields an original work?

We cannot resolve these issues here, but how one determines the parameters of intellectual labor deserving of a property right will be decisive for deciding how such rights should be awarded. We cannot deny that the application of Locke's basic theory to intellectual property is subject to conflicting interpretations. Nonetheless, the core idea that intellectual labor is deserving of some sort of property right as long as the public domain is not impaired by the granting of such a right seems to be an important consideration for any all-encompassing theory of intellectual property rights.

To some extent, modern copyright law strives to be consistent with the Lockean paradigm because it limits intellectual property rights to concrete expression instead of ideas and allows creative works to be accessed or utilized on a "fair use" basis. The law is seeking to reward the deserving individual creator while fostering the augmentation of the public domain. For example, the idea/expression dichotomy recognizes that property rights should only be extended to concrete expressions but not to abstract ideas or algorithms. According to Yen (1990), the English natural law of property, rooted in the Roman doctrines of possession along with the Lockean principle of labor, strongly suggests that property rights cannot be awarded unless the author creates things that are "capable of possession under the law." English natural law, therefore, along with Locke's important proviso, can be interpreted to support a robust public domain along with individual property rights in concrete intellectual objects. We can affirm that a creator's mental labor leads to the production of intellectual objects that deserve some sort of property right, as long as we also affirm that this right must be prudently limited in scope and duration.

Hegel on Property and Personhood

Another normative justification centers on the intimate relationship between property and personhood. It assumes that, in order to become a person, one needs some control over the resources in one's environment. If this theory provides an adequate account for the granting of property rights in general, then it is plausible to assume that the personality theory could be extended to justify intellectual property rights as well.

This theory has its roots in the philosophy of Hegel. Despite a certain wariness about property in his earlier political writings, Hegel consistently argued for the importance of property rights. In several of those works, such as "The Spirit of Christianity and its Fate," he developed an ontology of life and evaluated Judaism and Christianity according to their fidelity to the spirit of life. In this context, Hegel criticized the teachings of Jesus because they renounced self-expression of the individual achieved through property and family. But according to Hegel (1948), "The fate of property has become too powerful for us … to find its abolition thinkable" (p. 221). The abolition of property is a denial of life, since life requires free self-expression, and so individuals must be able to invest themselves in things. Hence, individuals need private property as a vehicle of self-expression. On the other hand, property must be restricted since excessive property is also opposed to life. The Greek πolis under Solon developed the correct model, since it limited the acquisition of property among the Greeks. For Hegel (1948), the virtue appropriate to property is honesty — people must manifest enough integrity and restraint to develop (or acquire) property only when necessary for the sake of self-expression. But they should not acquire goods and wealth for their own sake, since those things merely "tacked on to life … cannot be its property" (p. 221).

In later writings such as *The Phenomenology of Spirit,* Hegel (1944) develops the notion of objectification, and in language reminiscent of Locke, he describes labor as an "outer expression in which the individual no longer retains possession of himself *per se*, but lets the inner get right outside of him, and surrenders it to something else …" (p. 340). Hegel (1952) continues to emphasize the importance of property rights in works such as the *Philosophy of Right,* where he argued with insistence that "property is the first embodiment of freedom and so is in itself a substantive end" (§ 45). One cannot be free without property, since property allows one to overcome the opposition between self and world and to freely put one's personality into external objects beyond the inner self.

Hegel elaborates on the theme anticipated in his earlier works: selfhood is achieved by self-expression, by objectifying or embodying one's will in external objects and thereby appropriating those objects into the sphere of one's possessions. Acting upon things is necessary for self-actualization (or self-expression). Without property there can be no self-expression, and without self-expression there can be no freedom. And once we accept that self-actualization is manifest in physical objects, property rights take over to prevent people "from forever being embroiled in an internecine conflict of each individual trying to protect his first forays at self actualization from the predation of others" (Hughes, 1997, p. 144).

The core insight of Hegel is this notion of "embodied will," a reminder that we have intimate relationships with objects that give our lives meaning and value. And these relationships justify ownership, since without ownership there will be no continuity in the way we relate to these valuable objects. According to Merges, Mennell, and Lemley (2000), "one's expectations crystallize around certain 'things,' the loss of which causes ... disruption and disorientation" (p. 9).

Hegel has consistently maintained, then, that property is an expression of personality, a mechanism for self-actualization. This theory seems particularly apposite for intellectual property. If physical property is the "embodiment of personality" (Hegel, 1952, § 51), then the same can surely be said for intellectual property. As human beings freely externalize their will in various intellectual objects such as novels, works of art, or poetry, they create "property" to which they are entitled because those intellectual products are a manifestation or embodiment of their personality. Each of these creative works is an extension of their being and as such belongs to them. If a person has invested or "poured" himself or herself into an intellectual object, then it follows that the object should belong to that person.

To be sure, not all types of intellectual property entail a great deal of personality or self-expression. But the more creative and expressive are one's intellectual works — the greater one's "personality stake" in that particular object — the more important the need for some type of ownership rights and the stronger the justification for those rights (Hughes, 1997). Perhaps in keeping with Hegel's early views on property we should add that the creator who aspires to honesty should not seek absolute control but rather seek enough control over his or her work to prevent its unfair alienation (or exploitation).

Like the Lockean framework, a Hegelian approach to intellectual property has notable shortcomings. Once again we are confronted with the difficulty of defining and quantifying self-expression if we want to use it as a basis for granting intellectual property rights. To what extent does expression of one's personality justify increased property protection? What happens if inventions, reflecting the personality of their respective inventors, are developed simultaneously? When does imitative artwork or music manifest sufficient unique personality to qualify for a copyright? What should be done about computer software programs that rarely manifest the personality traits of their authors? On the other hand, what about works that are highly expressive and infused with personality and yet are deemed to be derivative according to current U.S. copyright law? For example, *The Wind Done Gone*, a clever takeoff on Margaret Mitchell's classic novel, *Gone with the Wind,* initially ran afoul of that copyright law due to its lack of literary originality. Yet this work would seem to qualify under an Hegelian approach, since it is a highly personal, revisionistic portrayal of the main characters in *Gone with the Wind* that borrows from the original text for the sake of parody and criticism.

In summary, then, Hegel espouses the principle that property is a natural right or end in itself because it provides freedom for the self, which, through the exercise of that freedom, objectifies itself in the external world—that is, gives its personality a reality outside of itself. And Hegel's notion that property is an expression of personality is well suited for intellectual property, since abstract objects can also be invested with personality.

Hughes (1997) has suggested that the theories of Locke and Hegel are complementary, especially if we consider the biggest weakness of each paradigm: Locke's theory cannot account for "the idea whose inception does not seemed to have involved labor," and the Hegelian personality theory is hard to apply to "valuable innovations that do not contain elements of what society might recognize as personal expression" (p. 164). But if an intellectual property right is construed as a right to the fruit of one's labor *and* individual expression, it may find a more sympathetic audience even among some intellectual property skeptics.

Utilitarianism

In contrast to intellectual property rights defended from a natural-rights perspective, we find the utilitarian approach, which assumes that the utility principle—often expressed as "the greatest good of the greatest number"—should be the basis for determining property entitlements. Intellectual property rights, according to this paradigm, are justified on the basis of their contribution to social utility.

The utilitarian argument for property rights in general is based on the premise that people need to acquire, possess, and use things in order to achieve some degree of happiness and fulfillment. Since insecurity in one's possessions does not provide such happiness, security in possession, use, and control of things is necessary. Furthermore, security of possession can only be accomplished by a system of property rights. Also, utilitarian philosophers such as

Bentham justified the institution of private property by the related argument that knowledge of future ownership is an incentive that encourages people to behave in certain ways that will increase socially valuable goods.

The utilitarian argument for intellectual property rights is equally straight-forward: those rights are necessary to maximize social utility by providing authors, inventors, and other creators with rewards for their work. Without those rewards, which in the Anglo-American system take the form of heavily protected monopolies of limited duration, there would be fewer such creations or inventions. This version of utilitarianism—known as incentive theory—has been articulated in many works, including those of Nordhaus (1969), who sought to demonstrate that an increase in the longevity or robustness of patents would stimulate more innovations.

Following Moore (2001) and others who have explicated this theory, it can be summarized as follows:

1. Society should adopt legal regimes or institutions if and only if they are expected to yield the optimization of aggregate social welfare.
2. A legal regime that provides authors, creators, and inventors with limited rights or control over their productions is expected to act as a strong incentive for the creation of intellectual works.
3. Stimulating the production and creation of intellectual works contributes to the maximization of aggregate welfare.
4. Therefore, a legal regime for intellectual property protection should be adopted.

The presumption, of course, is that the development of scientific, literary, and artistic works will promote general utility or social welfare. This seems to be reasonable, since it is hard to quarrel with any culture's need for such intellectual works. And it was precisely this need that was recognized in the U.S. Constitution that confers upon Congress the power "to promote the Progress of Science and the useful Arts, by securing for limited Times to Authors and Inventors the exclusive Right to their respective Writings and Discoveries" (Article I, § 8, clause 8).

In contrast to Locke and Hegel, utilitarian philosophers argue that intellectual property rights are not a natural entitlement or a matter of natural justice. Rather, they should be awarded purely for pragmatic purposes as a means of inducing creative or inventive activity. This line of reasoning is echoed in influential cases such as *Wheaton v. Peters* (1834), which denies that an author's intellectual property rights in published works are a matter of common law. Such a right is based purely on statute and is contingent on the consensus of lawmakers. Western societies, of course, have provided an ample level of intellectual property protection in order to promote future innovation and creativity. They have tended to presume that without such protection creators would not always be able to recover their initial investment and thus would refrain from creative activity. If society wants quality movies and technological innovation, it will have to protect those items from free riders. Precisely how that level of protection is calibrated in order to maximize productivity, however, is a matter of debate.

The primary problem with utilitarianism is the lack of empirical data available that will support those policy choices aimed at maximizing social welfare (measured as society's total wealth). To what extent will an increase or change in copyright or patent protection stimulate greater productivity of intellectual objects? Can we be sure of the effects of extending the duration of copyright protection or increasing the life of a patent from 17 to 20 years? What impact will these policy changes have on authors, inventors, and consumers? Consider Priest's (1986) trenchant observation about this problem:

[t]he inability of economists to resolve the question of whether activity stimulated by the patent system or other forms of protection of intellectual property enhances or diminishes social welfare implies...that economists can tell lawyers very little about how to enforce or interpret the law of intellectual property. (p.27)

Given these problems, one wonders whether copyright or patent jurisprudence should be based solely on utilitarian considerations. But despite its shortcomings, the utility argument should not be discounted. There are, for example, credible studies citing empirical evidence that strongly suggests a link between patent protection and innovation (Mansfield, 1986; Merges, 1992). However, a more stable basis for intellectual property rights might come from the *deontic* (or duty based) moral principles articulated in the philosophies of Locke and Hegel.

But rather than privilege one theory over another, a pluralistic approach seems more sensible. These normative theories should be seen as mutually supporting one another as they offer guiding principles for determining intellectual property policy and the validity of specific entitlements. The theories are not competitive, but complementary. A corollary principle that also emerges in these normative frameworks (especially Locke's) is the need to respect the intellectual commons or public domain. All of these prescriptive principles —

utility, labor-desert, self-expression, and respect for the commons — should function in our reasoning and deliberations about intellectual property issues as a system of checks and balances.

THE CASE AGAINST
INTELLECTUAL PROPERTY RIGHTS

So far, we have focused on normative justifications of intellectual property rights, which some see as morally inviolable and economically essential. But what about the case against assigning these rights? There is a strong tradition supporting a radical skepticism about property rights that deserves our careful consideration. Antipathy to private property often springs from opposition to the capitalist market system on the grounds that it sometimes leads to gross inequities in the acquisition of property.

Some philosophers such as Karl Marx have expressed great uneasiness about the notion of private property. Marx regarded such property in the capitalist context as a form of alienation and a blunt instrument of the ruling class to protect its interests. According to the Marxist tradition, private property is the end result of alienated labor. Marx agreed with Hegel that labor was an expressive activity. For laborers in a capitalist economy, however, while the object produced embodies their personality and nature, this object is sold by the producer, and hence is not under the laborer's control. These objects, therefore, are reduced to the status of mere commodities.

While Marx did not explicitly consider intellectual property, his theory has relevance for it. For those sympathetic to Marx, there is abundant evidence that in capitalist economies, creative labor is another instance of exploited labor. According to Drahos (1996), "it is capitalists rather than workers that end up owning most of the intellectual property that is produced within a capitalist economy" (pp. 99-100). A Marxist perspective then would not regard intellectual property rights in a benign light, as a socially useful instrument to stimulate creativity. Rather, those rights are regarded as yet another sinister means by which one class organizes and controls the production undertaken by another class. Hence, intellectual property rights, which give corporate producers sovereignty over many intellectual objects, should be repudiated or at least radically revised.

Furthermore, Marx subscribed to the Hegelian idea that labor could be part of the subject's self-actualization and thereby can be viewed as a means to achieve freedom. But for Marx (unlike Hegel), production and property do not always lead to authentic self-realization. Some individuals, for example, freely create music or art as a means to express their deepest emotions. In the capitalist system, however, this type of labor becomes easily commodified and thereby alienated. As Drahos (1996) explains, "capitalism seeks out creative labor and integrates such labor into its system of production, [and] the task of integration is achieved through intellectual property law" (p. 105). Capitalism assimilates creative labor in order to gain control over these desirable intellectual objects. Intellectual property law, therefore, performs a disservice by commodifying intellectual objects and creative labor and by integrating them into the capitalist structure. According to this line of reasoning, society would be better off with a system that avoided the commodification of intellectual and creative works, so that they are not alienated from their actual creators and openly available to anyone. This system would encourage and reward the sharing of information and the advancement of scientific knowledge.

Contemporary critics of intellectual property rights such as Martin (1995) argue that these rights lead to unjustifiably harmful consequences such as the exploitation of developing countries, which are at the mercy of companies holding patents for pharmaceutical products or copyrights for important software technologies. Moreover, many plants and microorganisms found in developing countries are key starting ingredients for new drugs and crops, but these substances are usually patented by companies from developed countries. In India, the neem tree has been used by that country to develop medical products, yet U.S. and Japanese companies have patented neem-based material. Some critics argue that, because intellectual property rights such as patents only exacerbate present inequities, it would be fairer if intellectual products produced in privileged countries be made available to poor countries at no cost.

The alternative to intellectual property rights is to ensure that all intellectual products remain unowned, either by individuals or organizations. Language, for example, can be freely used by anyone, and most scientific research is public knowledge. Proponents of this view, which we might label "information socialism," argue that the elimination of intellectual property rights will lead to the expansion of the intellectual commons and the fostering of creativity.

The justification of intellectual property rights has also been questioned by recent post-modern scholarship, which has expressed doubts about the true origin of intellectual objects. There are echoes of Marx in the writings of some post-modernists, who describe a crisis of human subjectivity and who see the structures of social and economic domination inscribed in that human subject. These doubts about the immediacy of the self have led to philosophical questions about authorship. Locke never questioned the unitary self that was the source of labor and the bearer of the property right. Similarly, the assumption had always been that the correlate of the creative work (such as the novel or poem) is the creative subject, who is responsible for his or her work. But is it not arbitrary to assume that this isolated subject is the ultimate responsible source? Why not revert to something more primordial such as social or familial antecedents?

Many post-modern philosophers and their followers now contend that the notion of authorship is "socially constructed" and that we must be wary of associating any creative work with a single, discrete, individual "author." Despite the author's labor, that work is not a product of this one individual but of the community's intellectual forces, which have mightily contributed their ideas and thoughts to the author's work. Halbert (1999), for example, argues that our notions of "literary work" and the "author function" must be thoroughly deconstructed: "[t]he author is so embedded in our thought processes that we look to the author as owner instead of looking behind the role of authorship to the production of discourses in society" (p. 126). Similarly, Vaidhyanathan (2001) claims that "authorship is theoretically suspect, texts are unstable, and originality is more often a pose or pretense than a definable aspect of a work" (p. 8).

Of course, if the notion of authorship is so inchoate, and if the author is more illusory than real, it makes no sense to award "rights" to this fictional entity. And if originality is a "pretense," there would be no valid copyrights, at least as the copyright statute is currently configured. But is there any plausibility to these unorthodox viewpoints?

In order to answer this question we must consider the reflections of the philosopher Michel Foucault (1969) who describes how the "author function faded away" in the 18th Century, replaced by scientific discourses "received for themselves ... in anonymity." For Foucault and other post-modern thinkers, the process of deconstruction or *différance* exposes the multiplicity of "differences" or different elements of reality that cannot be organized into categories or classified according to metaphysical species. It is the reader of a text who puts different elements together in order to create his or her own meaning. This process of *différance* represents "acategorial" thinking and has no center or author. And if a text is without an author, it must be without a unitary subject: "the subject is constituted only in being divided from itself, in becoming space, in temporizing, in deferral" (Derrida, 1981, p. 29). Thus, this questioning of authorial identity is part of the larger post-modern endeavor to raise doubts about the existence or continuity of the stable self.

It was Nietzsche who first saw the self as a *dividuum*, lacking unity and coherence, where one force temporarily dominates. Nietzsche (1962) described the self as "a plurality. . .a war and peace, a herd and a shepherd" (p. 27).[1] Following the philosophy of Nietzsche, Foucault (1969) and Derrida (1981) also regarded the human self not as a unified being but as fissured and divided. For the post-modern tradition, then, the self is not an immediate unity nor the ultimate source of activity.

Yet behind the discourses and the narrative must there not be such a stable self, an "I" who perdures through the evolving narrative in order to provide its coherence? Without a unitary subject as a personal focal point, how can there be serious and sustained engagement with an important topic or artistic theme? Moreover, in telling the tale of how he came to propound this or that view about the nonexistent self, isn't the post-modern narrator forced "to fall back into a mode of speech in which the use of personal pronouns presupposes just that metaphysical conception of accountability which [postmodernism] disowns?" (MacIntyre, 1990, p. 210). Discourse or narration requires an efficient cause, an author who may be deeply indebted to multiple sources but who nonetheless engages the topic at hand as an intentional subject and who is ultimately accountable for what is said or done.

When Foucault (1969) refers to the impersonality of these discourses, he assumes the presence of an individual who takes on the authorial function and who is contingently related to that discourse (MacIntyre, 1990). But Foucault fails to consider the intentions of this individual (author) as he or she actively expresses meaning through preexisting linguistic structures and endows that discourse with some measure of originality and uniqueness. When, for example, Jane Austen narrates a tale about marriage and love in early 19th Century England, this "discourse" has distinct qualities thanks to her intentional use of language in a certain way and with a certain style. The true artist or great novelist could never be reduced to an impersonal or passive purveyor of shapeless, amorphous discourse where the relationship of the author to that discourse involves only an unintentional dependence on or use of language.

We concede that the concept of "author" has been overly romanticized, as Boyle (2004) claims, and is surely subject to some degree of revision or re-conceptualization. Yet it seems impossible to emancipate the literary text or musical composition from the intentionality of a stable, originating author in the way that some post-modern legal scholars have proposed.

At the same time, cultural history and common sense should prevent us from accepting the spurious notion that all creative works lack originality. While it is undoubtedly true that even the giants have stood on the shoulders of their predecessors and borrowed from their cultural heritage, they have still produced works of remarkable freshness and novelty that opened up great possibilities and new perspectives for others. Can anyone deny the native talent or artistic genius of a Mozart or a Shakespeare? Can we gaze at a VanGogh painting depicting a pair of farm shoes without recognizing that this artist has created a profound and luminous truth out of bare materials in an ingenious way that sets him apart from ordinary artisans? Yet if we accept the claims of Vaidhyanathan (2001) and others, if we insist that the author is no more than a vague "cultural entity" (p. 10), it will not be possible to give true creators like VanGogh their due or to distinguish them from those who simply imitate and appropriate the works of others.

Thus, we conclude that while the critics of strong intellectual property rights have valid concerns, the case against intellectual property rights is unpersuasive for both practical and theoretical reasons. Let us first consider the practical problems. While patents can hurt developing countries, there is another side to this issue. Without those rights, developing countries would not be able to optimize their innovations. In India, for example, biotech entrepreneurs have developed innovative products, but they have not been successful at commercialization. The reason is that Indian patent law does not adequately cover pharmaceuticals, so "the fruits of their costly research are hard to protect from copycats" ("Patents and the Poor," 2001). The world intellectual property system needs revision to deal with biopiracy and clear-cut cases of exploitation, but while new property models are called for, the entire system should not be abandoned. Most developing countries perceive the need for a proper patent system that suits their needs. If configured fairly and managed properly, intellectual property rights can be an opportunity even for developing countries, since they will incentivize key domestic industries and enhance foreign investment ("Patents and the Poor," 2001).

From a theoretical standpoint, it is worth noting that Marx's idealistic philosophy cannot solve the incentive problem. Will people produce great quantities of intellectual work without the incentive of a tangible reward as Marx and his followers presumed? Can they risk investing in creative projects (such as big budget movies or biotech innovations) without the assurance of being able to safeguard their end products from free riders? It is no coincidence that most major innovations come from countries like the U.S. where the market system is strong and the incentive system is so generous. In addition, as we have argued, the notion that there is no discrete author and hence no basis for awarding intellectual property rights is incoherent. In our view, one is on firmer ground in proposing that property rights be moderate and balanced, recognizing the need to reward creative effort in a measured way that avoids impairment of the public domain.

LEGAL INFRASTRUCTURE TO PROTECT INTELLECTUAL PROPERTY RIGHTS IN THE UNITED STATES

To protect the rights and interests of "owners" of intellectual property, including computer software programs and applications, many nations have enacted specific laws and statutes. To some extent, the inspiration for these laws can be found in the normative frameworks. In an allusion to the Lockean paradigm, the U.S. Supreme Court indicated that "the immediate effect of our copyright law is to secure a fair return for an 'author's' creative labor" (*Harper & Row Publishers v. Nation Enterprises*, 1985). In this section, we examine four different types of schemes for protecting intellectual property rights in the U.S.: *copyright law*, *patents*, *trademarks*, and *trade secrets*. We begin with a look at copyright law.

Copyright Protection

The protections covered under U.S. copyright law are often referred to as a "bundle of rights" (Moore, 1997; Warwick, 2004) whose aim is to protect limited monopoly for certain kinds of intellectual objects. Section 106 of the U.S. 1976 Copyright Act (Title 17 of the U.S. Code) defines the set of exclusive rights granted to copyright owners under the law. Copyright holders have the exclusive right to make copies of the work and to produce derivative works, that is, translations into other languages, movies based on the book, and so forth. They also have the exclusive right to make and distribute copies of their works, display their works in public (for example, art works), and perform works in public (musicals, plays, and so forth).

In effect, a copyright is a form of legal protection given to an *author*. The author can be an organization or a corporation (such as Disney) or an individual person. Copyright protection is given to an author for the *expression* of an idea, which can be manifested in a book, poem, musical composition, photograph, dance movement, motion pictures, audiovisual works, or computer software. For a literary or artistic work to be protected under copyright law, it must satisfy three conditions. First, the work must be *original* in the sense that it "owes its origins to the author." Second, it must be *nonfunctional* or non-utilitarian in nature. Functions and processes, including inventions, are protected by patents, and, typically, are not eligible for copyright protection. Third, in order to qualify for a copyright, the work must be *fixed* or expressed concretely in the form of some *tangible medium* such as a book, poem, or musical score. So ideas, concepts, facts, processes, and methods are not, in themselves, protected by copyright law. The distinction between an idea and its expression is not always obvious. As Justice Hand (1930) observed, "Nobody has ever been able to fix that boundary [between idea and expression], and nobody ever can."

A Short History of Copyright Law in the United States

Copyright law in the Anglo-American world generally traces its origins to the Statute of Ann, passed by the English Parliament in 1710. The first copyright law in the United States, enacted in 1790, applied primarily to books, maps, and charts. Later, the law was extended to include newer forms of media such as photography, movies, audio recordings, and so forth. The duration of copyright protection was 14 years with the possibility of renewal for another 14 years.

In 1909, the copyright law was amended to include any "form that could be seen and read visually" by humans. This modification was motivated by a challenge involving a new technology—namely, the player piano. In particular, the change was prompted by a case in 1908 involving a song that was copied onto a perforated piano music roll. Since the musical copy could not be read visually (by humans) from the piano roll, the copy was not considered a violation of the song's copyright. The "machine readable" vs. "human readable" distinction would later have implications for decisions about whether software programs could qualify for copyright protection. Although a program's source code can be read by humans, its "executable code," which "runs" on a computer, cannot. The 1909 Act also extended copyright protection to an initial term of 28 years along with 28 additional years on renewal.

Copyright law was modified once again in 1976. This Act expanded the scope and duration of copyright protection. Any work that could be "fixed in a tangible medium of expression" was eligible for a copyright. At the same time, the 1976 Act codified the idea-expression dichotomy. In addition, copyright's duration became the life of the author plus 50 years for individual authors and 75 years for corporate authors.

Under the 1976 Copyright Act, computer programs still did not clearly satisfy the requirements necessary for making them eligible for copyright protection. The Copyright Act was amended again in 1980, specifically to address the status of software programs. That year, the concept of a literary work was extended to include programs, computers, and databases that "exhibit authorship." A computer program was defined under the U.S. Copyright Act as a "set of statements or instructions to be used directly in a computer in order to bring about certain results." To be granted a copyright for a computer program, however, the author had to show that the program contained an original expression (or original arrangement) of ideas and not simply the ideas themselves.

The Copyright Act of 1976 has since been amended on a number of occasions, primarily to keep pace with significant changes involving digital technology. For example, it was amended in 1984 with the Semiconductor Chip Protection Act. That Act was enacted to protect proprietary rights in semiconductor chips, specifically protecting the design layout of these chips.

There have been many controversies involving the role of copyright protection for computer programs, but the most noteworthy of these concerned the status of the "look and feel" of computer software. Some argued that, in addition to the software code itself, the "look and feel" of a software program — that is, the user interface, which consists of features such as icons and pull-down menus — should also be protected by copyright law. Initially, Lotus Corporation won a copyright infringement suit against Paperback Software International and Borderland International Inc., whose user interfaces included menus and buttons that resembled Lotus' 1-2-3 product. However, this decision was reversed on appeal in 1995. In a somewhat similar case, Apple lost its suit against Microsoft and Hewlett Packard for using features that Apple believed were similar to its icon-based, graphical user interface. In ruling against Apple and Lotus, the courts determined that icons and menus in a computer interface were analogous to buttons on a VCR or to controls on a car.

In 1998, two important amendments were made to the 1976 Copyright Act: the Copyright Term Extension Act (CTEA) and the Digital Millennium Copyright Act (DMCA). Both Acts have been regarded as controversial and both are examined in detail in a later section of this chapter.

Balancing Schemes in Copyright Law: Fair Use and First Sale Principles

Principles have been developed to balance the exclusive controls given to copyright holders against the broader interests of society. Two such principles are *fair use* and *first-sale*. Fair use means that every author or publisher may make limited use of another person's copyrighted work for purposes such as criticism, comment, news reporting, teaching, scholarship, and research. There are four factors that help the court determine fair use: (1) the purpose and character of the use [for example, commercial use weighs against the claim of fair use]; (2) the nature of the copyrighted work [for example, creative works receive more protection than factual ones]; (3) the "amount and substantiality of the portion used" in relation to the work as a whole; and (4) the effects of the use on the market for the work ("fair use, when properly applied, is limited to copying by others which does not materially impair the marketability of the work which is copied" [*Harper & Row v. Nation Enterprises*, 1985]). All of these factors are weighed together and decisions are made on a case-by-case basis.

Thus the fair use principle restricts the total control that the copyright holder would otherwise enjoy. The fair use principle has also been invoked to defend the practice of "reverse engineering." This practice has been very important in the computer industry in particular and in engineering in general, because it allows someone to buy a product for the purpose of taking it apart to see how it works.

Another balancing scheme in copyright law has been the principle of first sale, which applies once the original work has been sold for the first time. At that point, the original owner loses rights over the work of art. For example, once you purchase a copy of a book, audiotape, painting, etc., you are free to transfer (resell, give away, or even destroy) the copy of that work. It is not clear, however, that one can give away software that is licensed for use but not owned, strictly speaking, by a user. Some argue that the fair use and first sale principles are now threatened because of recent legislation such as the Digital Millennium Copyright Act along with growing reliance on technological schemes of protection known as digital rights management. We examine these arguments in detail in a later section of this chapter.

Software Piracy as a Form of Copyright Infringement
When personal computers became widespread in the 1980s, many users discovered how easy it was to copy software programs. Concerns about the amount of unauthorized copying of proprietary software rose as personal computer use proliferated. Some software manufacturers claimed to have lost millions of dollars of potential revenue because of software piracy. On the face of it, these software companies would certainly seem to be justified in their concerns regarding the pirating of proprietary software by individuals and organizations, both nationally and globally. However, some critics have responded by maintaining that claims made by American software manufacturers about the loss of revenue involving the use of pirated software in developing countries are either greatly exaggerated or altogether bogus. They point out, for example, that many people and organizations in developing countries who currently use American software products would not be able to pay the high prices for these products that have been set by American pricing standards. So, in this case, American software companies have not lost any (real) revenues

because their software would not be sold on the open market in most developing countries. And worse yet, these critics argue, individuals and organizations in those nations would not have access to software, if it were not for the unauthorized copies that have become available to them.

Corporations also worry about revenues lost in developed nations, including the United States, through the practice of copying software illegally. Some people believe that a distinction should be drawn between cases in which an individual makes an unauthorized copy of a friend's software program for personal use and practices in which corporations and criminals pirate software in a systematic way for profit. In terms of the economic and social consequences that can result from these two different modes of software piracy, the differences are materially significant. From a moral point of view, however, this factor may not make much of a difference.

Jurisdictional and International Challenges for Copyright Law

The copyright laws and amendments described in this section apply specifically to intellectual property in the United States. However, their implications are global because of the use of American-manufactured software products internationally. One obvious problem, of course, is how to enforce U.S. copyright law, or for that matter any nation's copyright laws, in an international arena. Some international treaties pertaining to intellectual property and copyright have been signed in recent years. For example, the Trade Relationship Aspects of Intellectual Property Standards (TRIPS) agreement implemented requirements from the Berne Convention for the Protection of Literary and Artistic Works. This international agreement is recognized by signatories to the World Intellectual Property Organization (WIPO), and it enunciates minimal standards of legal protection for intellectual property.

Nonetheless, intellectual property laws have been very difficult to enforce not only at the international level, but even within certain countries, such as the U.S., where different states can have different laws affecting the sale of goods and contracts involving goods and services. This has become especially apparent in e-commerce activities, where laws applicable to the sale of goods as well as to contracts involved in those sales, often vary from state to state. Recently, some legislative attempts have been made to improve uniformity across states in the U.S. One attempt has been through the Uniform Commerce Code (UCC), a law aimed at clarifying the rights and obligations of parties to the "sale of goods and contracts" and to the "lease of goods." Two other important pieces of legislation that could also significantly affect contracts are the Uniform Computer and Information Transactions ACT (UCITA) and the

Uniform Electronic Transactions ACT (UETA). Whereas UCITA is designed to govern computer information transactions, UETA applies to electronic contracts in general. We discuss UCITA in greater detail in a later section of this chapter.

Patents

How is patent protection different from the kind of protection granted by copyright law? A patent is a form of legal protection given to individuals who create an invention or process. Patent protection is covered in Title 35 of the U.S. Code. As in the case of copyright law, the basis for patent protection can be found in Article 1, Section 8 of the U.S. Constitution. Unlike copyright protection, patents offer a 20-year exclusive monopoly over an expression or implementation of a protected work. Patent law provides "thicker" protection than copyright protection, but for a shorter period. The first explicit U.S. patent law, the Patent Act of 1793, was passed when Thomas Jefferson was the administrator of the patent system. The present U.S. patent statute is based on the Patent Act of 1952, as amended in 1995.

Patent protection applies to inventions and discoveries that include utilitarian or functional devices such as machines, articles of manufacture, or "compositions of matter." The Patent Act requires three conditions to be satisfied for a patent to be granted. First, an invention must have a certain *usefulness* or utility in order to be awarded a patent. Inventing a machine that does nothing useful would not merit the inventor of such a machine a patent. Second, the invention must be *novel* or new in order to qualify for a patent. One cannot simply modify an existing invention and expect to be given a patent for it. The modification would have to be significant enough to make a "qualified difference." Third, the invention or process must be *non-obvious*. For example, it is possible that no one has yet recorded directions for how to travel from Ithaca, New York to Montreal, Canada, via Columbus, Ohio. However, describing the process for doing this would not satisfy the condition regarding non-obviousness.

Three different kinds of patents have been distinguished: design patents, utility patents, and plant patents. Only the first two of these, however, are of particular interest for computers and computer software. Whereas design patents protect any new, original, and ornamental design for an article of manufacture, utility patents protect any new, useful, and non-obvious process, machine, or article of manufacture. Patent protection provides a firm or individual inventor with the right to exclude others from making, using, or selling or importing the claimed invention for a twenty-year period.

The goal of the patent system's exclusionary, output-restricting monopolies is to reward and stimulate inventive efforts, which often require considerable investment. The presumption is that tight (or "thick") property protection will give the innovator the incentive to invent and provide an environment "conducive to securing the complementary assets, capital, manufacturing, marketing and support" that are necessary in order to bring that invention to the marketplace (Kieff, 2000).

Patenting Computer Programs

While computer hardware inventions clearly satisfied the requirements of patent law, this was not initially the case with computer software. In the 1960s, discussions involving the protection for software focused mainly on patents (Snapper, 1994). However, the U.S. Patent Office and the courts established a strong opposition to patents, beginning with the *Gottschalk v. Benson* (1972) decision. Benson had applied for a patent for an algorithm he developed that translated the representation of numbers from base 10 to base 2. Such an algorithm is an important feature of all programs. If granted a patent for his algorithm, however, Benson would have controlled almost every computer in use for 12 years. The patent was denied to Benson on the basis of a policy that bars the granting of patents for mere mathematical formulas or abstract processes, which are such that they can be performed by a series of "mental steps" with the aid of pencil and paper.

In the controversial court case *Diamond v. Diehr*, whose outcome was the result of a 5-4 decision, a patent was finally awarded in the case of a computer program. In this instance, the program assisted in a process of converting rubber into tires. On the one hand, Diehr had developed a new process that physically transformed raw rubber into rubber tires. On the other hand, it seemed that Diehr had only a new computer program, since all of the parts of the machine used in the conversion process consisted of traditional technology except for the computer program. Initially, Diehr's request for a patent was denied by Diamond, the director of the Patent Office. Diehr appealed, and this case was then taken to the U.S. Supreme Court. Although the Court ruled in favor of Diehr, the justices, in their decision, continued to affirm the view that computer algorithms themselves are not patentable. They pointed out that the patent awarded to Diehr was not for the computer program but for the rubber tire transformation process as a whole.

Since the decision reached in the Diehr case, patents have been granted to computer programs and software applications. Some fear that patent protection has now gone too far. Consider that the U.S. Patent and Trademark Office (PTO) currently issues approximately 20,000 new software patents every year. Aharonian (1999) points out that between 1993 and 1999, the number of patents issued represented a tenfold increase. He also points out that between 1979 and 1999, more than 700,000 patents had been issued for electronics inventions, including software products.

Because of what some critics believe to be an overly generous granting of patent protections in the case of computer programs and user interfaces, many have recently expressed concerns about how far patent protection should be extended in this area. For example, some specific concerns have recently been raised about which kinds of features in the user interfaces should be eligible for patent protection. Should the "look and feel" of the interface or other amorphous features be eligible for protection?

Proliferation of Patents

It should be underscored that the scope of patent protection has been steadily expanding. In addition to software, it is now possible to obtain patents for gene fragments, biological material, and living organisms (see *Diamond v. Chakrabarty*, 447 U.S. 303, 1980). Even mundane "business methods," such as a hub-and-spoke mutual fund accounting system, have become patentable subject matter. These patents have been particularly popular for online businesses. We consider the possible abuse of such patents in the context of reviewing the Amazon.com case in the section on current controversies.

Given the steady growth in the number of patents awarded, it is no surprise that patents have come under increasing criticism in recent years. The patent system's detractors argue that the patent monopoly and the right to exclude gives the patent owner control over price, which normally creates a deadweight loss for society. While these detractors recognize the need for rewards as incentives, they propose other possibilities besides a property right. For example, Shavell and van Ypersele (1999) propose a system of government-sponsored cash payouts as an alternative to awarding patents. According to this system, inventions would immediately become part of the public domain. The amount of the reward would depend on the demand for the innovation as ascertained by its sales or other relevant data. But as Kieff (2000) observes, this reward system runs the risk of neglecting commercialization activities subsequent to the actual invention; these activities include raising capital for production facilities, creating distribution channels, marketing to consumers, and so forth. A limited property right and the exclusivity that it engenders, however, provides the incentive for both the invention and commercialization.

According to Kieff (2000):

The patent right to exclude competitors who have not shared in bearing these initial costs provides incentives for the holder of the invention and the other players in the market to come together and incur all costs necessary to facilitate commercialization of the patented invention. (p.715)

The U.S. patent system is not perfect and there are valid concerns about the expanding scope of patent protection. However, the case for alternatives to the current system that confer a property right of limited duration must adequately deal with critical post-invention issues such as commercialization.

Trademarks

Trademarks are a form of intellectual property protection that differs in key respects from both patents and copyrights. A trademark is a word, name phrase, or symbol that identifies a product or service. The Lanham Act, also referred to as the Trademark Act of 1946, was passed to provide protection for owners of registered trademarks. One purpose of this Act was to help ensure that the quality associated with a certain logo or symbol used by a business actually represents the quality that consumers expect. So for example, when a consumer sees a Mercedes Benz or a BMW emblem, he or she can expect that the product will live up to the standards of the Mercedes Benz or the BMW industry. Some common trademarks in the United States are the golden arch-like "M" that has come to symbolize McDonald's restaurants, and the expression "coke" that symbolizes Coca-Cola. A corporation, or for that matter an individual, can typically acquire a trademark when it either: (a) is the first to use the word or expression publicly, or (b) explicitly registers the trademark with the U.S. Patent Office.

In order to qualify for a trademark, the "mark" or name is supposed to be *distinctive*. However, Halbert (1997) points out that a trademark for "uh-huh" was granted to Pepsi. Because of decisions such as this, Halbert and others have argued that trademark protections are being expanded in ways that are inappropriate and potentially damaging to the market place. A recent example that tends to support such a concern can be found in a case involving America On-Line (AOL), a major Internet Service Provider (ISP). AOL attempted to register as official trademarks a number of its symbols, including the following expressions: "You've Got Mail," "Buddy List," and "IM" (for Instant Messenger). If granted these trademarks, other ISPs who used these expressions could be charged with infringing on AOL's registered trademarks. When AT&T challenged AOL, however, the court decided that the expressions in question were not unique to AOL and thus could not qualify for registration as trademarks.

Trademark Controversies Involving Internet Domain Names

One particularly contentious issue concerning trademark disputes in cyberspace has involved the registering of Internet domain names. A *domain name* is an alphanumeric string of characters that identifies a unique address on the Web. The domain name is included in the address of a Universal Resource Locator (URL), e.g., http://www.usersite.net. The actual domain name itself immediately follows the hypertext transfer protocol (http://) and the Web (www) portions of the URL. Google.com, stanford.edu, and ABC.org are examples of domain names. Before 1998, the registration of domain names in the United States was administered by the National Science Foundation (NSF). This organization set up a network division (NSFNET) to oversee certain aspects of Internet governance. When Congress approved commerce on the Internet in 1992, it charged NSFNET with the task of working with Network Solutions, a private organization, to develop a scheme for determining how domain names would be assigned in the future. In the original NSF system, domain names were typically registered on a first-come, first-served basis. There was neither a clear nor a systematic policy for deciding which domain names one was eligible or ineligible to register. And this practice resulted in some confusion for Web users, especially those who assumed that there would be a correlation between a website's domain name and its corresponding content. However, if a user wished to access the website for the White House (in Washington, DC) via the URL www.whitehouse.com, he or she would connect to a pornographic site (since the White House site is www.whitehouse.gov.).

At first glance, one might assume that the confusion that resulted over Internet domain names was little more than a minor nuisance. From the perspective of property rights and commerce, however, a serious issue arose when certain individuals registered domain names containing key phrases or symbols that were previously registered as legal trademarks in physical space, such as the words "Disney," or "Playboy." One controversial case involved the domain name "candyland." It turned out that the first applicant for the candyland.com domain name was not Hasbro, the toy manufacturer who marketed the Candyland game, but instead was the operator of a pornographic website. Many trademark owners were outraged by the ways in which their registered trademarks were being co-opted and "abused" in cyberspace, and some filed trademark infringement suits against owners and operators of websites whose domain names included symbols identical to their trademarks.

In the early 1990s, there were no explicit laws in place to prevent an individual or an organization from registering a domain name that potentially conflicted with a registered trademark in physical space. Nor was it altogether clear that trademarks registered in physical space necessarily applied to cyberspace. Because there were no laws or policies governing domain name registration, there was also nothing to prevent some individuals and companies from registering as many domain names as they could afford. A few individuals who did this became wealthy when they later sold the rights to their registered domain names to corporations who wished to procure domain names that were either identical to or closely resembled the trademarks they had registered in physical space. However, not all individuals and corporations were willing to pay an exorbitant price for the right to use a domain names, especially since they believed they already had the legal right to own the name by virtue of their registered trademarks in physical space. In the legal disputes that ensued, those who had registered domain names that were either identical to or closely resembled the names of trademarks previously registered in physical space were referred to as "cybersquatters." Many trademark owners argued that these cybersquatters were unfairly using a mark that already had been registered, and they petitioned Congress for legislation to protect their trademarks. In 1999, the Anticybersquatting Consumer Protection Act was passed, which enables trademark holders to file suit against anyone who uses or registers a domain name that is identical to or "confusingly similar" to their trademark.

Arguably, trademark owners had a legitimate concern about the ways in which certain symbols or "marks" with which they had come to be identified by millions of people were now being abused. Among these concerns was the issue of "trademark dilution," where a trademark becomes less effective because of similar sounding marks used by competitors and adversaries. This was especially apparent in a case involving Amazon.com, who claimed that its trademark would be diluted if some variation of the "Amazon" trademark were allowed to be registered by a "bricks-and-mortar" bookstore that had also used the "Amazon" name. Initially, one would assume that Amazon.com would have a good case for registering "Amazon" both as a trademark and a domain name. Before the Amazon.com e-commerce site had been developed, however, a bookstore named Amazon had been operating in Minneapolis, Minnesota. This bookstore was fairly well known to many people who lived in the Minneapolis area. In April 1999, the Amazon bookstore sued Amazon.com for trademark infringement. It is important to note that the "bricks-and-mortar" Amazon bookstore had never formally registered the "Amazon" trademark. However, in the U.S. there is also the concept of a "common law" trademark, which would apply to the physical bookstore as long as the store simply used the "Amazon" mark. Because the Amazon bookstore had not formally applied to register the "Amazon" trademark, it is quite conceivable that Amazon.com was unfamiliar with the existence of this store. Defenders of Amazon.com questioned why the Amazon bookstore waited so long in filing its suit. In litigation involving trademark disputes, "delay in filing a suit" can be a relevant factor in determining the suit's legal outcome.

We should note that the policy for assigning domain names has tightened considerably since 1998, when the Federal Government directed the Commerce Department to supervise the administration of the Domain Name System. The Internet Corporation for Assigned Names and Numbers (ICANN) has since become responsible for assigning and registering domain names. However, ICANN has been criticized for implementing policies that some believe to be heavily biased towards those who owned trademarks previously registered in physical space.

Trade Secrets

Trade secrets as a form of property protection are significantly different from trademarks, patents, and copyrights. A trade secret is usually defined as information used in the operation of a business or other enterprise that is "sufficiently valuable and secret" to afford an actual or potential economic advantage over others. Included in the kind of data that trade secrets can be used to protect are: *formulas* (such as the one used by Coca-Cola), *blueprints* for future projects, *chemical compounds*, and *process of manufacturing*.

Trade secrets are generally recognized as "secrets" on which a company has expended money and energy and that are shown only to a select few major persons within an organization. Owners of a trade secret have exclusive rights to make use of a secret. However, they have this right *only as long* as the secret is maintained.

Many states in the U.S. have adopted the Uniform Trade Secrets Act (UTSA). According to this Act, a trade secret is defined as "information, including a formula, pattern, compilation, program, device, technique, or process" that (1) derives independent economic value from not being generally known to … other persons who can obtain economic value from its disclosure or use, and (2) is the subject that are reasonable under the circumstances to maintain its secrecy.

A major problem with protecting trade secrets is that trade secret law is difficult to enforce at the international level. Not only have corporate spies in the U.S. tried to steal secrets from their corporate rivals, but there is evidence to suggest that international industrial espionage has become a growing "industry." Recently, the world community has acknowledged the need for member states to protect against the disclosure of trade secrets. The Agreement on Trade-Related Aspects of Intellectual Property Rights (TRIPS), which was part of the World Intellectual Property Organization (WIPO) agreements (described in a preceding section), provides a platform for protecting trade secrets at the international level. Specifically, Article 39 of the TRIPS Agreement protects trade secrets by stating explicitly that disclosure of trade secrets "comes within the meaning of unfair competition in the global community."

RECENT LEGISLATION

In the previous section we noted that two recent amendments to United States copyright law, the Copyright Term Extension Act (CTEA) and the Digital Millennium Copyright Act (DMCA), have been highly controversial. In this section, we consider critical aspects of each act in more detail. We also examine recent legislation involving the No Electronic Theft (NET) Act and the Uniform Computer and Information Transactions Act (UCITA), which also have been subject to controversy.

Copyright Term Extension Act (CTEA)

The Copyright Term Extension Act represents the fourth major extension of the duration for copyright protection. This Act, passed by Congress and signed by President Clinton in 1998, maintained the general structure of the 1976 Copyright Act as it expanded the term for copyrights by 20 years. For creative works created by identifiable persons, the term is now 70 years after the author's death. For anonymous works and works "made for hire" (usually commissioned by corporations), the term is now 95 years from publication or 120 years from creation, whichever expires first (17 U.S.C. § 302 (c)).

Critics of the controversial CTEA did not fail to note that the law was passed just in time to keep "Mickey Mouse" from entering the public domain. Many of these critics have also pointed out that the Disney Corporation lobbied very hard for the passage of this act. In a subsequent section we examine a recent case that illustrates one way in which the CTEA threatens the communication of information that once had been in the public domain but is now protected by copyright law. The case (*Eldred v. Ashcroft*) involves Eric

Eldred of Derry, NH, who operated a personal (nonprofit) website on which he included electronic versions of classic books that have been in the public domain. With the passage of the CTEA in 1998, some of the books that were previously included in the public domain and also included on Eldred's site came under copyright protection. So Eldred found himself in violation of the new copyright law. Rather than remove books from his site, however, Eldred decided to challenge the legality of the amended Copyright Act, which he argued is incompatible with the fair-use provision of copyright law and in violation of Article 1, Section 8, Clause 8 of the U.S. Constitution (see above).

At issue is whether or not Congress exceeded its legislative authority as bestowed upon it by the Copyright Clause of the Constitution. Does the CTEA violate the Copyright Clause's "limited Times" restriction? Another concern is whether the CTEA conflicts with First Amendment rights. We will consider these issues in more depth in the next section which treats the *Eldred v. Ashcroft* case.

Digital Millennium Copyright Act (DMCA)

We noted in a previous section of this chapter that the DMCA has been a heavily disputed piece of legislation, particularly because of its "anti-circumvention" clause (1201(a)). This anti-circumvention provision prohibits the circumvention or bypassing of any technological measure (such as encryption mechanisms) that controls access to protected works. The DMCA (1998) also forbids the manufacturing, providing, distributing or otherwise "trafficking in" any software or hardware technology that is designed to facilitate *circumvention* of a protected work (§1201 (a) (2)). While the DMCA prohibits the circumvention of *access* control measures, it does not prohibit the circumvention of *use* control measures. Access controls deter unauthorized access to a protected work, but use controls help prevent unauthorized use. A user might have legitimate access to a work, but a "use control" may limit that user's ability to print or copy that work. Paradoxically, however, it is also forbidden to manufacture, distribute, or traffic in devices that circumvent use control measures (§1201 (c)).

There are exceptions to these provisions. Reverse engineering in order to achieve interoperability is allowed (subject to certain conditions). The DMCA also incorporates an exception for "good faith encryption research" or for security research. The researcher must make every effort to obtain permission from the copyright holder before implementing the circumvention device.

Despite these exceptions, critics have highlighted many problems with the DMCA, such as its implicit subversion of the fair-use exemption. The DMCA makes it virtually impossible to circumvent encryption measures for fair use of protected works. For example, it threatens our ability to use electronic books in many of the same ways that we have been able to use physical books. Consider the case involving Dimitri Sklyarov. While working for a Moscow-based company called ElcomSoft, Sklyarov had written a program that was able to decrypt the code for an electronic book reader ("e-book reader") developed by Adobe, an American-base software company. Adobe's Acrobat e-Reader product was designed so that computer users could read digital books. Adobe was very concerned that with Sklyarov's program, users would be able to read e-books for free.

The United States Government was eager to test the DMCA, especially the Act's anti-circumvention clause. Although the Act was passed in 1998, it was not enforceable as a law until 2000. So the Sklyarov incident in the summer of 2001 provided an opportune time for law officials to prosecute a case under the provisions of the DMCA. When Sklyarov attended a computer security conference in Las Vegas, Nevada in July 2001, he was arrested by federal authorities who immediately seized his briefcase containing the controversial program. Sklyarov's arrest sparked considerable controversy and protest, especially among software engineers who realized, perhaps more than most ordinary users, the significance of the controversy at issue. A "Free Sklyarov" movement developed on the part of some protesters. Even some conservatives, who tend to be proponents of strong copyright protection, believe that the DMCA may have gone too far. While many protesters in the Sklyarov case believed that Adobe had a legitimate concern, they were also troubled by the fact that the principle of fair use was being technologically undermined by Adobe and legally undermined by the DMCA.

Some critics also pointed out the DMCA violates the principle of first sale, another element in the balancing scheme embodied in current copyright law. These critics correctly pointed out that in the case of a physical (paper and glue) book, one could do whatever one wishes after purchasing it. For example, one could lend the book or parts of the book to a friend. Also, one could make a photocopy of a chapter in that book. And, finally, one could resell that book in compliance with the first-sale principle provided under copyright law. In the case of e-books, however, one does not have the right to sell or even to give away the digital book because of the kind of protection granted to copyright holders of digital media under the DMCA. Adobe eventually dropped its charges against Sklyarov. However, most critics believe that the fundamental principles underlying the Sklyarov incident have not yet been challenged and ultimately will need to be resolved through future litigation.

The No Electronic Theft (NET) Act

The NET (No Electronic Theft) Act makes the dissemination of copy-righted information by electronic means a criminal act. In other words, it criminalizes behavior involving the distribution of copyrighted material, which traditionally could only be contested in a civil court. This Act was passed, in part at least, in response to an incident involving MIT student Robert LaMacchia who had facilitated the distribution of copyrighted software over an electronic bulletin board system in the Spring of 1994. When authorities tried to prosecute LaMacchia, they found that they were unable to do so because no explicit laws existed that made the unauthorized distribution of copyright material over a computer network a criminal act.

Prior to the NET Act, a person had to "infringe a copyright willfully and for purposes of commercial or financial gain" in order to be punished under the criminal provisions of the Copyright Act. The NET Act, however, has made criminal the "reproduction or distribution, including by electronic means...of one or more copies or phonorecords of one or more copyrighted works, which have a total retail value of more than $1,000." Grosso (2000) believes that the meaning of "copyright infringement" has been expanded under this act. For example, he points out that in addition to a copyright infringement occurring in "fixation" (in print or paper), an infringement can now occur in virtual space as well. In other words, a possible infringement can occur by means of a mere electronic distribution, regardless of whether that work is ever printed on paper or downloaded onto a diskette or CD. According to the NET Act, the mere viewing of a copyrighted work posted on the Internet can be interpreted as a violation of copyright that is criminal. In one possible interpretation, a "fixation" occurs in online viewing, because a temporary copy is "fixed" in the memory (i.e., in RAM) of the host computer, no matter how briefly the information may be stored. While many agree with the spirit of the Net Act, others believe that it goes too far.

UCITA

Earlier in this chapter we noted that in the United States, the various states have different laws affecting the contracts that govern the sale of goods and services. Electronic commerce and software licenses have been directly affected by this lack of uniformity. We also noted that recently some legislative attempts, such as UCITA (the Uniform Computer and Information Transactions Act), have been designed to improve uniformity across states and to govern computer/information transactions, including contracts for the development, sale, licensing, maintenance, and support of computer software. This Act, which extends to all shrink-wrap and "click-wrap" agreements, is an attempt to develop a single national framework that would help states address issues such as warranties and software licenses. For example, the law would turn the consumer license that comes with shrink-wrapped software into a binding contract.

To date, UCITA has been enacted into law only in the states of Virginia and Maryland. Even though UCITA is not law in most states, its effects can be felt in all states because contracts involving electronic goods and services can span multiple states and thus potentially involve Virginia and Maryland law in the process. Although there is general agreement that a uniform law across states pertaining to electronic contracts would be desirable, many worry about the effects that universal passage of the current version of UCITA would have for consumers in the United States.

UCITA's critics are concerned that the further enactment of this law by additional state legislatures will have negative consequences for consumers and for the general public. Thus far, UCITA has been criticized by the Software Engineering Ethics Research Institute and the American Library Association, as well as by many consumer advocacy groups. Many critics believe that this act overreaches because it would (a) give software vendors the right to repossess software by disabling it remotely if the vendor perceived a violation of the licensing agreement, and (b) prevent the transfer of licenses from one party to another without vendor permission. Some critics also worry that UCITA would undermine existing consumer protection laws and would threaten current copyright exceptions for the principles of fair use and first sale (Tavani, 2004).

UCITA's defenders, however, which include companies such as Microsoft and AOL, have lobbied hard on behalf of UCITA. They have tried to persuade lawmakers that UCITA would be good for e-commerce and would create more jobs, especially in the computer industry. Critics, however, believe that these companies simply want increased control over the products they license — controls that UCITA's opponents argue would further ensure that these products cannot be passed along from one party to another without vendor approval. Other critics of UTICA point to a certain irony by noting that at the same time software vendors argue for the need for greater control over the licensing of their products, they have lobbied for the right to be exempt from responsibility and liability for those products.

DIGITAL RIGHTS MANAGEMENT AND TRUSTED PLATFORMS

Intellectual property can be protected by other means than the law. There are the community's social norms that inhibit copying another's original work. And there is what Lessig (1999) calls "code." In this context, code refers primarily to software programs (such as an encryption mechanism) that limit access and use of a protected work. It is instructive to consider the implications of the more widespread diffusion of these software architectures.

DRM Technology

Copyright and patent law may be difficult to enforce especially in cyberspace, but a code-based solution has the potential to be a more powerful substitute for the law. The content industry believes that Digital Rights Management (DRM) systems can be an important tool for preventing copyright infringement by imposing restrictive rules on end users.

As noted earlier, the music and movie industries need new business models since their traditional way of doing business has been disrupted by digital technology. Effective DRM will enable those new models by allowing digital content to be sold and distributed on a more secure basis. DRM encompasses a range of technologies that will give content providers varying degrees of control over how content will be accessed and utilized. At a most basic level, DRM will prevent access to creative works, usually by means of encryption. Access is enabled for legitimate users through the use of passwords or similar mechanisms.

Thus, DRM can lock up content and prevent unauthorized access. It can also control how that content is used once it is legitimately accessed. DRM systems can embed rules that restrict the user's ability to copy that content and to transmit it to someone else. For example, a DRM technology might be configured so that it allows a user to make only a single copy of a CD. Or in the case of digital books, it may allow viewing of the book but forbid printing and transmission to another user. According to McSwain (1999), DRM (or "trusted") systems perform two basic functions: first, these systems make sure that the content is maintained "in a secure 'container,' either hardware or software, which performs encryption and decryption on the digital software"; and second, this container "stores precise instructions detailing which uses to permit, which uses to deny, and how much to charge for each, thereby 'managing' the rights relationship between the user and content provider."

A DRM application can run on an ordinary operating system such as Windows or Macintosh, but it's also possible to incorporate this functionality directly into the operating system itself. In 2002, Microsoft announced that it was working on a new operating system known as Palladium, a trusted computer platform that provides a secure environment for other applications. A machine running an OS such as Palladium would obey instructions of the programs that forward data to this machine. If an online music store sends a song with an instruction "play this one time," the Palladium OS would ensure that this command was automatically followed.

DRM technology can work hand-in-hand with the Digital Millennium Copyright Act, which bans circumvention of access controls along with the production of technologies that facilitate circumvention. Since all code is prone to attacks by hackers, the DMCA serves as a legal fallback in case DRM code is penetrated. Those who dare to bypass these DRM controls will run afoul of § 1201 of the DMCA, which gives victims the opportunity to sue for damages and to seek injunctive relief.

Standardizing DRM Controls

A universal DRM standard for computers systems can emerge in one of several ways. In one scenario, the PC industry and its complementors (for example, the content providers) could simply agree on the adoption of a single de facto standard. This process took place in the late 1990s when the movie industry settled on Content Scrambling System (CSS) as a standard for DVDs and DVD players. Encrypted DVDs could only be played on CSS-compliant machines. If this type of industry consensus fails to occur, it's possible that federal legislation will be enacted to demand the implementation of a standard DRM technology.

If there are multiple versions of DRM technology, the end result will be consumer confusion and chaos. Thus, agreeing upon or mandating a standard for DRM would undoubtedly overcome this chaos and hasten its acceptance. One U.S. senator has proposed the Consumer Broadband and Digital Television Promotion Act that would require the relevant industries to reach such a standard. That bill would also require digital media devices to include DRM architecture. Under this law, failure to make a digital media device without DRM would constitute a felony (Samuelson, 2003).

But without government intervention, a de facto standard could still quickly emerge, given the potential for significant network effects. Manufacturers of DVD and similar equipment will have a big incentive to make their systems compliant with the emerging standard, or they may find themselves excluded from major content markets. Once the content and entertainment equipment industries begin "tipping" toward such a standard, it will rapidly dominate the marketplace as more and more companies rush to adopt that standard.

Critical Concerns

Despite the fact that DRMs will undoubtedly be susceptible to counter-measures, this scheme for automation of copyright enforcement is unsettling. For one thing, "DRM permits content owners to exercise far more control over uses of copyrighted works than copyright law provides" (Samuelson, 2003). For example, DRM systems prohibit access even for fair use purposes.

One way to resolve this problem is to construct DRMs that incorporate provisions such as fair use. The legal conception of fair use, however, is fuzzy and open to subjective interpretation. Hence it will be difficult to develop mathematical models that will allow for fair-use exceptions to protected works. However, despite the vagueness of fair use, it may be possible to develop a subset of fair-use possibilities that can be embedded in DRM code, such as allowing for the creation of single copy of a digital work expressly for personal use. Fox and LaMacchia (2003) explain that this set of "always available" licenses (that is, fair-use rights expressed in a policy language) becomes "the first safe harbor for DRM implementers."

In addition, some DRM technologies are designed to report back to content providers, especially in pay-per-use contexts. Other systems might be set up to collect data regarding user preferences for content provided. There is some danger, therefore, that DRM could threaten privacy rights by invading a user's private space and recording his or her intellectual interests.

Finally, some economists contend that DRM technology could potentially harm innovation. These economists maintain that a considerable amount of innovation comes from the users themselves, who will be less able to experiment on a trusted platform. Thus, user-based innovation is apt to be curtailed if software usage is restricted and monitored after the software has been purchased.

CONTROVERSIAL ISSUES AND LEGAL CASES

We have so far considered normative theories defending property rights along with theoretical questions about the moral viability of these rights which, for some scholars, threaten the intellectual commons. We have also reviewed the legal infrastructure, recent legislation, and new technologies designed to safeguard those rights. We turn now to the more practical dimensions of intellectual property issues.

The commercialization of the Internet along with challenges to recent legislation have led to a number of important legal cases regarding intellectual property protection. In this section we will review some of the more significant cases and thereby highlight several major current controversies.

Napster and Peer to Peer Networks

The meteoric rise of digital music has been made possible by a standard known as MP3, an audio-compression format that creates near-CD-quality files that are as much as 20 times smaller than the files on a standard music CD. Thanks to MP3, digital music can now be accessed and transmitted over the Web without the need of a physical container such as a compact disk.

Napster was one of the first companies to take advantage of this new distribution method. This software, created by a young college student, functioned by allowing a Napster user to access the computer systems of other Napster users to search for a particular piece of music as long as they had installed Napster's free file-sharing software. Once that music was located, it could be downloaded directly from that system in MP3 format and stored on the user's hard drive. Napster did not store or "cache" any digital music files on its own servers, and it was not involved in any copying of music files. Napster's role was confined to the maintenance of a central directory of the shareable music available among all Napster users.

In December 1999, the Recording Industry Association of America (RIAA) claimed that Napster was culpable of secondary liability for all of the copyright violations taking place on its system. Secondary liability refers to liability for acts of copyright infringement performed by another person. It can encompass contributory liability, which occurs when one party encourages or assists the infringement of another party, and vicarious liability, which occurs when one party has the ability to control the infringer's activities and enjoys direct financial benefits as a result of those activities.

The RIAA sued Napster for both vicarious and contributory copyright infringement, demanding $100,000 each time a copyrighted song was downloaded by a Napster user. In the summer of 2000, a federal district court granted the RIAA's request for a preliminary injunction ordering the company to shut down its file-sharing service. But two days later the U.S. Court of

Appeals for the Ninth Circuit stayed the injunction so that Napster could have its day in court.

At trial, the plaintiffs argued that a majority of Napster users were downloading and uploading copyrighted music and that these actions constituted direct infringement of the musical recordings owned by the plaintiffs. And since Napster users were culpable of direct copyright infringement, Napster itself was liable for contributory copyright infringement, that is, for materially contributing to the direct infringement.

In its defense, Napster presented several key arguments, invoking the protection of the 1998 Digital Millennium Copyright Act (DMCA), which provides a "safe harbor" for Internet Service Providers (or search engines) against liability for copyright infringement committed by their customers (§ 512). Napster also argued that its users often downloaded MP3 files to sample their contents before making a decision about whether or not to make a CD purchase. Napster cited the precedent of *Universal City Studios* v. *Sony Corp. of America* (1979) litigation. In that case, Universal had sued VCR manufacturer Sony for copyright infringement, but the Supreme Court ruled in favor of the defendant, reasoning that a VCR is capable of substantial noninfringing uses and that its manufacturers should therefore be immune from secondary liability when infringement does occur. One such noninfringing use would be "time-shifting," that is, taping a movie or television show so that it could be viewed at a different time. Thus, manufacturers of "staple articles of commerce" (like VCRs) that have "commercially significant noninfringing uses" cannot be held liable for contributory infringement just because they have general knowledge that some of the purchasers of that equipment might use it to make unauthorized copies of copyrighted material. Napster analogized itself to a VCR—since Napster could also be used for noninfringing purposes (e.g., downloading non-copyrighted music), the company should be immune from liability when its users infringe copyrights.

But in the end, all of these arguments were to no avail. Napster's lawyers failed to persuade the U.S. Court of Appeals for the Ninth Circuit, which found that "the district court did not err; Napster, by its conduct, knowingly encourages and assists the infringement of plaintiffs' copyrights" (*A&M Records, Inc. v. Napster*, 2001).

The demise of Napster, however, did little to impede the rapid growth of file sharing as the Napster service was replaced by true peer-to-peer (P2P) networks. Unlike server-based technology, with peer-to-peer software such as KaZaA, any computer in the network can function as the distribution point. In this way, one central server is not inundated with requests from multiple clients. P2P systems, therefore, enable communications among individual personal computers relying on the Internet infrastructure. For example, a user can prompt his or her personal computer to ask other PCs in a peer-to-peer network if they have a certain digital file. That request is passed along from computer to computer within the network until the file is located and a copy is sent along to the requester's system.

Thus, peer-to-peer networks differ from Napster technology in several salient respects. There is no central server that maintains a list of files that users can download. In addition, these networks allow for the exchange of a wide range of material in addition to MP3 music files, including movie files, books and other text files, and even photographs. This fact has been seized upon by defenders of P2P who insist that its proprietors should be protected by the Sony ruling, since these networks are capable of significant noninfringing uses.

KaZaA is the most popular music sharing software with approximately 275 million users (as of September 2003) and about three million new users added each week (Delaney, 2003). The software was created under the leadership of Niklas Zennstrom who cofounded a Dutch company called KaZaA, BV in order to distribute the KaZaA software. Zennstrom sold the software to Sharman Networks (located on a South Pacific island called Vanuatu) in early 2002, partly out of concern over impending lawsuits. Sharman's servers are in Denmark and its employees are contracted through an Australian company called LEF.

KaZaA, BV was sued in a Netherlands court for contributory copyright infringement. In the U.S., liability for contributory infringement can be imposed on anyone who "with knowledge of the infringing activity, induces, causes, or materially contributes to the infringing conduct" of the guilty party (*Gershwin Publishing v. Columbia Artists Mgmt*, 1971). KaZaA, BV lost the first round of the case, but in March 2002, a Netherlands court of appeals overturned the lower court ruling and held that KaZaA should not be held liable for the unlawful acts of those who use its software. According to the Amsterdam Appellate Court (2002),

The KaZaA application does not depend on any intervention by KaZaA, BV. The program is expanded and functions even better by means of the services provided by KaZaA plus it can be better controlled that way. These services, however, are not necessary for the locating and exchanging of files. . . With the present state of standardization, it is not possible to technically detect which files are copyrighted and which are not. Thus,

it is not possible for KaZaA (or any other software) to incorporate a
blockage against the unlawful exchange of files.

This ruling seems generally consistent with the U.S. *Sony* decision, which appears to immunize the manufacture and distribution of technologies like P2P networks for which there are substantial noninfringing uses.

In addition, in the United States, the music and movie industries have also filed suit against Grokster and StreamCast for contributory and vicarious copyright infringement. Grokster uses the FastTrack networking technology that it has licensed from KaZaA, and StreamCast uses a variation of the Gnutella P2P network. The plaintiffs (which include MGM, Disney, Universal City Studios, Warner Music, Motown Records, Arista Records, et al.) contended that both of these networks were employed for the purpose of swapping copyrighted music and movie files: "90% of the works available on the FastTrack network demonstrably were infringing, and over 70% belonged to Plaintiffs" (Plaintiffs' Joint Excerpts of Record, 2003). The plaintiffs lost the first round of this case when a California district court granted the defendants' motion for summary judgment. The case has been appealed to the Ninth Circuit and a decision is pending.

At issue in this case is the applicability of previous rulings in the Napster and Sony cases. The defendants argue that the Sony precedent works strongly in their favor; i.e., they are immunized from liability since they are simply providing a "staple article of commerce." In *Sony v. Universal* (1984), the Supreme Court had concluded that a judgement in favor of Universal would give copyright holders some measure of control over non-copyright markets: "It seems extraordinary to suggest that the Copyright Act confers upon all copyright owners collectively, much less the two respondents in this case, the exclusive right to distribute [VCRs] simply because they may be used to infringe copyrights."

It is instructive to review why the *Sony* standard did not rescue Napster from secondary liability. The District Court ruled that Napster could not be construed as a "staple article of commerce" because of Napster's ongoing relationship with its users. According to the Court, "Napster's primary role of facilitating the unauthorized copying and distribution [of] established artists' songs renders *Sony* inapplicable" (*A&M Records v. Napster*, 2000). The Ninth Circuit, however, was not so quick to dismiss the *Sony* precedent: "The *Sony* Court declined to impute the requisite level of knowledge where the defendants made and sold equipment capable of both infringing and 'substantial noninfringing uses' ... We are bound to follow *Sony* and will not impute the requisite level of knowledge to Napster merely because peer-to-peer file-sharing technology may be used to infringe plaintiffs' copyrights" (*A&M Records v. Napster*, 2001). However, since Napster had actual notice of infringing activities and made no effort to prevent those activities, the Ninth Circuit found that this rule for "imputing knowledge" did not apply.

One critical question for the *Grokster* case is the applicability of the *Sony* case. In an Amici Curiae Brief, forty law professors argued that the standard set by the Sony case should immunize from secondary liability those who develop technologies that have the capability for substantial noninfringing uses. They argue for the soundness of this "mere capability rule," since it accommodates the fact that uses of a technology "may evolve significantly over time" (Amici Curiae Brief, 2003). According to this simple rule, if the technology has or is capable of having substantial noninfringing uses, there should be no secondary liability regardless of what the purveyor of that technology knows or should have known about infringing uses of that technology. The Brief goes on to criticize the Napster decision because the Ninth Circuit made the mistake of "subordinat[ing] the substantial noninfringing use requirement to the knowledge requirement," and it urges that the courts separate "the substantial noninfringing use inquiry" from the "knowledge inquiry." One can infer that the presence of substantial noninfringing use should not be trumped by the knowledge of current infringement on the part of the technology provider.

This Brief, however, fails to consider some of the unresolved issues that linger from the *Sony* decision and make it a problematic standard. How should we define a "staple article of commerce"? Does it only apply to sales of physical equipment such as VCRs or DVD players? Can we be so sure that the court intended to include in this category software programs such as Napster and peer-to-peer programs such as KaZaA? What level of noninfringing use is enough to qualify as "substantial?" (see Dogan, 2001).

The vagueness of the *Sony* standard also manifests itself in other aspects of this ruling. For example, according to the Amici Curiae Brief, if a technology is merely *capable* of substantial noninfringing uses, it passes the *Sony* test, which virtually immunizes purveyors of that technology from liability for copyright infringement. But what if a technology is being used predominantly or perhaps even exclusively for infringement, yet it is recognized that the technology has the capability for noninfringing use on a significant scale in the future? Given the plasticity of computer software, it would not be hard to envision such a use for almost any single technology. That technology may *never* in fact be used in a noninfringing way by a substantial number of people, but as long as the possibility for such use is present, it passes the *Sony* test. Can we really predict how technology will be used and differentiate between hypothetical uses and ones that are likely to occur on a significant scale? This reasoning would have us prescind from *actuality,* the present use of this technology, and focus instead on nebulous potentialities, that is, the *possible* noninfringing uses for future adopters of this technology and how substantial such uses are apt to be. In this case, those who argue against the plaintiffs contend that the *Sony* precedent cannot be ignored, and, as a consequence, the fact that 90% of the files available on the FastTrack network are copyrighted should be overlooked. Should the fact that there is minimal noninfringing use with the potential for an increase in the future immunize the defendants from dealing with a massive level of current infringing use? If this is so, any purveyor of technology will be able to promote piracy unencumbered by law as long as it can point to the possibility of some substantial noninfringing use at some future time.

In addition, there are certainly some asymmetries between *Sony* and *Grokster.* In the latter case, the Plaintiffs are not trying to undermine peer-to-peer technology; they are merely seeking to deter the infringing uses of that technology. Deterring infringement on these networks does not necessarily imply that the networks will be shut down, only that they will be used for legitimate purposes. Even Napster has not disappeared but has reinvented itself as a law-abiding service providing access to music tracks by charging a fee for each download. Moreover, in *Sony* (1984), the "only contact between Sony and [its] users ... occurred at the moment of sale," but developers of peer-to-peer networks maintain a more ongoing relationship with users. This relationship does not enjoy the same level of proximity as the relationship between Napster and its users, but it is far more than merely incidental. First-time users on FastTrack must register and provide a username and password. That username and password is checked in every subsequent login so that servers can block access to unregistered users or to users who have violated the rules. Also, as soon as the user logs in, the software sends to an index the list of digital files on the user's computer that are available for downloading by other FastTrack users. And Grokster continues to interact with users after they have installed this software by sending messages about software upgrades and by disseminating ads and other web content that users encounter when they exchange files. Grokster also reserves the right to terminate users and to block files that contain viruses or "bogus" content.

This ongoing relationship is much different from the onetime, mediated relationship established when a customer makes a purchase of a Sony VCR from one of many retail stores where these products are sold. It is worth noting that in similar cases the court has concluded that *Sony* is inapplicable when the defendant "went far beyond merely selling" a staple article of commerce (*A&M Records, Inc. v. Abdallah*, 1996).

The District Court acknowledged that the defendants "clearly know that many if not most of [their users] who download their software subsequently use it to infringe copyrights" (*Metro-Goldwyn-Mayer Studios, Inc. v. Grokster*, 2003). The court ruled that the defendants' liability hinges on actual knowledge of specific infringing acts occurring at a time when the infringement can be deterred. Plaintiffs contend, however, that this standard raises the bar too high, since it precludes from liability a wide range of conduct that facilitates and even encourages infringement. Moreover, in the Napster decision no such evidence of specific knowledge was required.

Space constraints prevent us from considering many other nuances of this complicated case. Our key concern has been trying to find the right standard for secondary (i.e., contributory and vicarious) liability in a dynamic networked environment. Should we follow the *Sony* precedent and drop or mitigate the knowledge requirement for these technologies with substantial noninfringing uses? If not, how specific does knowledge have to be and does one need to know about infringement *ex ante*? We tend to agree that the district court in this case has raised the bar too high. If Grokster and StreamCast know that 90% of the file sharing on their respective networks involves copyrighted files, if the magnitude (in terms of lost revenues) is material enough, there is at the very least a firm moral obligation to take action and prevent continuance of harm to the music and recording industries. Such action might require reconfiguring the architecture of these networks so they can block the sharing of infringing material once the network provider has been informed by the copyright holder of the impermissible sharing. As mentioned, these networks already block certain files (such as those that contain pornography or viruses), so they have the general capability to block infringing content.

Before concluding this discussion of peer-to-peer networks, we should reiterate that the legality of sharing copyrighted material over these networks is still a murky area. Some forms of file sharing that are "noncommercial" and do not harm the potential market for the work being shared would most likely constitute fair use. On the other hand, there is a strong case to be made that placing a large quantity of music or movie files on one's computer system for many others to copy (via a P2P network) is tantamount to direct copyright infringement. The music and movie industries have made this assumption, and they are most likely on solid legal ground. Certainly, rulings in relevant cases would tend to confirm that assumption: "[d]efendants ... apparently believe that the ongoing, massive, and unauthorized distribution and copying of Plaintiffs' copyrighted works by Aimster's end users somehow constitutes 'personal use'; this contention is specious" (*In re Aimster Copyright Litigation*, 2002).

But even if peer-to-peer file sharing on this scale were perfectly legal, it would still be morally problematic. From a normative standpoint, the sharing of a large volume of these files to people all over the Internet is difficult to justify, since the creators and producers of movies, music, and other copyrighted material are not being compensated for their creative efforts. As we have observed, the design of these networks is especially troublesome, since once a user downloads a file onto his or her computer, that file is made available for other users in a widening cycle of viral distribution. Given the harm to creators caused by this rampant copying, it is difficult to absolve those engaged in this level of file sharing of any moral culpability.

Property Disputes over Cyberpatents

As observed above, the scope of patent protection has been steadily expanding, leading some legal analysts to justifiably complain about dense "patent thickets" (Shapiro, 2001). In one benchmark patent case, *State Street Bank & Trust Co. v. Signature Financial Group* (1998), the court ruled in favor of business method patents. In that case, the U.S. Court of Appeals for the Federal Circuit ruled that an innovation or invention was patentable as long as it achieves "a useful, concrete and tangible result," even if such a result amounts to no more than a "the transformation of data." Thus, patent protection for new systems or methodologies for conducting business were now possible. This opened the floodgates for many new patents, especially in cyberspace where new methods of online business were being devised in this unfamiliar terrain. These patents became known as *cyberpatents*.

One such patent that has been particularly controversial was granted for Amazon's "one-click" ordering system, which was introduced by Amazon.com in September 1997. As the name connotes, one-click ordering enables a consumer to complete a transaction over an electronic network by utilizing only a "single action." Amazon.com, the leading purveyor of online books, videos, music, and many other products, developed this model to improve upon its shopping-cart model of making online purchases whereby users would add items to the virtual shopping cart, proceed to a checkout screen, fill in (or check) billing and credit card information, and then click to execute the order. The one-click system reduces these final steps to one step after the user has selected the items for purchase. The user, of course, must have previously visited the Amazon site in order to provide necessary shipping and credit card data.

Shortly after Amazon introduced one-click, Barnes & Noble (BN), Amazon's main competitor in the online book business, followed suit with its own expedited ordering system known as "Express Lane." Like Amazon's model, only one single action needs to be taken in order for the consumer to complete his or her order.

Amazon immediately took Barnes & Noble to court and sought a preliminary injunction preventing the bookseller from using this Express Lane functionality since it was in violation of Amazon's patent. Barnes & Noble claimed that there were serious questions about the validity of the Amazon patent, and it argued that the injunction was not warranted since there was not a reasonable likelihood of Amazon's success based on the merits of its case. But to the surprise of many in the industry, the U.S. District Court for the Western District of Washington granted the preliminary injunction sought by Amazon. As a result, Barnes & Noble was forced to add a second step to its checkout process in order to preserve the Express Lane feature, pending the outcome of the trial.

There was considerable backlash against Amazon, but the company persisted in defending business-method patents. According to one unsympathetic account of the one-click patent: "When 21st Century historians look back at the breakdown of the United States patent system, they will see a turning point in the case of Jeff Bezos and Amazon.com and their special invention" (Gleick, 2000).

Barnes & Noble immediately appealed this ruling, and the Federal Circuit concluded in February 2001 that Barnes & Noble had indeed raised substantial questions concerning the validity of the Amazon patent. One-click may not have the requisite novelty to qualify for a patent. According to the Court, "When the heft of the asserted prior art is assessed in light of the correct legal standards, we conclude that BN has mounted a serious challenge to the validity of Amazon's patent" (*Amazon.com v. Barnesandnoble.com*, 2001). Consequently, it vacated the injunction and it remanded the case for trial to U.S. District Court. One year later, the parties settled the case out of court with a confidential agreement. However, the Barnes & Noble Express Lane option still requires two clicks instead of one.

The obvious question raised by this case is the validity of cyberpatents. Do companies like Amazon.com truly deserve patent protection for developing business methods like the "one-click" system? The normative frameworks considered above might be of some assistance in addressing this question. First, it is unlikely that the development of these minor innovations would entail a substantial investment of labor and money. Developing this sort of software innovation takes a fraction of the time required to build a full software application or an operating system, which do deserve some type of intellectual property protection. The Lockean rationale, therefore, is not so strong in this case. Second, companies are probably inclined to make this type of incremental service improvement without the stimulus of a patent, as they strive to provide better service to their customers in a competitive marketplace. Consequently, it is hard to argue that such patent protection is necessary on utilitarian grounds. Third, when considered from the Hegelian perspective, it seems hard to claim that this simple new methodology is imbued with the "personhood" or personality of its creator(s). The theories strongly suggest the invalidity of such patents from a purely normative viewpoint. Cyberpatents represent a form of overprotection, and if possible, the law should be swiftly modified so that minor innovations like "one-click" are no longer patentable.

Copyright Extension

Eldred v. Ashcroft

This case was a challenge to the 20-year copyright term extensions enabled by the CTEA. The CTEA was relatively uncontroversial when it unanimously passed the Senate, but its nullification has become a *cause celebre* for some legal activists, who saw the Eldred case as an opportunity to challenge this law on constitutional grounds.

The main petitioners were Eric Eldred, founder of Eldritch Press, and Dover Publications, which both publish works in the public domain. Eldred had set up a website (www.eldritchpress.org) for online versions of classic books so that individuals interested in accessing these kinds of books could avoid the frustration that he experienced in helping his daughters locate some older and out-of-print books for a high school literature project. Among the works included on his site are the complete works of Nathaniel Hawthorne. It was perfectly legal for Eldred to include these books on his site because their copyright protection had expired or they had always been in the public domain. With the passage of the CTEA in 1998, some of the books that were previously included in the public domain and also included on Eldred's site came under copyright protection and their inclusion on that site was in violation of the law.

The main argument of these plaintiffs was that the CTEA hurts individuals and corporations who leverage works in the public domain. Popular culture itself also depends heavily on a public domain that is being renewed with new creative works for others to fully draw upon as source material. Eugene O'Neill's great play, *Morning Becomes Elektra*, would have been impossible without the inspiration of *The Oresteia* written by the Greek playwright, Aeschylus. And Disney, which advocated passage of the CTEA, has benefited immensely from works in the public domain such as Hans Christian Andersen's *Little Mermaid*. Without a natural flow of enhancements to the public domain, certain types of future creativity is impaired, since works like this fairy tale cannot become the basis for new creative projects.

The case was first heard by the U.S. District Court for the District of Columbia which ruled in favor of the defendant, the U.S. Government. The case was then appealed to the D.C. Circuit Court and this court also ruled that the 20-year extension did not exceed Congress's power. Finally, appeal was made to the U.S. Supreme Court, and in early 2003 that court also upheld the 20-year extension. The Court reasoned that the CTEA "complies with the limited Times prescription" and that it "[is] not at liberty to second-guess Congressional determinations and policy judgments of this order, however debatable or arguably unwise they may be" (*Eldred v. Ashcroft,* 2003).

It may be that, based purely on the law, the Supreme Court's 7-2 decision represents a reasonable resolution of this case. Congress apparently has the prerogative to extend copyright protection, and, although the duration is excessive, the term is still "limited." One wonders, however, where is the breaking point to this authority to extend copyright duration in accordance with the "limited Times" restriction? In addition, even if the CTEA is not unconstitutional and the extension is within the authority of Congress, this law is bad policy. When one examines the CTEA through the lens of intellectual property theory, its justification is dubious. The current term seems like an ample reward for one's work, and utilitarian reasoning is unlikely to yield positive arguments on behalf of the CTEA. It is difficult to argue that this retrospective increase in copyright protection will provide a further inducement to creativity and innovation. According to one Court decision, "[a] grant of copyright protection after the author's death to an entity not itself responsible for creating the work provides scant incentive for future creative endeavors" (*United Christian Scientists v. Christian Science Board of Directors,* 1987). Further, the weakening of the public domain by delaying the introduction of creative works for a 20-year period seems to far outweigh any of the meager incentives engendered by this law. Arguably, the Hegelian personality theory also does not seem to warrant this extension. Individuals surrender property when they die and no longer require it for the exercise of freedom. There may be other reasons why we want property rights to extend beyond someone's death, but this theory intimates that intellectual property rights are only essential for free, living beings. A creator who has objectified himself or herself has no reason to expect the ability to control that objectification beyond death.

The CTEA, therefore, is an unambiguous example of Congress's failure to discern the proper level of intellectual property protection, since this law overprotects property and is not in the public interest. This legislation appears to be the result of capture by the entertainment industry's most powerful players, such as Disney. Some have called it a "hijacking of technology policy by lobbyists" ("Free Mickey Mouse," 2002). As a result, this copyright extension should be repudiated by Congress.

Challenging the DMCA

Universal City Studios v. Corley

The next controversy for consideration involves a major challenge to the DMCA, which thus far has been resolved in favor of the content and entertainment industries. This case involves the encryption system used to protect DVDs from illicit copying. This system is known as the Content Scramble System or CSS. Manufacturers of DVD players along with the major content providers (i.e., the movie studios) have jointly adopted this standard. All movies in this digital format are distributed on DVDs protected with CSS.

Personal computer users can also view DVD movies as long as they are running a Mac or Windows operating system. CSS does not support any other operating system at the present time. In the fall of 1999, Jan Johansen of Larvik, Norway, created a software program that would play DVDs on a Linux system. In order to write this software, Johansen had to crack the CSS encryption code. The resultant decryption program was called DeCSS (or *De*code *CSS*), and it allows a user to decode a DVD disk. Johansen immediately posted the executable object code of DeCSS on the Web. As both the DeCSS source code and object code proliferated through cyberspace, the movie industry decided to seek injunctions against certain offenders.

The industry filed a lawsuit against Eric Corley and others responsible for the 2600 "hacker" website associated with the print magazine, *2600: The Hacker Quarterly*. Corley had written a piece for the website about DeCSS, and he included copies of the source code and object code of DeCSS. The 2600 website also contained links to other websites with DeCSS. Corley contends that the code and the links were incorporated in his story because "in a journalistic world, ... you have to show your evidence, ... and particularly in the magazine that I work for, people want to see specifically what it is that we are referring to" (Trial Transcript, 2000).

The movie industry demanded the immediate removal of the DeCSS code and sought an injunction against Corley (along with two other defendants, Remeirdes and Kazan). In January 2000, a Federal District Court issued a preliminary injunction preventing the 2600 website from posting the DeCSS code. The defendants complied, but they continued to post links to other websites where the DeCSS code could be found. At the plaintiff's request, the scope of the preliminary injunction was broadened to include those hyperlinks, which were then removed from the 2600.com website by the defendants (Spinello, 2004).

A trial was held in the summer of 2000. The plaintiffs argued that DeCSS was the equivalent of a "digital crowbar" that could be used to decrypt copyrighted DVDs. The movie industry's case centered on its claim that DeCSS violated the anti-trafficking provision of the DMCA, which prohibits the dissemination of technologies that allow for the circumvention of encryption technologies (§1201(a)).

In their defense against these accusations, Corley's lawyers claimed that the DMCA was unconstitutional. The defense team argued that computer programs like DeCSS, including both object and source code, represent a form of expressive free speech that deserves full First Amendment protection. The defense also argued that the ban on linking was tantamount to suppressing another important form of First Amendment expression. Hyperlinks, despite their functionality, are a vital part of the expressiveness of a Web page and therefore their curtailment clearly violates the First Amendment.

The District Court, however, was unmoved by these arguments, and ruled in favor of the movie industry. According to the court, DeCSS "was created solely for the purpose of decrypting CSS" and its distribution was tantamount to "publishing a bank vault combination in a national newspaper" (*Universal v. Remeirdes*, 2000). The court also asserted that by linking to sites with DeCSS code the defendants were "trafficking" in DeCSS, so that the defendants were also liable for these linking activities. A permanent injunction was issued prohibiting the defendants from posting DeCSS or linking to websites containing DeCSS code.

The case was appealed by Corley and 2600 Enterprises (the other defendants dropped out). The appeal was based on two constitutional arguments: (1) the DMCA violates the First Amendment since computer code such as DeCSS is a form of protected speech; and (2) it violates both the First

Amendment and the Copyright Act by restricting fair use of copyrighted works. But in November 2001, the U.S. Court of Appeals for the Second Circuit affirmed the judgment of the District Court. The Appeals Court agreed that posting DeCSS or hyperlinking to sites with DeCSS violated the DMCA, and it left the permanent injunction in place.

Like the District Court, the Second Circuit Court did not disagree with the categorization of the DeCSS code as a form of speech, but it reasoned that this code also has a functional component. The purpose of the DMCA is to regulate the functionality of DeCSS. Thus, any restriction on the dissemination of DeCSS is content-neutral because the intent is not to suppress the content of the expression but to advance a particular government interest, that is, the protection of copyrighted material. According to the Appeals Court:

*As a communication, the DeCSS code has a claim to being "speech" and as "speech," it has a claim to being protected by the First Amendment. But just as the realities of what any computer code can accomplish must inform the scope of its constitutional protection, so the capacity of a decryption program like DeCSS to accomplish unauthorized — indeed, unlawful — access to materials in which the Plaintiffs have intellectual property rights must inform and limit the scope of its First Amendment protection (*Universal City Studios v. Corley, *2001).*

The Appeals Court also agreed with the restrictions on linking to other sites containing DeCSS on the same grounds: "The linking prohibition is justified solely by the functional capability of the hyperlink" (*Universal City Studios v. Corley*, 2001).

The DeCSS case illustrates the difficulty of resolving conflicts between property and free speech rights. While the courts were undoubtedly constrained by the language of the DMCA, there is something disconcerting about this ruling, especially the prohibition on linking to other websites. The defendants have a right to critique the DMCA without fear of retribution, even if part of that critique is pointing to websites that contain rogue code such as DeCSS. Expressiveness on a web page is inextricably connected with hyperlinks that are interwoven with textual matter, and such expression would be incomplete without links. Therefore, liability against linking under these circumstances is a major burden for free speech in cyberspace. The defendants rightly argued that the court failed to adequately consider whether the DMCA "burdens substantially more speech than is necessary to further the government's legitimate interests" (Appellant's Brief, 2001).

If Congress intended to suppress links to websites with decryption code, since links are a form of "trafficking" in anti-circumvention code, it has erred on the side of overprotecting property rights to the detriment of free expression. If not, the DMCA needs revision and more precise language to guide the courts in cases like this one.

Intellectual Property and Anti-Trust

U.S. vs. Microsoft

Intellectual property rights confer monopoly power, but to what extent should those rights supersede or compromise antitrust laws? Granting a property right appears to give a company an exclusive prerogative to exclude competition, yet antitrust law exists to ensure that competition is fair and that monopoly power is held in check. What happens when companies like Microsoft aggressively leverage their intellectual property rights? Does this type of competitive behavior fulfill copyright law, which bestows property rights in software, or does it undermine that law?

This was one of the key questions at the core of the Microsoft antitrust case. Because of the phenomenon of "network effects," Microsoft's proprietary Windows platform became the standard for PC operating systems (OS). Network theory applies when the value of a product for each user increases with the number of users. The more people using the same operating system, the easier to communicate with other users and the more software applications such a platform will attract (the so-called complement effect). These network effects bias industries (such as operating systems) to monopoly status. Intellectual property rights strengthen that power by giving monopolies like Microsoft the right to exclude others from use of their property. But can antitrust law be invoked to curtail core intellectual property rights? Where is the appropriate balance between an intellectual property holder's right to exclude and the public's right to fair competition?

Microsoft sought to leverage its dominance in the OS market in order to strengthen its position in the browser market. A Web browser enables personal computer users to navigate the World Wide Web and to display or scan various Web pages. Netscape's Navigator browser had gained momentum in this new market, and Microsoft was anxious to fight back with its own Internet Explorer (IE) browser. Navigator was a threat to its operating system monopoly because a browser is a type of *middleware,* which exposes its own application programming interfaces (APIs). This means that applications can be written to run on the browser platform instead of the OS platform. If third-party vendors began writing applications for Navigator and users could get many of their key applications through a browser (instead of an operating system), the Windows OS would be effectively commoditized.

In its zeal to defeat Navigator, Microsoft engaged in several exclusionary acts that were later determined to be anti-competitive. One such act involved the company's exclusionary dealings with its Original Equipment Manufacturers (OEMs), such as Dell and Compaq, that distribute that operating system. Microsoft imposed restrictions on OEMs that prevented them from removing desktop icons, Start menu entries, etc. This prohibition precluded the distribution of a rival browser because OEMs could not remove visible access to IE. And OEMs were loath to install another browser in addition to IE since "preinstalling more than one product in a given category ... can significantly increase an OEM's support costs, for the redundancy can lead to confusion among novice users" (*U.S. v. Microsoft*, 2001). OEMs were also forbidden to modify the initial "boot sequence" that occurs the very first time a user turns on his or her computer. In the Microsoft-approved boot sequence, users were given a chance to choose a Microsoft-approved Internet Access Provider that used IE (but not Navigator) for website access.

The Justice Department argued with some insistence that these restrictions were anti-competitive. But Microsoft contended that the restrictions were justified since the company was "exercising its rights as the holder of valid copyrights" (Appellant's Opening Brief, 1998). Microsoft was arguing for the right to dictate how its property would be used, and this might appear to be a reasonable imposition for a property holder. According to Microsoft's lawyers, "[I]f intellectual property rights have been lawfully acquired, their subsequent exercise cannot give rise to antitrust liability" (Appellant's Opening Brief, 1998). But the Appeals Court unequivocally rejected this line of reasoning, as it cited the Federal Circuit's conclusion in a similar case: "Intellectual property rights do not confer a privilege to violate antitrust laws" (*In re Independent Service Organization*, 2000).

Thus, the Court affirmed this clear constraint against leveraging intellectual property rights in a reckless fashion that suppresses fair competition and yields anti-competitive consequences. The problem is that such leveraging could easily stifle innovation by preventing competitors from distributing their competitive products. The essential conclusion of the Microsoft case is that intellectual property rights do not give copyright holders immunity from obeying antitrust law. Microsoft's anti-competitive actions, which it defended by citing its copyright protection for Windows, had the effect of denying the interoperability of the Navigator program and this helped defeat Navigator in the marketplace.

Windows is a gateway to the Internet, and left unanswered in this dispute is the extent to which Microsoft must share control of that gateway by licensing or opening its code so that complementary applications (such as a browser or Internet access software) are assured equal access. The Microsoft case highlights the sharp distinction between two competing visions of the Internet and its extensions. One approach sees the Internet as an information commons built primarily on open technologies that encourage access and support interoperability. Consider the open communication protocols of the Internet itself: "No one owns the Internet protocol [IP], no one licenses its use, and no one restricts access to it" (Oxman, 1999). Indeed, these open protocols have been critical to the Internet's success as an "innovation commons" (Lessig, 2001). The other approach favors the proprietary development model adopted by companies like Microsoft. Lessig argues that the Internet must continue to function as a commons built on open technologies such as TCP/IP, and avoid being held captive by the proprietary systems of companies like Microsoft. And one antidote to proprietary control is open source software, where users are free to use the software as they see fit and modify its source code. If Windows were an open source code platform, Microsoft's bundling strategy for Internet Explorer would have been futile, since users (and OEMs) could easily have removed this functionality and substituted another browser. As Lessig (2001) writes, "the source code for open source projects is therefore a check on the power of the project; it is a limit on the power of the project to behave strategically against anything written to the platform."

The primary problem with mandating open access (that is, interoperability between a platform and complementary or rival applications) *or* open source code is that it directly conflicts with intellectual property rights, which have been instrumental in stimulating software development. Such a policy would neglect the need to provide adequate incentives for investment. A law, for example, requiring that all software be "open" (with freely available source code) would destroy the market-based incentives that induce software developers to create innovative new software products. Such a requirement could have an adverse effect on future software development with a corresponding net loss for consumer welfare.

But perhaps a middle ground between the proprietary and the commons models is possible. Weiser (2003) proposes the model of a "limited commons." This model calls for proprietary standards where there is rivalry between different platform standards (for example, an operating system or browser), but favors open standards when a single standard wins and reaps "sufficient rewards." Weiser recognizes that property rights will stimulate investment while network effects will encourage the development of a standard that permits interoperability. This model "respects the need to provide incentives for investment and permits access when necessary to facilitate competition and innovation" (Weiser, 2003).

CONCLUSIONS

At this point we draw this overview to a close. Our purpose has been to illuminate theories underlying intellectual property rights, while exposing the difficulties involved in implementing those rights fairly and responsibly. The primary problem that has preoccupied us is the proper scope of intellectual property rights in a digital environment and a networked world. We have critiqued laws and court decisions that tend to underprotect or overprotect those rights. We have argued instead for a prudent level of protection that approximates the ideal of the Aristotelian mean, that is, property rights that are measured and proportionate to the need to reward and induce creative effort. Property rights, properly constructed, should mediate two polarities. One polarity overemphasizes the exclusive, private ownership of intellectual objects, while the other polarity is represented by the radical viewpoint that all intellectual objects should belong to the "commons" or public domain from the moment of their creation.

We began with theory. Locke was the first philosopher to seriously thematize the problem of property. For many intellectual property scholars, Locke's meditation on labor is the key to comprehending the meaning of property and the normative justification for a right to own property. The importance of property rights is also discernible in the writings of Hegel, as well as in utilitarian philosophers such as Bentham and Mill. While these philosophers did not explicitly discuss intellectual property rights, their insights have laid the foundation for those rights. For Locke and Hegel, intellectual property rights are natural entitlements, necessary as a reward for labor or as a means to achieve free self-expression. This approach contrasts with utilitarian reasoning where those rights are regarded as useful social instruments with a rationale grounded in the need for incentives to spur the steady production of intellectual objects. But both approaches demand that rights be limited by concern for the public domain and the common good. As we have seen, Lockeans may insist on the need for a property right as a just dessert of one's labors, but the bestowal of such a right cannot harm the commons by depriving it of intellectual objects (such as ideas and algorithms) that others will need as raw material for their own creations. Property rights should be neither thick nor thin, but hale and sound.

But what about the case against intellectual property — why should intellectual objects be "owned" by anyone, especially given their non-rivalrous nature? We find the case against property rights to be weak. Even if one rejects the notion of a "natural" property right, there is compelling evidence that intellectual property protection is crucial stimulus for the economy. There is also evidence that developing countries could optimize their own resources more efficiently if they had stronger property systems, albeit ones suited to their particular needs.

We reviewed the legal infrastructure that protects intellectual property, noting that the law's validity depends to some extent on the normative frameworks. We also highlighted more recent controversial laws such as the DMCA and the CTEA, and we briefly considered technological solutions such as digital rights management (DRM), which could be more efficacious than the law in protecting digital content. If enforcement of copyright law continues to be sporadic and expensive, content providers will turn to technological schemes that offer a more Draconian solution that could absolutize property rights by ignoring user rights and "safety valves" such as fair use and limited term.

Finally, we discussed some of the more prominent current controversies. These cases enabled us to perceive how the issue of intellectual property is closely interconnected with issues such as free speech, secondary liability, and even fair competition. We saw some examples of intellectual property's vulnerability in certain contexts, because of ingenious software architectures and inadequate enforcement. At the same time, several other case studies made apparent the problems and social costs that ensue when intellectual property is overprotected.

In the case of peer-to-peer networks, intellectual property is too vulnerable if precedents such as *Sony* are strictly applied and users are allowed to share files on a massive scale. On the other hand, cyberpatents and arbitrary 20-year extensions of the copyright term have no justification, especially when objectively evaluated in light of the normative frameworks. In addition, the Microsoft case revealed some of the problems with the proprietary model for software development, which, for certain critics, threatens to *enclose* the Internet commons. Open source code and open access have been proposed as possible alternatives.

As our discussion of the Microsoft case demonstrated, there are two basic property models in cyberspace. There are some content providers and software developers who seek almost absolute control (proprietary model) over intellectual objects. On the other hand, some legal scholars and cyberspace libertarians advocate a dissipation of property controls since the current system of rights is so disadvantageous to the robustness of the public domain (commons model). Those who embrace the commons model see an enclosure movement "fencing off" intellectual objects. They also worry about how the insistence on application of property rights in cyberspace will interfere with the evolution of the Internet and related technologies like peer-to-peer networks.

What the commons model and its adherents downplay is the dynamic incentive effects of intellectual property rights. As the Supreme Court has observed, the "ultimate aim" of copyright and similar protections is "to stimulate [the creation of useful works] for the general public good" (*Harper & Row Publishers v. Nation Enterterprises*, 1985). Critics of intellectual property rights also fail to fully appreciate the concept of "incomplete capture," that is, "an intellectual property owner cannot possibly appropriate all of the information (and thus social value) generated by her creation" (Wagner, 2003). Even if an intellectual object is copyrighted, there can never be complete control of that object. A protected intellectual object is not hermetically sealed off from public access. Rather, there is usually a positive spillover effect as this information is disseminated throughout society. Copyrighted works, once they are disclosed to the public, convey information, ideas, and suggestions to many others who can utilize those ideas or follow up on these suggestions without violating that copyright. Some of the information stimulated may be only indirectly or obliquely affiliated with the new creation. For example, a successful novel (and subsequent movie) like *Cold Mountain* engenders new investigations and discussions of the civil war. Thus, even "fully propertized intellectual goods" can contribute to the spiraling growth of information resources and thereby enhance in some limited way the public domain (Wagner, 2003).

But while this fixation on control and enclosure may be exaggerated, flawed legislation such as the DMCA and particularly the CTEA remind us that policy makers are subject to capture. This leads to the unwarranted expansion of intellectual property rights that is not in the public interest. In their zeal to thwart piracy and to protect fragile digital content, there is also a threat that content providers will insist on greater control than the intellectual property system has tolerated in the past. Policy makers must find that elusive middle way that balances legitimate concerns about protecting intellectual objects with the need for a robust and renewable public domain.

We admit that discerning and legislating the "right" or proportionate amount of intellectual property protection is a difficult process. A full exposition of what a moderate protection scheme would look like is beyond the scope of this chapter. But we have offered some recommendations in the course of this analysis: software platforms as a limited commons under certain conditions, shorter duration for copyright protection, more limited scope of patent coverage, thick patent protection for genuine inventions that are costly to commercialize, and so forth. Finally, as we have been at pains to insist here, while the normative frameworks may be indeterminate, they can still guide policy makers in making prudent choices that will reward creative labor and stimulate creativity while avoiding further erosion of the intellectual commons.

ENDNOTES

[1]   Eine Vielheit,. . . ein Krieg und ein Frieden, eine Herde und ein Hirt.

REFERENCES

Aharonian, G. (1999). Does the Patent Office respect the software community? *IEEE Software*, 16 (4), 87-89.

Amazon.com v. BarnesandNoble.com. (2001). 239 F. 3d 1343 [Fed. Cir.].

Amici Curiae Brief. (2003). *Metro-Goldwyn-Mayer Studios, Inc. v. Grokster, Ltd*. 259 F. Supp. 2d [C.D. Cal], on appeal.

Amsterdam Appellate Court (2002). BUMA & STEMRA v. KaZaA, March 28.

Appellant's Opening Brief. (1998). *United States of America v. Microsoft Corporation* 253 F 3rd [D.C. Cir.].

A&M Records, Inc. v. Abdallah, (1996). 948 F. Supp 1449 [C.D. Cal.].

A&M Records, Inc. v. Napster, (2001). 239 F. 3d 1004 [9th Cir].

Becker, L. (1977). *Property rights*. London: Routledge and Kegan Paul.

Boyle, J. (2004). A politics of intellectual property: Environmentalism for the Net. In R.A. Spinello & H.T. Tavani (Eds.), *Readings in CyberEthics (2nd ed.)*, pp. 273-293. Sudbury, MA: Jones and Bartlett Publishers.

Delaney, K. (2003). KaZaA founder peddles software to speed file sharing. *The Wall Street Journal*, (September 8), B1.

Derrida, J. (1981). *Positions*. Trans. A. Bass. Chicago, IL: University of Chicago Press.

Diamond v. Diehr (1981). 450 U.S. 175.

Digital Millennium Copyright Act (DMCA), (1998) U.S.C., § 103, Title 17, § 1201.

Dogan, S. (2001). Is Napster a VCR? The implications of Sony for Napster and other Internet technologies. *Hastings Law Journal*, 52, 939.

Drahos, P. (1996). *A philosophy of intellectual property*. Aldershot, UK: Dartmouth Publishing.

Easterbrook, F. (1990). Intellectual property is still property. *Harvard Journal of Law and Public Policy*, 3, 110.

Eldred v. Ashcroft (2003). 123 U.S. 769.

Fisher, W. (1998). Theories of intellectual property. Available at: http://cyber.law.harvard.edu/ipcoop/98fish.html.

Foucualt, M. (1969). Qu'est-ce qu'un Autuer? In *Textual Strategies*. Trans. J.V. Harari. Ithaca, NY: Cornell University Press.

Fox, B. & LaMacchia, B.A. (2003). Encouraging recognition of fair uses in DRM systems. *Communications of the ACM*, 46(4), 61-63.

"Free Mickey Mouse." (2002). *The Economist*, (October 12), 67.

Gershwin v. Columbia Artists Management (1971). 443 F. 2d 1150 [2d Cir.].

Gleick, J. (2000). Patently absurd. *New York Times Magazine*, (March 12), 44.

Gordon, W.J. (1992). Asymmetric market failure and prisoner's dilemma in intellectual property. *University of Dayton Law Review*, 17, 853.

Gordon, W.J. (1993). A property right in self-expression: Equality and individualism in the natural law of intellectual property. *Yale Law Journal*, 102, 1533.

Gottschalk v. Benson (1972). 409 U.S. 63.

Grosso, A. (2000). The promise and the problems of the No Electronic Theft Act. *Communications of the ACM*, 43 (2), 23-26.

Halbert, D. (1999) *Intellectual property in the information age*. Westport, CT: Quorum Books.

Hand, L. (1930). Opinion in *Nichols v. Universal Pictures* 45 F. 2d 119, [2nd Cir.].

Hand, L. (1936). Opinion in *Sheldon v. Metro-Goldwyn Pictures Corp.* 81 F. 2d 49, [2nd Cir.].

Harper & Row Publishers, Inc. v. Nation Enterprises. (1985). 471 U.S. 539, 85 L. Ed. 2d 588.

Hegel, G.W. F. (1944). *The phenomenology of mind*. Trans. J. Baille. New York: MacMillan & Co. (Original work published 1806).

Hegel, G.W.F. (1948). *Early theological writings.* Trans. T. Knox. Chicago, IL: University of Chicago Press. (Original work published 1800).

Hegel, G.W.F. (1952). *Philosophy of right.* Trans. T. Knox. London: Oxford University Press. (Original work published 1821).

Hettinger, E.C. (1989). Justifying intellectual property. *Philosophy and Public Affairs,* 18, 31-52.

Hughes, J. (1997). The philosophy of intellectual property. In A. Moore (Ed.), *Intellectual property,* (pp. 107-177). Lanham, MD: Rowman & Littlefield.

In re Aimster Copyright Litigation, (2002). 252 F. Supp 2d 634 [N.D. Ill], aff'd No 01 C 8133 [7th Cir, 2003].

In re Independent Service Organization's Antitrust Liability. (2000). 203 F. 3d 1322 [Fed. Cir.].

Kieff, F.S. (2000). Property rights and property rules for commercializing inventions. *Minnesota Law Review,* 85, 697.

Lemley, M. (1997). Romantic authorship and the rhetoric of property. *Texas Law Review,* 75, 873.

Lessig, L. (1999). *Code and other laws of cyberspace.* New York: Basic Books.

Lessig, L. (2001). *The future of ideas.* New York: Random House.

Locke, J. (1952). *The second treatise of government.* Indianapolis, IN: Bobbs-Merrill. (Original work published 1690).

MacIntyre, A. (1990). *Three rival versions of moral enquiry.* Notre Dame, IN: University of Notre Dame Press.

Mansfield, E. (1986). Patents and innovation: An empirical study. *Management Science,* 32, 783.

Martin, B. (1995). Against intellectual property. *Philosophy and Social Action,* 21(3), 7-22.

McSwain, W. (1999). The law of cyberspace. *Harvard Law Review,* 112, 1574.

Merges, R. P. (1992). Uncertainty and the standard of patentability. *High Technology Law Journal,* 7(1), 10-12.

Merges, R. P., Mennell, P., & Lemley, M. (2000). *Intellectual property in the new technological age.* New York: Aspen Law.

Metro-Goldwyn-Mayer Studios, Inc. v. Grokster, Ltd. (2003). 259 F. Supp. 2d [C.D. Cal].

Moore, A. (2001). *Intellectual property and information control.* New Brunswick, NJ: Transaction Publishers.

Negroponte, N. (1995). *Being digital.* New York: Alfred A. Knopf.

Nietzsche, F. (1962). *Also Sprach Zarathustra.* Stuttgart: Philipp Reclam. (Original work published 1892).

Nimmer, D. (2001). *Nimmer on copyright.* New York: Matthew Bender.

Nordhaus, W.D. (1969). *Invention, growth and welfare: A theoretical treatment of technological change.* Cambridge, MA: MIT Press.

Olivecrona, K. (1974). Appropriation in the state of nature: Locke on the origin of property. *Journal of the History of Ideas, 35,* 211-235.

Oxman, J. (1999). The FCC and the unregulation of the internet, OPP Working Paper, No. 31. Available at: http://www.fcc.gov/Bureaus/Opp/working_papers/oppwp31.txt.

Palmer, T. (1997). Intellectual property: A non-Posnerian law and economics approach. In A.E. Moore (Ed.), *Intellectual property: Moral, legal, and international dilemmas,* (pp. 179-224). Lanham, MD: Rowman and Littlefield.

"Patents and the Poor" (2001). *The Economist,* June 23, 21-23.

Plaintiffs' Joint Excerpts of Record (2003). *Metro-Goldwyn-Mayer Studios, Inc. v. Grokster,* Ltd. 259 F. Supp. 2d [C.D. Cal].

Priest, G. (1986). What economists can tell lawyers. *Research in Law and Economics, 8,* 19.

Samuelson, P. (2003). DRM {and, or, vs.} the law. *Communications of the ACM, 46* (4), 41-45.

Shapiro, C. (2001). Navigating the patent thicket: Cross licenses, patent pools and standard-setting. [Unpublished manuscript, on file with *Columbia Law Review*.].

Shavell, S. & van Ypersele, T. (1999). Rewards versus intellectual property rights. National Bureau of Economics Research Working Paper, No. 6956.

Snapper, J. (1995). Intellectual property protections for computer software. In D. G. Johnson & H. Nissenbaum (Eds.), *Computing, ethics and social values,* (pp. 181-189). Englewood Cliffs, NJ: Prentice Hall.

Sony Corp of America v. Universal City Studios, Inc. (1984). 464 U.S. 417.

Spinello, R. (2004). Note on the DeCSS Case. In R. A. Spinello & H. Tavani (Eds.), *Readings in cyberethics (2nd ed.),* pp. 264-268. Sudbury, MA: Jones and Bartlett.

State Street Bank & Trust Co. v. Signature Financial Group (1998). 149 F. 3d 1368 [Fed. Cir.].

Tavani, H. (2004). *Ethics & technology: Ethical issues in an age of information and communication technology.* Hoboken, NJ: John Wiley & Sons.

Trial Transcript (2000). *Universal City Studios v. Remeirdes* 111 F. Supp. 294 [S.D.N.Y.].

United Christian Scientists v. Christian Science Board of Directors (1987). 829 F.2d 1152 [D.C. Cir.].

Universal City Studios v. Corley (2001). 273 F. 3d 429 [2d Cir.].

Universal City Studios v. Remeirdes (2000). 111 F. Supp. 294 [S.D.N.Y.].

Universal City Studios v. Sony Corp of America (1979). 480 F. Supp. 429 [C.D. Cal.].

U.S. Constitution, Article I, § 8, clause 8.

United States of America v. Microsoft Corporation (2001). 253 F. 3d 34 [D.C. Cir.].

Vaidhyanathan, S. (2001). *Copyrights and copywrongs: The rise of intellectual property and how it threatens creativity.* New York: New York University Press.

Volokh, E. (1998). Freedom of speech and injunctions in intellectual property cases. *Duke Law Journal,* 48, 147.

Wagner, R. P. (2003). Information wants to be free: Intellectual property and the mythologies of control. *Columbia Law Review,* 103, 995.

Warwick, S. (2004). Is copyright ethical? In R.A. Spinello & H.T. Tavani (Eds.), *Readings in cyberethics (2nd ed.),* pp. 305-321. Sudbury, MA: Jones and Bartlett Publishers.

Weiser, P. (2003). The Internet, innovation, and intellectual property policy. *Columbia Law Review,* 103, 534.

Wheaton v. Peters (1834). 33 U.S. 591.

Yen, A. (1990). Restoring the natural law: Copyright as labor and possession. *Ohio State Law Journal,* 51, 517.

Section II

Theoretical Perspectives

Chapter II

Intellectual Property Rights in Software — Justifiable from a Liberalist Position?
Free Software Foundation's Position in Comparison to John Locke's Concept of Property

Kai Kimppa
University of Turku, Finland

ABSTRACT

This chapter offers a new view on how justifiable the current liberalist view on intellectual property rights (IPRs) in software actually is if based on Locke's Second Treatise and especially on Chapter V, "Of Property" (2002), which has traditionally been seen as the starting point of liberalist argument for property — be it immaterial or material. This chapter will show how in Locke, the possibility of property in the immaterial is denounced and how that, in fact, fits the position of the Free Software Foundation for both patents and copyright in software, GNU General Public License (GPL) being the main example of this.

INTRODUCTION

Locke (2002) bases his arguments for property in freedom of a person to do as he or she pleases with his body and thus his possessions, which are extensions of his ownership of his body through labor. The reason ownership is needed is that material resources are scarce, and thus everyone cannot necessarily own everything they would want to. This does not hold true for the immaterial. The immaterial is unlimited, and everyone can own as much as they want to at the same time. No one is deprived of ownership in what he or she has if someone else owns the same immaterial as well. Locke implicitly argues for this view in his writing by never assuming that the method used to gain access to something material would be owned. Quite the contrary, Locke assumes that the method of picking acorns or apples or drawing water from a fountain is anyone's right to use. The reason for this is that no one is worse off if someone else uses the same method as the other has used. Even though Locke proposes that the material commons should be divided between owned and not owned, he or she never seems to intend this for the immaterial commons. From the immaterial commons, anyone may draw what he or she needs for personal purposes. Anything in the immaterial commons can be shared by as many people as happen to have a need for it. Again, we return to the first argument, i.e., that Locke needed the material to be divided amongst people because it can not be owned by many at once, but that the immaterial need not be owned as it can be used by as many as have a need for it.

Richard Stallman is an avid proponent of individual freedom — the freedom to learn, share, copy, sell, or trade what one has to another, for the benefit of any and all people. The Free Software Foundation seems to agree with the view of the immaterial not needing ownership. If something is given, traded, or sold to another, the other has as much ownership in it as the first. Thus, no one needs ownership in the immaterial, but only the instances he or she happens to hold. The method for software, namely the source, and, as pointed out by Richard Stallman, for other digitally deliverable material (be it pictures, text, or anything else immaterial) should be free to be redistributed by anyone having it. The immaterial commons would be available to all via the World Wide Web or even digital media such as floppy disks, CDs or DVDs. The distinction from material items is that there is a clear difference in the duplication of the material and the immaterial. Again, one cannot own the same car another owns at the same time, but one can own the user's manual, especially in digital form, of the car with another.

LOCKE'S ARGUMENTS FOR PROPERTY: AN INTERPRETATION

Locke's Second Treatise on Government (TTG II) (2002) is a widely used text when property rights are considered. Some attention has been paid to what kinds of intellectual property rights (IPRs) can be derived from Locke (see, e.g., Kramer, 1997; Long, 1995; Simmons, 1992), but what seems to be missing from this discussion is how it could be argued that Locke never intended his definition of property rights to include IPRs.

Locke's (2002) main arguments on property stem from one's right to one's preservation:

"Whether we consider natural reason, which tells us that men, being once born, have a right to their preservation, and consequently to meat and drink and such other things as Nature affords for their subsistence" (TTG II, 24).

And thus, to ensure this, one must have a means to appropriate something for the benefit of oneself:

And though all the fruits it naturally produces, and beasts it feeds, belong to mankind in common, as they are produced by the spontaneous hand of Nature, and nobody has originally a private dominion exclusive of the rest of mankind in any of them, as they are thus in their natural state, yet being given for the use of men, there must of necessity be a means to appropriate them some way or other before they can be of any use, or at all beneficial, to any particular men. (TTG II, 25)

Everyone has property to oneself. Property is owned through mixing of labor—which is of oneself—to what one works upon.

"[...] every man has a 'property' in his own 'person.' [...] For this 'labor' being the unquestionable property of the laborer, no man but he can have a right to what that is once joined to[.]" (TTG II, 26).

The major issues connecting TTG II to intellectual property are unstealability of immaterial objects, the rights of a person to that which he or she has from a liberalist perspective, the Lockean proviso, and that as much and as good ought to be left to others. These issues rise through the liberalist tradition. Locke is considered to be the first person to concisely present the liberalist chain of thought and most (if not all) further writings on the liberalist tradition are based on his work in the Treatises. Thus, if an inconsistency can be shown from what Locke has said to the derivations from his work within the tradition, a strong case can be pointed out against an implementation of that derivation. In this case, the derivation is rights to the immaterial, as the term is used in the European tradition, or, as the term is used in the Anglo-American tradition, intellectual property or intellectual property rights (or privileges).

Of Deprivation

When property is mentioned in liberalist discourse, Locke's labor theory of ownership is most often brought forth in one form or another (see, e.g., Kinsella, 2000; Kramer, 1997; Simmons, 1992). Labor is undoubtedly essential for defining what one can own when considering how one may appropriate property, but in Locke, it is only a means to an end. Labor gives one right to property, property, which when it is one's, is one's fully. If one chooses to trade, give, or sell one's property to another, the other then has full ownership of the property (Long, 1995).

[...] If he gave away a part to anybody else, so that it perished not uselessly in his possession, these he also made use of. And if he also bartered away plums that would have rotted in a week, for nuts that would last good for his eating a whole year, he did no injury; he wasted not the common stock; destroyed no part of the portion of goods that belonged to others, so long as nothing perished uselessly in his hands. Again, if he would give his nuts for a piece of metal, pleased with its colour, or exchange his sheep for shells, or wool for a sparkling pebble or a diamond, and keep those [...] he invaded not the right of others [...] (TTG II, 46)

If someone else would be granted power over what one may do with one's property, others would be given access to what one has purchased, traded for, or obtained as a gift, which would clearly compromise one's right to what one has (Long, 1995).

Man being born, as has been proved, with a title to perfect freedom and an uncontrolled enjoyment of all the rights and privileges of the law of Nature, equally with any other man, or number of men in the world, hath by nature a power [...] to preserve his property — that is, his life, liberty, and estate, against the injuries and attempts of other men. (TTG II, 87)

But labor gives one right to material property (see, e.g., Kinsella, 2000; Simmons, 1997). The reason for needing ownership of the material property is scarcity—there is only a limited amount of material things to be owned and they can't be had by multiple parties at one time.

As is pointed out by Long (1995) and Kinsella (2000), immaterial property does not suffer from this restriction. Immaterial things can be owned by as many at one time who have a need or a want to own them. The immaterial is not away from one if shared with another. Thus the immaterial can be sold, traded, or given to another with no less being left to the first, or another can discover, invent, or create the same immaterial thing without lessening one from his or her ownership. This is in sharp contrast to material things, where, for example, if one tills a piece of land, another can not till the same piece of land without the first loosing it; one can not take away from another what is his or hers.

*But the chief matter of property being now [...] the earth itself, as that which takes in and carries with it all the rest, I think it is plain that property in that too is acquired as the former. As much land as a man tills, plants, improves, cultivates, and can use the product of, so much is his property. [...] He that [...] subdued, tilled, and sowed any part of it, thereby annexed to it something that was his property, which another had no title to, **nor could without injury take from him.** (TTG II, 31, Emphasis mine).*

There are many other places where Locke emphasizes that the taking away from another is the main issue, for example:

"That was his property, which could not be taken from him wherever he had fixed it." (TTG II, 34)

[...] not [...] to [...] take away or impair the life, or what tends to the preservation of the life, the liberty, health, limb, or goods, of another." (TTG II, 6.)

If one mixes labor to what has previously not been owned, that which was not owned then becomes owned by one. But, with the immaterial, there is not something not owned, but rather undiscovered or uninvented, which can be discovered or invented by others without lessening the opportunity for the first to use what he or she has. Thus, the argument—which can easily be seen to follow from Locke — that one owns something due to the fact that it can not be owned by another at the same time is obviously flawed when it comes to the immaterial and since depriving another of something is essential, rights to the immaterial are difficult to justify.

Of Method

There are plentiful examples in Locke where a person uses a method to acquire property. But if a person mixes his or her labor with something from the commons that something becomes his or hers; this in no way implicates that the method used will become the person's property. None of Locke's examples considered the method to be something to be protected. Quite the contrary, in all of his examples, Locke seems to take it for granted that anyone can pick apples from the ground, drink from a stream, and so forth, and he or she does not even seem to give thought to the possibility that if another person sees the first picking apples from the ground, he or she should ask for permission from the first to replicate the act.

He that is nourished by the acorns he picked up under an oak, or the apples he gathered from the trees in the woods, has certainly appropriated them to himself. Nobody can deny but the nourishment is his. [...] the taking of this or that part does not depend on the express consent of all the commoners. Thus, the grass my horse has bit [...] the ore I have digged in any place, where I have a right to them in common with others, become my property without the assignation of consent of anybody. (TTG II, 27)

[...] this law of reason makes the deer that Indian's who hath killed it; it is allowed to be his goods who hath bestowed his labor upon it, though, before, it was the common right of every one. (TTG II, 29)

Thus the right to one's labor doesn't apply to methods of work, and methods of work can not be said to be of oneself. The reason for this is that using the method is not away from another's opportunity to use the same method, unlike if the other would take material goods away from the first, which would be away from the first (Long, 1995). Thus it could be argued that, contrary to the limited material commons, Locke instead presumes an unlimited immaterial commons from which one may draw new ideas or ideas already found as one wishes.

Of Immaterial Commons

In most liberalist tradition, immaterial commons are compared to material commons. In this kind of thinking, one can "till a piece of land" from the immaterial commons as one would from the material commons, thus gaining patent or copyright to the immaterial discovery, invention, or creation as one would to a material piece of land. In pure liberalist thinking, this would lead to full ownership of the immaterial one has discovered or invented, not to a limited one, as provided by today's copyright and patent laws in Western society, due to a compromise with the consequentialists.

In Locke's thinking, one may take as much as one needs from the natural state as long as one leaves as much and as good for others to take. In a world of limited resources this clearly becomes impossible after the population increases to such an extent that as much and as good can not be left for others.

[...] in some parts of the world, where the increase of people and stock, with the use of money, had made land scarce, and so of some value, the several communities settled the bounds of their distinct territories, and, by laws, within themselves, regulated the properties of the private men of their society, and so, by compact and agreement, settled the property which labor and industry began. (TTG II, 45)

Scarcity, however, is not a problem with the immaterial. There are two differing views on what "as much and as good" should be interpreted to mean in the immaterial: (1) the immaterial is infinite, thus there can be as much and as good left for others anyway; or (2) one can't appropriate something exclusively for oneself from the immaterial, because the same (cf. Apples) that would be as much and as good is not left for others.

The first view is that the immaterial is infinite, and thus, by definition, as much and as good is left there even if rights to something one discovers or invents are given to the person finding it. In such a case, "as much and as good" is just other things than the ones already discovered or invented (see Figure 1).

Thus, if I labored for it, i.e., discovered, invented, or created it, it is mine. But if we return to why ownership is needed, we again note that it is needed to protect ownership in a situation where ownership is limited. This is not the case when immaterial things are considered.

The second view differs from this in pointing out that the immaterial is not scarce and can thus be owned by many without lessening the possibility of anybody else owning it. Also, the latter part of the statement, namely "as good,"

Figure 1: The largest infinite area is the area of all of the immaterial commons. The smaller infinite area is the area of actually usable immaterial objects. The black dots represent actual immaterial objects, like one-click-shopping and the small area around them represents similar objects, often especially in the case of patenting patented as a bundle with the object intended for use.

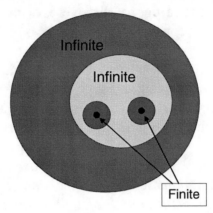

doesn't necessarily fulfil (for similar argument, see, e.g., Friedman, 2000), and thus rights (or privileges) to the immaterial shouldn't be given; rather, since no one is (directly) worse off by distributing the immaterial, all immaterial should be free for anyone to use. The contrary, that if someone has something that could be freely used but "'will spoil'" if not used, namely not benefit others while in the possession of one, they are falsely taken by that person.

[…] but if they perished in his possession without their due use; if the fruits rotted or the venison putrefied before he could spend it, he offended against the common law of Nature, and was liable to be punished: he invaded his neighbour's share, for he had no right farther than his use called for any of them, and they might serve to afford him conveniencies of life. (TTG II, 37)

That is, if one doesn't share what is sharable and what one can't all use oneself, one is at fault. And again:

But if either the grass of his enclosure rotted on the ground, or the fruit of his planting perished without gathering and laying up, this part of the

Figure 2. The instance of an immaterial object can be used by as many as have need to it at any one time.

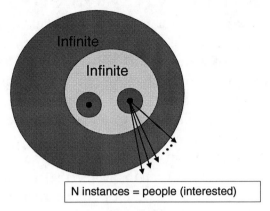

earth, notwithstanding his enclosure, was still to be looked on as waste,
and might be the possession of any other. (TTG II, 38).

Immaterial objects are hardly scarce. Anyone can make a copy of an
immaterial object without taking it away from another. Therefore, any number
of people can share the same immaterial object without it being taken away
from another in any way. Thus, the immaterial should indeed be seen as
commons, but unlike the material commons, which is limited, the immaterial
commons should be seen as an infinite commons, products of which can each
be shared an unlimited number of times (see Figure 2).

Even though Locke addresses this to the state of nature, in IPRs we have
a situation in which there still is "as good and as much" left for others, if others
are given the opportunity to use that as good and as much. Now, the immaterial
if not used would be a good spoiled, since it would "perish" in the possession
of one and be taken away from the use of others. If everyone had enough
imperishable goods to purchase it, this would not be a problem.

The deprivation argument is of course strongly tied to this argument. The
counterargument to the deprivation argument would be the deprivation of
potential profits. Potential profits are a difficult question, which needs a
consequentialist approach rather than a liberalist approach. This is not a
Lockean problem, but rather a liberalism vs. consequentialism problem (see,
however, Kimppa, 2004).

FREE SOFTWARE FOUNDATION: A CASE FOR A LIBERALIST VIEW ON SOFTWARE?

As an example on how a system for the immaterial would work if the views presented were applied, the Free Software Foundation (FSF) stands out. The FSF does not propose that software should be given away for free, but it does support the idea that once a piece of software is obtained, the one possessing that piece of software should be able to do with it as he or she pleases (Free Software Foundation, 1996). This, in my view is in accordance to Locke's views presented in the previous chapter.

The FSF is interested in freedom, freedom to do with software one has as one pleases. Freedom is more important to the FSF than is utility (Vadén & Stallman, 2002), as it is for Locke. If it fits the purposes of ones needs, use it, if it doesn't, modify it or have it modified by another. If one likes it and supposes someone else might as well, one ought to have freedom to give it to another, to sell it to another, or trade it with another (Free Software Foundation, 1996; Stallman, 1992, 2001).

"'Free software' is a matter of liberty, not price. To understand the concept, you should think of 'free' as in 'free speech,' not as in 'free beer'" (Free Software Foundation, 2001).

The long-term goal of FSF is to make the post-scarcity world possible by trying to ensure that at least software will be non-scarce (Free Software Foundation, 1993). Now, software is artificially made scarce by IPRs, even though the immaterial is by nature non-scarce, unlike the material.

One is not Deprived of One's Software

What is software? Our ideas of software are muddled by our thoughts of the material objects, as pointed out in previous chapter. Stallman (1994) and the FSF agree with this:

Our ideas and intuitions about property for material objects are about whether it is right to take an object away from someone else. They don't directly apply to making a copy of something. But the owners ask us to apply them anyway.

FSF's view is that software differs from material goods in a fundamental way; namely, it can be used by as many people as want to use it at once, without it being taken away from any one user. It is a good that can be copied to as many users that have a need for it; thus, it is an unstealable good in the Lockean sense. It isn't necessary to deprive someone else from the same by getting one for oneself. The material component is irrelevant from this point of view, be it a CD, a hard drive, or a floppy disk among other possible storage media (Free Software Foundation, 2001a).

Stallman (1994) opposes the right of the IPR owners to restrict the direct rights of the purchaser of software to do with the software as he or she pleases. Creators of programs should not have the right to order what others can do with what they possess when it is in the creator's possession at the same time. On the contrary, the users should be able to do with what they have as they please.

According to Stallman (1994), the main reason for our intuition for having property rights in software comes from a misguided implication from the material objects needing ownership, because material objects can only be owned by someone other than the current owner if they are taken away from the current owner. If one loses a material object, it hurts the one who loses it equally to the gain by another getting it. The owners of IPRs expect others to apply this thinking to their products even though they do not ever lack the "property," even if others have copies. There is a clear mistake in this thinking from the intuition of taking away an object to the thinking of having rights to something another possesses.

When I cook spaghetti, I do object if someone else eats it, because then I cannot eat it. His action hurts me exactly as much as it benefits him; only one of us can eat the spaghetti, so the question is, which? The smallest distinction between us is enough to tip the ethical balance.

But whether you run or change a program I wrote affects you directly and me only indirectly. Whether you give a copy to your friend affects you and your friend much more than it affects me. I shouldn't have the power to tell you not to do these things. No one should. (Stallman, 1994)

Who is the owner of a piece of software — the person who has purchased it or the person who has written it? If there are no IPRs on software, one need not worry about what one may or may not do with the software, so the question really becomes moot (Free Software Foundation, 1993).

Owners of IPRs claim to suffer a potential harm by letting others do as they please with what they possess (Stallman, 1994). Now this may or may not be true, but that is a consequentialist argument that is irrelevant if the freedom of a person to do as he or she pleases with his or her possessions is considered to be of more importance.

The FSF doesn't claim that one may not sell, trade, give away, or share software; rather, it actually claims just the opposite, i.e., that one may do all that, independent of whether the creator of the software wants it or not. One doesn't need to pay for permission to use the software, although one may have to pay to get the software. Software can be delivered in many different forms, and it can be ready made or made to the specifications of the ordering party. Thus one gets paid for the work, but not for the software itself, which need not be limited in use (Free Software Foundation, 1993).

Although the FSF takes no direct stance on other digitally distributable information, it does notice strong similarities with software, because again, it is not taken away from someone if it is shared, but giving someone else the right to dictate what one may do with one's possessions is at least problematic (Free Software Foundation, 2000).

Method Should Be Free

There is a crucial difference between material objects and immaterial objects, namely, that the method for a material object is at times hard to copy (not that this would justify IPRs on material objects, but it lessens the argument for IPRs on immaterial ones). But as we saw previously, some of the methods to acquire material objects aren't hard to copy either, and Locke seems to support copying of methods for material objects. The method for creation of an immaterial object, however, is easy to copy. It should be clear that unnecessary artificial fences shouldn't be erected to obstruct others from using immaterial objects. Competition for competition's sake — without giving thought to the ways how and why it is done — can be destructive rather than constructive. Destructive competition is what follows from putting up artificial fences around immaterial objects and restricting people's use of the immaterial (Stallman, 1992). Intellectual property rights are privileges given to promote the amount of immaterial goods in the world, but if instead they adversely affect one's freedom, they should be abolished (Free Software Foundation, 1998).

According to the FSF, one ought to be able to make as many copies of one's program as one wants, be they for personal use or for distribution either for free or for sale. One ought to also have the right to modify the software one possesses to better fit the purposes for which it is intended. The reason for these arguments being that one should have the freedom to use the method and the freedom to do with what one has as one pleases. For this, one ought to not only get the executable but also the source code, so that one really has what one has gotten either by free or by purchasing the software (Free Software Foundation, 2001; Stallman, 1992).

One should be able to learn the method to use it, to improve on it, and to be able to fix it (Stallman, 1992). This is especially crucial with scientific knowledge. The main purpose of scientific knowledge is just dissemination of knowledge, and if copyright restricts rather than promotes this, it should be abandoned with regard to scientific articles or books (Stallman, 2001b). This is a form of freedom to do with what one has as one pleases. Again, we are faced with the same basic thought that applying this freedom to the immaterial (e.g., software) doesn't deprive anyone else from what they have. "[C]opyright cuts into the natural rights of the public — and that ... can only be justified for the public's sake" (Stallman, 1994). Now, if that can't be justified for the public's sake (See e.g., Kimppa, 2004) and if this argument is not also very compelling, it shouldn't be the case. Natural rights are not something that can be arbitrarily overdriven.

When it comes to software, one needs the software sources to be able to either self modify the software or have it modified by someone else as one sees necessary (Free Software Foundation, 1993). Source, in software, is the method; it is what creates the immaterial commons — if it is available for others to use.

How to Get Immaterial Commons

Free software can be seen as a part of the immaterial commons derived from Locke. As is pointed out by the FSF, this doesn't need to be limited to software alone but could include any and all digitally distributable media (Free Software Foundation, 2000). Especially critical would be to get scientific knowledge distributed via the World Wide Web, so that its dissemination would not be hindered by the efforts of publishing houses to make a profit rather than spread knowledge (Stallman, 2001b). For example, Prentice Hall PTR Publishing (among many others) is joining in this either fully or partly by making publications available directly from websites or publishing digitally delivered works some time after the publication in retail form: "[The books] are legal to copy, modify, and redistribute" (Perens, 2003). Of course, the FSF both sells printed copies and delivers manuals digitally (Free Software Foundation, 2002). This is a viable start towards a real immaterial commons, but there is still a way to go.

Copyleft is a viable way to promote the immaterial commons, because it ensures that any material done or modified under the copyleft license remains copylefted. To get viable immaterial commons, anything that one wants to belong to it should be copylefted (Stallman, 2001a). More consistent with the idea of the immaterial commons would be to cease thinking of the immaterial as something that can be owned, but this will require serious reconsideration of the Western law tradition.

CONCLUSIONS

Most of liberalist thinking is in one way or another based in Locke, and thus either a new justification needs to be found for IPRs — other than Locke's, since it seems that Locke can't be used in defense of them — or a new insight to IPRs must be adopted.

Now what kind of a world of software creation would combining Locke's and Stallman's arguments lead to? Likely to a world where there would be less mammoth software and more modular software, from which one (or a company) could compile fitting programs for oneself (or the users). More tailored programs would likely exist, since programs would be made to fit the needs of the one ordering them rather than the created needs of the marketing department. But most of all, it would imply that the user, the person actually having the software, could modify the software to his or her own needs if necessary or have that done by an outside party. For a method of how to actually implement this, refer to the FSF website at http://www.fsf.org.

Even though Locke promotes the need for ownership of property, he does it from the point of necessity; one can't have something material that another has. This thinking should not be taken for granted, however, when we move to the world of the immaterial, since the aforementioned is not the case there. Rather other values, such as cooperation should be promoted, and I fail to see Locke not agreeing on this.

Locke's goal was for a world in which there would be as much justice and good for all as possible. Stallman's aim for a post-scarcity world (Free Software Foundation, 1993) would indeed seem to be an aim towards Locke's world, and in my opinion, it is a goal worth pursuing.

REFERENCES

Free Software Foundation. (1993). The Gnu Manifesto. Retrieved January 13, 2003, at: http://www.gnu.org/gnu/manifesto.html.
Free Software Foundation. (1996). Overview of the GNU Project. Retrieved January 13, 2003, at: http://www.gnu.org/gnu/gnu-history.html.

Free Software Foundation. (1996a). Selling Free Software. Retrieved January 13, 2003, at: http://www.gnu.org/philosophy/selling.html.

Free Software Foundation. (1998). Reevaluating Copyright: The Public Must Prevail. Retrieved January 14, 2003.

Free Software Foundation (2000). Regarding Gnutella. Retrieved January 13, 2003 at: http://www.gnu.org/philosophy/gnutella.html.

Free Software Foundation (2001). The Free Software Definition. Retrieved January 13, 2003, at: http://www.gnu.org/philosophy/free-sw.html.

Free Software Foundation (2001a). Philosophy of the GNU Project. Retrieved January 13, 2003, at: http://www.gnu.org/philosophy/.

Free Software Foundation (2002). Free Software and Free Manuals. Retrieved January 13, 2003, at: http://www.gnu.org/philosophy/free-doc.html.

Friedman, D.D. (2000). Law's order: What economics has to do with law and why it matters. Princeton, NJ: Princeton University Press. Retrieved January 10, 2003, at: http://www.daviddfriedman.com/laws_order/index.shtml.

Kimppa, K.K. (2004). Consequentialist considerations of intellectual property rights in software and other digitally distributable media. In press. *Proceedings of Ethicomp 2004, Challenges for the Citizen of the Information Society*, April 14-16, University of the Aegean, Syros, Greece.

Kinsella, N. S. (2001). Against intellectual property. *Journal of Libertarian Studies*, 15(2) (Spring 2001), 1-53. Retrieved January 10, 2003, at: http://www.mises.org/journals/jls/15_2/15_2_1.pdf.

Kramer, M. H. (1997). *John Locke and the origins of private property: Philosophical explorations of individualism, community, and equality.* Cambridge, UK: Cambridge University Press.

Locke, J. (2002). Two treatises of government. Originally published in 1690, various publishers used. London: Everyman, Orion Publishing Group. Second Treatise of Government available online, for example, retrieved January 10, 2003, at http://www.swan.ac.uk/poli/texts/locke/lockcont.htm.

Long, R.T. (1995). *The Libertarian case against intellectual property rights. Formulations, Autumn.* Libertarian Nation Foundation. Retrieved January 9, 2003, at: http://www.libertariannation.org/a/f3111.html.

Perens, B. (2003). *Bruce Perens' Open Source Series, with Prentice Hall PTR Publishers.* Retrieved January 13, 2003, at http://perens.com/Books.

Simmons, A.J. (1992). *The Lockean theory of rights.* Princeton, NJ: Princeton University Press.

Stallman, R. (1992). *Why software should be free.* Retrieved January 13, 2003, at: http://www.gnu.org/philosophy/shouldbefree.html.

Stallman, R. (1994). *Why software should not have owners.* Retrieved January 13, 2003, at http://www.gnu.org/philosophy/why-free.html.

Stallman, R. (2001). *The GNU GPL and the American way.* Retrieved January 13, 2003, at: http://www.gnu.org/philosophy/gpl-american-way.html.

Stallman, R. (2001a). *The GNU project.* Retrieved January 13, 2003, at: http://www.gnu.org/gnu/thegnuproject.html.

Stallman, R. (2001b). *Science must "push copyright aside."* Nature webdebates. Retrieved January 14, 2003, at: http://www.nature.com/nature/debates/e-access/Articles/stallman.html.

Vadén, T. & Stallman, R. (2002). *Koodi vapaaksi (not translated).* Tampere, Finland: Tampere University Press.

Chapter III

Locke and Intellectual Property Rights

Michael J. Scanlan
Oregon State University, USA

ABSTRACT

This chapter considers certain features of Locke's account in Chapter V of his Second Treatise concerning how a natural right of ownership can arise in previously unowned goods. We note that some take this theory to be still applicable in our own day in situations of original acquisition of ownership in intellectual property. The chapter explains how a quasi-Lockean theory could support a very limited natural right to a species of intellectual property. But it also notes that this theory by itself is not strong enough to support a natural right in an intellectual property of the sort given by copyright. Such property rights must be provided as a result of positive law.

LOCKE ON PROPERTY ACQUISITION

Many people think that something like the theory of natural acquisition of property rights in John Locke's *Second Treatise of Civil Government* can provide a basis for an entitlement theory of property. Such an entitlement theory is defined by Robert Nozick in *Anarchy, State, and Utopia* (1974). As Nozick expresses the idea, an entitlement theory has three parts: one is an account of justice in original acquisition, i.e., making what had previously been unowned the property of an individual; a second is an account of justice in property transfer, e.g., through sale, inheritance, gift, forfeiture, etc. These first two elements embody a notion similar to the notion of "good title" in U.S. real estate laws; i.e., that I properly got my house and land from someone who properly got it from someone else, and so on back to some (perhaps mythic) original event when the previously unoccupied land was (somehow) justly appropriated. The idea is that if the original appropriation was good, and each step of transfer was good, then my "title" in my current property is good.

The third and last feature in an entitlement theory of justice in property ownership, according to Nozick, is an account of justice in rectification. This is rooted in the observation that in any actual long chains of entitlements, there are bound to be steps that don't meet the standards of justice. An account of justice in rectification is supposed to tell me what to do when I discover that my entitlement to my house and land is faulty because of an event that happened, unbeknownst to me, a hundred years ago.

Quite a few people have thought that Locke's ideas about acquisition of property in the state of nature (1690, Ch. V) can form the core of an account of the principles of original acquisition. This is often thought to be the trickiest of the three sets of principles. Nozick himself, while endorsing entitlement theories of property rights (as opposed to Rawlsian theories), declines to flesh out the content of the three sorts of principles. In particular, he argues that Locke's treatment of principles of original acquisition is inadequate. Whether or not Nozick or someone else could have provided us with a plausible entitlement account of ownership, Thomas Mautner (1982) made the important point that it wouldn't really matter. This is assuming that people engage in such discussions in order to throw light on the justice of actual property distributions in our present world. If we were to take seriously the multistep view of derived rights to property, few homeowners in North America, such as myself, could confidently assert a just title in their property.[1] One has, of course, the doubtful justice of the acquisition of territory by Europeans where Native Americans were already living. But even aside from that, given a 100- to 400-year history of property transfers, something questionable by reasonably strict standards of justice is bound to occur. As Mautner puts it:

A clean record can hardly ever be established. Force and fraud have reigned supreme in the history of mankind. And records without any known *unjust steps in them are in most cases not fully known and there is then an extremely strong presumption that they are fraught with iniquity somewhere along the line. (p. 267)*

Of course, the Nozickian account of entitlement theories includes a segment that gives principles of rectification in recognition of these sorts of problems. But, as Mautner suggests, "a moment's reflection" indicates that any serious quest for such principles will probably be unsuccessful. Even if we knew what really happened one hundred or two hundred or three hundred years ago, what does that tell us should be done about my and my neighbors' belief that we really own our houses and lots?

Given that in the present state of the world, any acquisitions of property from an unowned condition occurred in the distant past, Mautner (1982) concludes:

According to the approach now under discussion, a theory of original appropriation would be relevant only in combination with the principles of derivation and rectification. But as I have shown, we know that our knowledge of history and our ignorance of history are such that these principles cannot be applied as envisaged. Consequently, a theory of original appropriation is irrelevant to questions concerning contemporary property rights, and can be of no use in current debates on e.g. income tax, social welfare, or medical insurance. (p. 268)

Written in 1981, Mautner's account of the irrelevance of theories of original appropriation, such as Locke's, to contemporary debates about property rights seems to me perfectly accurate. However, since that date, we have had the rise of the information economy and, irrespective of its other problems, a goodly number of people have felt that here is an area where Locke's theory of justice in original appropriation has a role to play.

This is because, in the case of intellectual property, many people feel that there is a situation similar to what Locke presented as a distant historical period when the whole earth was a "common" held jointly by all humans. For the theorist of intellectual property, it is tempting to analogize the situation envisioned by Locke to the situation in the realm of thought. This is that (roughly) there is a realm of ideas that we humans are able to roam freely over, according to our abilities, picking up what interests us as we go, just as in Locke's picture early humans might have wandered the woods of Britain gathering acorns to eat.

This analogy between gathering ideas and gathering acorns is what attracts certain theorists to Locke's account. This is because Locke seeks to give a natural law account of ownership in the previously unowned acorns gathered by the primeval Briton. In a famous passage, Locke (1690) tells us that for the individual on the primeval earth when all land was held in common:

... the "labour" of his body and the "work" of his hands, we may say, are properly his. Whatsoever, then, he removes out of the state that Nature hath provided and left it in, he hath mixed his labour with it, and joined it to something that is his own, and thereby made it his property. It being by him removed from the common state Nature placed it in, it has by this labour something annexed to it that excludes the common right of other men. (Ch. V, sec. 26)

This labor mixing is supposed to give a natural right of ownership in the acorns separate from any "positive" law established by social compact and one which any such compact is obliged to respect. If we think of the acorns as ideas gathered from the common realm of thought, then this natural law account has some attractions for certain U.S. theorists. For them it provides an alternative account to the sort of frankly consequentialist treatment of intellectual property rights embodied in the U.S. Constitution's grant to Congress of the power to establish copyrights and patents. That document specified that such rights are to "promote the Progress of Science and Useful Arts, by securing for limited Times to Authors and Inventors the exclusive Right to their respective Writings and Discoveries" (Art. I, sec. 8).

What we have here is a provision for laws that are justified by their ability to provide for some aspects of the general welfare. This constitutional context in the U.S. neatly frames the question of whether intellectual property rights can be accounted for as natural rights on the basis of some quasi-Lockean[2] theory of original appropriation or if their ultimate justification is always going to be some judgment of overall social benefit as a result of some agreed upon system of positive law?

ON OWNING *HAMLET*

I will not attempt a detailed analysis of Locke's actual theory of original appropriation in his *Second Treatise on Civil Government*, but there is reason to use him as a reference point. This is mainly because so many others do.[3] He was following in a natural law tradition established by Grotius and

Pufendorf,[4] but, at least in English-speaking countries, his chapter on property has effectively become the *fons et origo* of subsequent learned discussion. Because of this, my strategy will be to consider the ideas that many have found in Locke, but not to attempt a total account of their relations in the *Second Treatise*. The labor principle seems to be what drives theorists back to Locke. They take him to provide a classic formulation of the principle in his attribution of ownership to "mixing one's labor" with unowned material. Nozick (1974) provides a compendium of problems involved in making sense of what becomes owned as a result of any such labor mixing (pp. 174-175). Nevertheless, some sort of "labor mixing" theory has a great deal of intuitive appeal. This seems most aptly summed up in the statement that people are entitled to the fruits of their labor.

I am perfectly willing to accept this intuition as true, as far as it goes. The problem is whether there is enough in this intuition to support a useful account of original ownership. Before we consider the original ownership problems, we should clarify that whatever a proponent of such a theory means by "labor," it seems that (1) it isn't limited to physical "sweat of the brow" labor, and (2) that ownership is not contingent on the amount of labor. I assume these two provisions must hold in connection with such a theory because I don't see how to get a workable account without them.

To see this, consider me with my (already owned) flour, water, yeast, salt, oven, and workspace setting up to make bread. I go through the usual process of mixing, kneading, rising, baking, and at the end have some nice loaves of bread. We say that these are clearly mine because I owned the original ingredients and equipment and put my labor into producing the finished loaves. But what if I instead own the flour, water, yeast, salt and also a magic wand? I wave this wand over the ingredients while chanting a short incantation (detailed in the wand instructions) and the ingredients are transformed into piping hot, lovely loaves of bread. My intuition is that I own these loaves of bread as much as I own the previous ones, even though I think it is safe to say that I put much less work/labor into producing these loaves. We can say I did work in this case. I did *something* that produced the transformation of the ingredients into bread. That seems all that is required here to make the resulting loaves fully mine. The nature of the something and the amount of the something don't seem relevant to the ownership claim.

Looking ahead, these features of any plausible version of a labor theory of ownership are attractive aspects if we are going to apply such a theory to intellectual property. Even though Thomas Edison said that genius is one-tenth inspiration and nine-tenths perspiration, it is clear that in most cases the sort of labor involved in generating intellectual products is different from that involved in plowing fields or digging ditches. Again, notwithstanding a general truth contained in Edison's dictum, there are a good number of cases where key ideas "come to" researchers in a time when they are not specifically focused on a problem on which they have been working, for example, while taking a stroll, drinking a beer, etc.[5] To be applicable to cases of intellectual property, it is clear that a labor theory of original acquisition will need to have the above two provisos; that is, the ownership is independent of the amount of labor involved or how "sweaty" the labor. With these provisos, many people see an exact parallel between the quasi-Lockean acquisition by labor scenario and the situation in intellectual production. Shakespeare goes to the public house across from the Globe Theater, buys a pot of ale, gets out his pen and ink and paper, sits down and starts writing out *Hamlet, the Prince of Denmark*. What he produces must be his.

The knowledgeable reader is probably aware already of a significant flaw in this analogy. This is that I already owned the flour, etc., with which I "mixed" my labor. Shakespeare did not, however, own the English language that he used to shape the play *Hamlet*. But there are resources in the quasi-Lockean theory to deal with this. Consider my earlier bread-baking example. It might have been that I am a baker who disdains buying packaged yeast in a store. Instead, I wish to create my own natural sourdough starter for my bread baking. To do this I "capture" naturally occurring wild yeast organisms floating in the air and incorporate them into a flour-water mixture where they happily go about reproducing themselves. If I had chosen to bake my loaves of bread in this way, I would take myself to own my loaves in a robust sense of ownership. But I am, in this case, appropriating a small, but essential, part of the ingredients from a resource that is either previously unowned or commonly owned.[6]

So it seems that there are cases where one can incorporate material that one doesn't own into a production and still own the resulting product. So, maybe Shakespeare was like the baker using wild yeast. As has been noted in the literature, the real force of Locke's theory of appropriation is not really in the "labor-mixing" portion. This we can take to be a necessary condition under a quasi-Lockean theory. The more interesting portion of Locke's view is what has come to be called the "proviso." This is that a person can appropriate material that is unowned by him or her from a common resource, "at least where there is enough and as good left in common for others" (1690, Ch. V, sec. 26). Locke's examples of such instances from his own day include catching fish from the ocean or hunting hares on common land. In terms of Locke's own time, these examples met the criterion of being an effectively unlimited resource. All of those in the population who want to take a portion of the resource for their own use do not effectively impair the abundance available to others. Similarly, when I appropriate free-floating yeast for my bread baking, I don't effectively diminish the resource for others.

This would seem to be exactly the situation we have with Shakespeare. Shakespeare's use of the English language in *Hamlet* did not diminish the resources available for others; all the words of English were still available to English speakers. So, here it seems that we can take a version of Locke's theory and use it to say that Shakespeare has a natural law ownership right in *Hamlet*. But, of course it isn't as neat as that. There are clear differences between hares and *Hamlet,* and we must see what difference they make. One important difference is that we've taken *Hamlet* to be a product produced from resources in an abundant common reserve. Hares and fish are not "produced" but are caught fully formed. Some might say that Shakespeare "caught" *Hamlet* in this way, but we have started with the producing metaphor and it seems more apt. Locke's set of examples has a comparison to handle this situation: he also speaks of "the ore I have digged in any place, where I have a right to [it] in common with others" (1690, Ch. V, sec. 27) becoming his own property (assuming there is an ample supply left for all others who may want it). So Shakespeare's case may be more like this, mining out parts of the English language to take and process into *Hamlet*. In the case of an ore deposit, one can wonder about limits to the resource even under primitive conditions of exploitation. But, given the nature of language, Shakespeare's appropriation of words to produce *Hamlet* seems to leave exactly as much behind for others. So now it seems we have a case that fits the Lockean proviso for appropriation even better than his own example of digging ore.

But we still have the problem of what is it that Shakespeare owns under this scheme of quasi-Lockean natural law. We are talking about *intellectual* property. The ontic status of such stuff is unclear, but we do know, at least, that it is not a physical object. Thus, we are not talking about the ale-stained manuscript that Shakespeare has written out. We might want to say that it is a certain combination or sequence of English words as an abstract object. But this won't really do. Consider the admittedly unlikely case that Ben Jonson sits down in a different pub with a different pot of ale at the other end of London on the night after that fateful night when Shakespeare had written down *Hamlet*. Jonson is also in search of a new play. With remarkable coincidence he writes out the same play *Hamlet* (by Ben Jonson). Does Jonson own *Hamlet?* All our previous reasoning tells us he does to the same extent that Shakespeare does. But if *Hamlet* is *the* abstract object consisting in a certain sequence of English words, then Jonson is too late — Shakespeare already owns it.

Now some might not object to this result. They may be happy with a "finders, keepers" view of intellectual property ownership. Shakespeare was skilled or resourceful enough to come across the previously unowned object that is the abstract sequence of words in *Hamlet*, recognize its value, and appropriate it. I doubt this theory is one we want to hold generally, but I'm not going to argue against it in general. What is important for our purposes here is that it is not quasi-Lockean. The "finders, keepers" approach does makes *Hamlet* a unique object. There is only one, and once it is appropriated from an unowned or commonly owned condition, there is nothing as good as it left for anyone else to appropriate. This clearly violates the Lockean proviso.

A Lockean approach can't treat Shakespeare as appropriating *Hamlet* as a whole abstract object, and so, just like Shakespeare, Jonson can go to the mine of the English language and dig out the ore from which to form his own *Hamlet*. But this, of course, is a puzzling result. In the ore case, Bill and Ben might have each dug the ore, smelted it down, and cast the metal into identically formed belt buckles. But there would still be two distinct buckles, one owned by Bill and one owned by Ben. In the *Hamlet* case, although the ontology is tricky, it seems that we want to stay committed to the idea that they each own the same thing. Here we start to reach some real limits in applying a Lockean theory of natural law ownership to intellectual property. Locke's theory is clearly crafted to deal with ownership only in the case of physical objects. When we start considering nonphysical objects, we are on our own and must face the fact that we are extending Locke's theory into a realm for which it was not crafted. The question is whether we can extend the theory in a way that doesn't violate its fundamental provisions ("owner action" and "enough remaining").

U.S. copyright law does provide for cases like the Bill, Ben, and *Hamlet* situation. What it grants in these cases is not a fully robust sort of ownership, but the right for each to keep others from copying from his own manuscript, but not the other's. Thus, if Ben decides to hold onto his manuscript and wait for the right producer to stage the play, while Bill rushes into the Globe Theater the next day waving his manuscript, saying how this is going to be a blockbuster, and gets it staged in a couple of weeks, then Bill has not violated Ben's copyright.

Of course, U.S. copyright law is far from being a natural law or even based on a notion of natural law. Although people speak of "owning" a copyright and these are bought and sold, it is really an ownership of a right that is at stake here and not the ownership of a thing, even a conceptual thing. The right is that one can exclude others from copying one's text (or other form of "expression") even after one has presented it in a public way that makes it practically possible for such copying to occur. But this right isn't a natural right. This is not simply because U.S. copyright law is positive law, it is because the copyright law is aimed at blocking the "natural" course of events. If the producer of a copyrightable work exposes this work to public view, as in a production of a play or publication of a text, it is "natural" for some other people to want their own copies. The copyright law blocks this from happening, legally, to provide an economic benefit to the producer from his product.

All this is to say that the copyright law protects the producer of a certain sort of intellectual product from certain economic consequences of his *use* of his product. This distinction of the use of the product from the product itself is significant here, because our previous quasi-Lockean reasoning has identified a natural right of ownership in the *product* of certain actions. Thus, our baker owned the loaves of bread he produced. To extend a quasi-Lockean theory of natural ownership rights to the case of intellectual property, we must identify what the intellectual analog is to the product that is "owned" in the case of material objects.

We have seen that we cannot give a Lockean account of ownership by appropriation of the full abstract text of *Hamlet*. We can only account for it by talking of a rightful appropriation from the resources of the English language of the raw material to "produce" the text of *Hamlet*. But in this case, if Bill and Ben produce each their own identical texts, they don't — as abstract objects — just match, they are the same text. One might say that this gives half-ownership to each in the full abstract text. But this really won't do, on our previous reasoning. The producer is naturally entitled to the full product of his actions and, on the account we are considering, the abstract text of *Hamlet* is produced fully by Bill and also produced fully by Ben.

But, of course, there is another way of looking at the ontology here. To some ears, it will sound strange to talk of either Bill or Ben "producing" the abstract text of *Hamlet*. Such a thing is an abstract object existing outside of time and is not produced or destroyed. Whether this view of the ontology of the text of Hamlet can be sustained in a general ontic theory is unclear to me, but I do find it intriguing that it provides a basis for a view of naturally owned intellectual product that has some correlation to U.S. intellectual property law.

This ontology is, of course, in accordance with our previous conclusion that neither Bill nor Ben own the abstract text of *Hamlet*, this because the abstract text cannot be produced and we have already seen the Lockean argument that it cannot be justly appropriated as a whole from the "commons." We have also previously accepted the view that, although Bill and Ben have each produced a manuscript of their play, it is a physical property of theirs and not an intellectual property. So, what is their intellectual product?

I would propose that it is the knowledge (in the sense of awareness) of the abstract text that is what the actions of Bill and Ben produce. We might say that they have produced a certain intellectual state in themselves and recorded it in their manuscripts. Here, the two intellectual states individuate nicely. Bill has produced his intellectual state and Ben has produced his own intellectual state. The two cases individuate in the way that the belt buckles that each might have produced individuate. We can also easily identify this knowledge or awareness as a product of their actions. So, here on a quasi-Lockean theory of ownership we have an "intellectual" product in which "intellectual workers" have a natural ownership right.[7]

This right to possess the knowledge/awareness that one has produced by one's own actions does provide for a natural right in intellectual property, but it is vastly weaker than the sort of natural ownership rights in intellectual property that some authors hope to find. Indeed, I suspect those who hold such a "natural rights" view will consider what I have come up with as a trivial sort of ownership. Shortly, I will explore how it indeed does fall short of the practical goals that generally motivate the work of natural property rights theorists. But first, I want to argue that what I have derived as a natural right of ownership (assuming the quasi-Lockean theory of natural ownership) is indeed a species of intellectual property.

My only argument for this is the existence of the poor relative of U.S. intellectual property law, the trade secrets doctrine. This roughly holds that an individual can hold certain sorts of knowledge secret, and if someone obtains that knowledge in violation of the holder's efforts to keep it secret, then his or her acquisition of that knowledge is illegitimate and the acquirer cannot use it. The standard example of a piece of intellectual property of this sort is the secret formula for Coca-Cola syrup. Legend has it that the exact secret formula is known only to a few people in the Coca-Cola enterprise. Others know only what they need to know to do their one part in the production processes.[8] In the quasi-Lockean account I have given, this one piece of positive U.S. intellectual property law represents a positive institution of a natural right.

COPYRIGHT PROTECTION OF SOFTWARE

So, I have found a natural right in intellectual property on a quasi-Lockean basis and have found it enshrined in one aspect of U.S. law. But as I mentioned, this is not the sort of natural ownership many would want to find. One way to see how this is so is to consider the motto of the Software and Information Industry Association, "Copying is Theft." As a somewhat crude and oversimplified statement of U.S. copyright law, this is true.[9] But, of course, many in the software and other industries want to see it not as "theft" because of a social "compact" (to put the matter in Lockean terms), but as theft in the context of natural right. This they will be unable to do on the basis of my quasi-Lockean account of natural right in intellectual property.

Indeed, on this account, the standard pro-copying argument finds a theoretic basis. That argument is that if I copy software from you, you have not lost anything that is naturally yours. Unlike the situation where Ben steals Bill's belt buckle and Bill no longer has anything to hold up his pants, if Ben had not thought up *Hamlet* himself but had instead copied a manuscript that Bill had carelessly left lying about, Bill still has his copy of *Hamlet*. In the terminology used previously, by his efforts Ben has acquired new knowledge, which is his, i.e., awareness of *Hamlet,* and he has certainly not taken away Bill's own knowledge of *Hamlet*, so he has not stolen Bill's intellectual property. Similarly, the proponents of software copying say that the original software owner has exactly the same intellectual property at the end of the software copying process, so he or she has not lost any intellectual property — there is nothing stolen.

But the officials of the Software and Information Industry Association will say, "Wait a minute! Ben has done something simply wrong by copying Bill's manuscript that he has left lying around." Many people will feel this way and that is because the case is incompletely described. A crucial element is Bill's state of mind with respect to his *Hamlet* knowledge. Most people will assume that Bill wishes to keep his knowledge of *Hamlet* secret, at least until he can stage it. If that is the case, then indeed (modulo some other details of the specific case) Ben has violated Bill's natural right to keep his knowledge secret. This is the natural right embodied in trade secret legal doctrine. For our purposes, it is important to note that this is a different natural right violation from theft. People speak of trade secrets as intellectual "property." But, as has been noted in the literature, property rights can be viewed as various bundles of rights, which can vary from one sort of property right to another. As noted above, I view the trade secret right as the right to keep one's knowledge secret. If someone attempts to breach that secrecy, then he or she has violated my right. We do speak of "stealing" secrets, but the point here is that the "stealing" is different from stealing a car or money. This means the moral rationale for what is wrong is different in each case. In the car or money case, the problem is depriving the owner of the use of the property. That isn't the case in the "stealing" secrets situation. The trade secret owner still has his or her knowledge and can use it. The problem, as diagnosed above, lies in some natural right to keep our knowledge to ourselves. But for our purposes, it is important to note that this is a different natural right violation from theft in a strict sense, although the fact that there is *some* natural right violation clouds our perception of this case. The quasi-Lockean theory does account for the perception of many people that there is a violation of some sort of right here.

Of course, Bill's state of mind (he wants to keep his play to himself until it can be staged) is the state of mind of members of the Software and Information Industry Association. There may be disks or files of their software "lying around," so to speak, but they don't want people to make copies of them to gain access to their knowledge. They want to keep their knowledge, embodied in their software, to themselves. So, that seems to be the end of the story; it isn't exactly theft in a strict sense, but there is a violation of natural right in the copying, if we work on analogy with Ben and Bill and the unauthorized manuscript copying.

But this neglects an important aspect of the use of certain sorts of knowledge, i.e., natural intellectual property. Some knowledge can by used and still kept secret, like the Coca-Cola syrup formula. But for other sorts of knowledge, e.g., a novel, a musical piece, a play, the way that most producers want to "use" their knowledge is by disseminating it, making others aware of it. Here one is not attempting to keep one's knowledge secret, one is indeed actively working to transfer it. What is the situation here under the quasi-Lockean natural law account?

To have a specific case, we will consider that Shakespeare has actually arranged for production of *Hamlet* by the Lord Chamberlain's Men at the Globe Theater. Ben buys a ticket and goes to attend the production. Ben happens to own the world's first video camcorder. Because his is the first and nobody else has heard of such a thing, the Globe management has not put small print on the back of his ticket about "all recording by electronic or other devices is expressly forbidden." We are, we suppose, operating in a state of nature with no positive law on these matters and no agreements between Bill, Ben, or the management. So, Ben videorecords the production of *Hamlet* and takes it home with him. By his actions, he has produced a physical object that gives him knowledge of the text of *Hamlet*. Has he violated Bill's natural right in his knowledge of *Hamlet*? To make the point sharper, we will also assume that Bill doesn't want copies made of his play. In this case, Ben has violated Bill's wishes, but has he also violated his natural right?

My answer is "no". This is because Bill can't have it both ways, despite the common human tendency to try. He can't both disseminate his knowledge, awareness, and ideas, and at the same time not disseminate them. This is an aspect covered in U.S. trade secret law. Coca-Cola can't take out an ad in the *Atlanta Journal-Constitution* publishing the secret formula for Coke and then complain that they are being robbed if readers clip it out or copy it. In the state of nature, it seems that if someone gives you access to his or her knowledge with no prior stipulation as to what you can or can't do with it, then if you take some action to acquire that knowledge, it is yours also.

How does this apply to software? Insofar as we think of it as analogous to the text by Shakespeare, that is, insofar as it makes sense to locate it under copyright law, then it would seem that as a matter of natural right as developed in a quasi-Lockean manner the software developer in the state of nature has two choices (leaving aside software licensing agreements): either keep the software only for her own use or disseminate the software, at which point people can make copies without taking from her something in which she has a natural right, i.e., her knowledge of the software. So, in a quasi-Lockean state of nature, absent software licensing agreements that bar copying, copying is not theft, even if the software developer doesn't want others to copy.

The problem here is the use to which people want to put their knowledge, more specifically, the way they want to make money from it. Just as the way in which people usually want to make money from plays, music, movies, novels, etc., is by "exhibition" of them in some fashion, many software developers intend to make money from their software by distributing to others, for a fee, copies to put on their own computers.[10] This subjects the software distributor to the danger of having additional copies made in the way that copies of movies, novels, etc. can be made. This is the "natural" course of human behavior. It is the contention of the quasi-Lockean theory that within a state of nature, the software distributor is expecting an impossibility. She wants to distribute copies and have the distributed material remain in her possession in the same way it would have if kept secret by her. She can, of course, seek agreements with the parties receiving copies of the software that require them not to make copies. But there is no general natural right that allows her to both disseminate the material and expect it, in effect, to be kept secret.

We can view copyright law as a societal device to remedy the perceived problems with this natural state. In this way, it is much like modern sewer and water systems. These are built to overcome the unsanitary conditions that "naturally" arise when large numbers of humans attempt to live in a restricted area. The copyright laws function in a different realm but aim to overcome the disadvantages for society that arise in the natural context of disseminating intellectual works, which would make it difficult for intellectual producers to make money from their knowledge. Since it is perceived to be a societal good that these producers have a road to riches, or at least remuneration, we create under positive law an artificial set of rights for the producers that forbids copying of their works under most circumstances.

On this quasi-Lockean theory, the U.S. Constitution gets the basis of copyright law just right in its frankly consequentialist treatment. It explicitly does not present the copyright provision as giving legal enunciation to a pre-existing natural right of property. This contrasts with provisions for such rights as free speech and freedom of religion, which many people see as natural rights being given positive legal status in the relevant constitutional provisions. On the quasi-Lockean theory, the framers of the constitutional provision were not for some ideological or political purpose invoking a consequentialist basis for copyright law and avoiding a natural right treatment. On this quasi-Lockean theory, there is no alternative justification for copyright law. There is no natural right to copyright protection of intellectual property.

ENDNOTES

1   This problem is obviated in most U.S. jurisdictions by statute. For instance, state law might only require that a property owner possess clear title dating back forty years from acquisition of the property. The property owner does not need to defend against claims from prior to that cut-off date.

2   I use quasi-Lockean to indicate that in general I am concerned with principles of right that subsequent authors have thought to find in Locke's *Second Treatise*. What Locke actually had in mind in his treatise is mostly outside the scope of this chapter.

3   A good example of such use of Locke for defending a natural right to intellectual property is in Moore (2001). For various reasons, I have chosen not to address the specific arguments of Moore or other authors in this exposition, but to discuss the issues more generally.

4   For excellent accounts of Locke's relations to Grotius and Pufendorf see Olivecrona (1974a, 1974b).

5   For instance, the basic idea for the polymerase chain reaction came to Kary Mullis while driving to a summer cabin. See the end of his Nobel prize biography at www.nobel.se/chemistry/laureates/1993/mullis-autobio.html.

6   In the *Second Treatise,* Locke is, generally, speaking of a situation where the earth's land and its produce is owned in "common" by all humans, perhaps in the sense of "common land" in English law. Many subsequent writers have taken his ideas to apply to a situation where something is, prior to appropriation, not owned in common but completely unowned. I follow that tradition in this chapter, although how it relates to Locke's actual thought is unclear.

6   On a true Lockean theory this result is overdetermined, since Locke considers people to have ownership in their "persons," and presumably this would include their mental states.

7   This corresponds to the practice in the Elizabethan theater of not giving actors the entire text of a play, but only a copy of their own words with cueing words from the other actors in a scene.

8   In this treatment, I am going to ignore patent protection. I believe that much of what I have to say about copyright can be transferred over to the situations covered by patents.

9   Of course, there are software developers who make their money developing software to run on one or a set of computer systems for a single, typically corporate, client. The corporate client would presumably have a right of ownership in the programming as a result of agreement with the software developer and, on the quasi-Lockean theory, be entitled to keep it secret.

REFERENCES

Locke, J. (1690). *Two treatises of government.* Many editions, standard edition is edited by Peter Laslett, 2nd ed. Cambridge, UK: Cambridge University Press, 1967.

Mautner, T. (1982). Locke on original appropriation. *American Philosophical Quarterly, 19,* 259-270.

Moore, A.D. (2001). *Intellectual property and information control.* New Brunswick, NJ: Transaction Publishers.

Nozick, R. (1974). *Anarchy, state, and utopia.* New York: Basic Books.

Olivecrona, K. (1974a). Appropriation in the State of Nature: Locke on the Origin of Property. *Journal of the History of Ideas, 35,* 211-230.

Olivecrona, K. (1974b). Locke's Theory of Appropriation. *Philosophical Quarterly, 24,* 220-234.

Chapter IV

Ideas, Expressions, Universals, and Particulars:
Metaphysics in the Realm of Software Copyright Law

Thomas M. Powers
University of Virginia, USA

ABSTRACT

The distinction in U.S. copyright law between ideas and their expressions is of particular importance in protecting software. In literary works and software alike, the ideas that underlie these forms of intellectual property do not enjoy copyright protection, whereas the tangible expressions of the ideas, in fixed media and of sufficient originality, can have copyright protection. The idea vs. expression distinction has been the focus of many cases in the courts, especially where there was an alleged infringement of non-literal parts of a software program, such as "structure, sequence, and organization" or "look and feel." I argue that this legal distinction relies on the metaphysical distinction between universals and particulars, one that has been a major topic of philosophical controversy for over two millennia. The unsettled nature of the philosophical debate serves as a good explanation of the meandering of case law in this area.

INTRODUCTION

Common-sense morality and philosophical ethics agree that stealing the property of another is prima facie wrong. The act of stealing can be defined as the intentional appropriation of property that one knows to belong to another, when the owner has not given permission for the appropriation. Stealing is not, for the most part, the appropriation of abandoned property, or property from the commons to which one is party, or property that is in the possession of another but not rightfully so. Where there is disagreement, the controversy centers not on stealing as an act, but on what counts as the property of another. Locke, despite his talk of natural rights, struggled with the question of property that could have been left for others to appropriate, if only the original laborer had left behind "enough and as good." Contemporary property-rights advocates, in complaints about "takings," assume that property covers not only what one owns but also what one has hoped for in terms of profits from the use of the property, even when such use threatens the interests of others. Similar conceptual difficulties over property and theft are alive as well within the special province of intellectual property. Were I to erase the true author's name on the draft of a novel and submit it to a publisher as my own, I would obviously be guilty of stealing. Short of that, what would count as stealing the novel?

It is not clear that every aspect of the novel is the property of its original author. Here too, then, the moral question concerns what exactly is owned, and not whether stealing is wrong. The interesting cases are almost never so bold nor so easy to decide as those involving outright, intentional theft. Do I steal the original author's property when I quote at length, without attribution, or when I incorporate parts of his plot in my own work, or when I imitate his style in an attempt at sincere flattery? In U.S. copyright law, the distinction between ideas and expressions is supposed to shed light on what can be protected by a limited property right. The received doctrine is that original, tangible expressions of literary works, broadly construed, gain legal protection for a limited period of time simply by the act of publication. The ideas from which those expressions stem, however, do not gain protection.

How does this distinction fare when applied to software as intellectual property? What exactly are software "ideas" and "expressions"? I will argue that case law in this area reveals, if mostly through its meanderings, the persistence of a major philosophical controversy lasting at least 2500 years. Every attempt by the courts so far to sidestep the deep philosophical issue of universals and particulars, while maintaining the distinction that embodies it, has only led to greater confusion. In particular, confusion reigns in the area of computer software as intellectual property.

DOCTRINES OF THE LAW

Statutory and case law in the U.S. have tried to give force and boundaries to the constitutional power of Congress to secure "to authors and inventors the exclusive right to their respective writings and discoveries." In *Baker v. Selden* (101 U.S. 99, 1879) the court makes clear that copyright only protects expression, and that copyright protection is both easier to achieve and less beneficial to the holder when compared to patent protection.

"The difference between the two things, letters-patent and copyright, may be illustrated by reference to the subjects just enumerated. Take the case of medicines. Certain mixtures are found to be of great value in the healing art. If the discoverer writes and publishes a book on the subject (as regular physicians generally do), he gains no exclusive right to the manufacture and sale of the medicine; he gives that to the public. If he desires to acquire such exclusive right, he must obtain a patent for the mixture as a new art, manufacture, or composition of matter. He may copyright his book, if he pleases; but that only secures to him the exclusive right of printing and publishing his book. So of all other inventions or discoveries." (101 U.S. at 102-103)

In settling on copyright as the form of protection for works of art or expression and reserving patent for processes, discoveries, and inventions, judges and legislators have not sought to protect every claim that an author or inventor might want. Specifically, it would be advantageous for authors if they could stake claim to the most general and abstract intellectual origins of their work, as well as to the literal expressions themselves. This notion of the intellectual origin, or what is "behind" or motivating the eventual expression, serves as the basis of the distinction between ideas and their tangible expressions. But for the law to grant protection for something so broad would be an excessive reward for authors and a serious hindrance to those who wish to enter the market. At most, the courts have allowed a "limited monopoly over the expression" (*Hoehling v. Universal Studios*, 1980).

Judges and legislators have tried to balance individual rights to intellectual property with the social good of healthy market competition. This balancing act has proven none too easy. As soon as a doctrine for copyright is worked out, one that tells authors and artists what can gain protection and what cannot, it seems that a new type of intellectual property — or in effect, a new technology — comes along to show that the "bright lines" of distinction are really not so bright. Hence the piano roll that plays another artist's song, the videocassette recorder that copies a rented movie, the computer program that reverse engineers a rival program, and, recently, the Internet or intranet application that facilitates the "sharing" of digital content by end-users have all strained the tidy distinctions of the law and provoked refinements where possible (*A&M Records v. Napster,* 2001; *Sony v. Universal Studios,* 1984; *White-Smith v. Apollo,* 1908). Here we are concerned with analyzing the series of refinements that attempt to separate legal from illegal copying of one particular kind of intellectual property: licensed software.

My contention is that the evolution of the idea/expression distinction in intellectual property law repeats the debate begun by Plato and Aristotle on the status of universals. Moreover, the various positions on what is and is not protected in software can be mapped onto subsequent doctrines of universals from medieval to contemporary philosophers. Despite the plausible connection between Plato's *eidos* (ideas, or universals) and the "ideas" in U.S. copyright law, the courts have been reluctant to engage the philosophical issue. One court sought explicitly to avoid an "approach to separating idea from expression in computer programs [that] relies too heavily on metaphysical distinctions and does not place enough emphasis on practical considerations" (*Computer Associates International v. Altai,* 1992). I will argue that the law cannot ignore philosophy on this topic. Aversions to philosophizing notwithstanding, the allegedly "practical" legal solutions merely restate the deep metaphysical problem of universals. In its persistence and ubiquity, the problem of universals effectively thwarts the hopes of a judiciary that wants to dodge metaphysics.

DOCTRINES OF METAPHYSICAL UNIVERSALS

What are universals? Most modern philosophers since Descartes have identified them with properties, characteristics, qualities ("redness"), and also with abstract ideas (the number "3"). Contemporary philosophers have also designated them as types and have used "tokens" to denote particulars. We might say that your neighbor has two tokens of the type "dog," and in this manner of speaking we would be committed to the existence of an entity beyond the two dogs. This way of speaking of universals seems to follow quite naturally from the consideration of language. Sentences like "Your neighbor has two dogs" or "The apple is red" betray the existence of more entities than particular dogs and apples. Doghood or redness are said to be entities because the terms "is a dog" and "is red" are predicable of all members of certain classes. If redness is predicable of any red thing, then it is the universal picked out by that class. Following from this clue given by language, a universal term is said to have an *extension*, or a class of particulars of which that term can truly be predicated. A universal, then, is an ontological entity corresponding to the universal term.

The key logical notion in the universal/particular distinction goes back to a doctrine that Aristotle attributed to Plato, that of the "one and the many." If there is some universal X, it is only "one" thing, though it may be instantiated by potentially "many" distinct particular x's. For example, many particular apples, scarves, and books could be red, though redness remains one color. Instantiating "being 3 in quantity" might be a set of geese, the balls in a tennis can, and the sum of one and two. The logical notion in all of these illustrations is the same: a universal is not a multiplicity, though instances of it are. A single universal might be instantiated in many spaces or at several times, but it is a point of contention whether the universal itself is an entity in space or time. Platonists believe that universals, properly speaking, are not in space and time. For this reason, a Platonist would hold that there can never be a convergence or "merger" of particular and universal — no particular that uniquely instantiated a universal — since at most we could say that there is only one thing (particular) of that type *right now*. Because universals, on the Platonic view, have an existence independent of space and time, they survive existents (and extinction) on earth. Particulars, on the other hand, are entirely in space and time. The everyday world of objects and properties consists entirely of them according to the Platonic view.

In Plato's dialogues *Phaedo*, *Republic*, and *Timaeus*, he develops a view of universals that posits their existence independently of the world of particulars in which they are instantiated. This "Platonic Heaven" is for him the realm of metaphysical significance; it is unchanging and the source of all truth. Later medieval philosophers referred to this strong realist view as positing universals *ante res* or "prior to things." In other words, universals or forms exist whether or not anyone knows them. They will continue to exist after our solar system implodes or grows cold. On the assumption that the ideas behind a software program are universals or abstract ideas of this sort, existing in perpetuity, we might be led by Plato to adopt a peculiar view of software as intellectual property. Namely, we would tend to see the act of creating software as the *discovery* of antecedently existing ideas, brought to human significance in the expressions of the software programmer or engineer. We would also tend to see a virtually limitless stockpile of ideas, owned by no one but accessed by the privileged few. There could be ideas for software that never get expressed, and also thousands or millions of numerically different expressions of one and the same idea. For the Platonist, even expressions that employ logical connectives (and, or, if-then) are trading in universals. Hence, from this view, programming and natural languages are full of terms denoting universals. A Platonist's perspective on software must hold that every program instantiates many universals or ideas. From this point of view, we cannot make software without mining the realm of transcendental ideas.

Bertrand Russell sought to defend a version of Platonic realism about universals, though "merely with such modifications as time has shown to be necessary" (Russell, 1997/1912). His view was heavily influenced by his early philosophy of language and partly explains why the issue of universals would be absent in writings on the law. References to these universals were, in Russell's view, so ubiquitous as to be easily overlooked. He states that "nearly all of the words to be found in the dictionary stand for universals," and notes that not only adjectives and substantives, but also verbs, prepositions, and relations commonly represent universals.

Aristotle held a more moderate realism about universals that denies their transcendent being. He believed that universals exist only *in rebus* (in the things) and not *ante res*. Later realists, who accept this "immanent" realism, effectively charge Plato (and Russell) with advocating an excessive ontology. But how does immanent realism about universals differ from transcendent (Platonic) realism when it comes to intellectual property? For the immanent realist, universals are only in existents, that is, only in tangible expressions.

While transcendent realists about universals must conceive of building software as a form of discovery, the immanent realist does not believe that the ideas exist independently of the expressions that are their manifestations. Rather, the immanent realist holds a kind of co-construction view; i.e., in writing software, the expression embodies, simultaneously, the ideas of the software engineer. That there can be similarity of ideas in two software products from two different engineers is no more surprising than that there can be two similar kittens from different cats. Immanent realists would also believe that some particular software program could uniquely express an idea. We will see later on that the "merger theory" of some jurists relies on this kind of realism.

A third position on universals was put forth by the 14th-century philosopher William of Ockham, who claimed that only particulars or individuals exist. This view, known as nominalism, is rarely defended in contemporary philosophy. Its adherents usually hold a version of an error theory, which states that common sense notions about characters, properties, and types are simply errors. Language, in this view, is no reliable indication of what exists. While it is true that pronouns, proper names, and definite descriptions refer to particulars, there is no reason to think that other parts of speech pick out existent (that is, abstract or universal) entities. On this view, *every* piece of software is unique. That is to say, each tangible copy is a particular. The backup copy of an application and the perfectly reverse-engineered piece of rival software are as distinct from their alleged origins as the operating system is from the screen saver. There simply are no ideas behind software, there are only expressions. Taking nominalism to the extreme, we might think that copying a program directly onto disk would create a second software program. On this view, it is hard to see that *any* form of software piracy exists. Though nominalism is an unlikely philosophical position, it does seem to have adherents in the realm of software use. For those who believe that each copy of a program is a new piece of software, the only view that justifies their position is nominalism.

GENERAL AND SPECIAL PROBLEMS OF UNIVERSALS FOR SOFTWARE

As a close analogue to literary work, software is susceptible to a general puzzle that confronts almost all human creations. Take, for example, the issue of what counts as software. Does it have to be written into ROM, or can it also be in RAM? Does it have to come on a floppy disk, or can it be embedded in a chip or game controller? Questions like these show that we have a presumption in favor of the term "software" picking out a type. They also show that the type has, at the least, vague identity conditions, or in other words that there are instances that test the boundaries of the category. Consider, also, the notion of the software bug. Can we define a software bug a priori, as it were, before we run any piece of software? A Platonist would have us think so, but is a bug a mistake in programming that reduces the functionality of the system as a whole? What about "unplanned features" that are not in the specification but are nonetheless in the behavior of the system when it runs the software? It has been said that harmless bugs "become" features. Is this notion of becoming of metaphysical or merely of technical significance? Are there instances of the type "software bug" that are clearly definable prior to their being experienced? In being open to these quandaries, computer science is not special. As Russell (1912, 1977) says, "We succeed in avoiding all notice of universals as such, until the study of philosophy forces them upon our attention." The general problem, then, infects almost every attempt at taxonomy or categorization.

The special problem of universals, on the other hand, brings our focus to the idea/expression distinction. In cases where some non-literal copying of software is alleged, attention turns to the supposed ideas embodied in the software. Such cases have involved claims of protection over the structure, organization, functionality, and "look and feel" of the software. On the assumption that it makes sense to talk of ideas being expressed in programming, the intellectual property protection of software (where we are concerned with copying non-literal aspects) admits of at least two views. On the one hand, the permissive view would follow from the belief that the non-literal parts of a computer program are all ideas, so they cannot have copyright protection. Therefore, only literal (line-for-line) copies count as theft. A more restrictive or protective view would follow from the belief that at least some non-literal parts of a computer program are expressions, and not the "ideas" themselves from which they allegedly stem. Those programmers who gain protection are the lucky ones who "discovered" the expressions and first wrote them down, and so they gain a limited property right to them, effectively keeping all others from using them.

The special problem of universals, as I have indicated, has no easy solution. It requires jurists to commit to a particular view on universals in order to adjudicate all non-obvious cases of software copying. This task is under-standably as hard for jurists as it is for philosophers. But in the law, we also expect doctrines to serve as means of clarifying and setting expectations for those who earnestly wish to abide by its constraints. The law should aid in prediction. As the following cases show, software copyright doctrine up to this point has not been a good means to these ends.

REFINEMENT OF IDEA/EXPRESSION

Developments in technology in the second half of the 20th Century produced tension in a copyright doctrine designed primarily for ordinary literary and artistic works. Eventually, Congress sought to clear up the confusions produced by the computer age. In the Copyright Act of 1976, Section 102(b) states the basic understanding of idea/expression:

In no case does copyright protection for an original work of authorship extend to any idea, procedure, process, system, method of operation, concept, principle, or discovery, regardless of the form in which it is described, explained, illustrated, or embodied in such work.

In several subsequent cases, the courts interpreted the new Copyright Act so as to answer questions about the protected status of different kinds of software. It was held that the distinction between protected expressions and unprotected ideas, concepts, and principles (what I earlier called "intellectual origins") holds for operating systems as well as applications. The ruling in *Apple v. Franklin* (1983) asserts that operating systems are not "methods of operation," in the language of Section 102(b):

Franklin argues that an operating system program is either a "process," "system," or "method of operation" and hence uncopyrightable ... However, Franklin's argument misapplies that distinction in this case. Apple does not seek to copyright the method which instructs the computer to perform its operating functions but only the instructions themselves ... Many of the courts which have sought to draw the line between an idea and expression have found difficulty in articulating where it falls. We believe that in the context before us, a program for an operating system, the line must be a pragmatic one, which also keeps in consideration "the preservation of the balance between competition and protection reflected in the patent and copyright laws. Unlike a patent, a copyright protects originality rather than novelty or invention." In that opinion, we quoted approvingly the following passage from Dymow v. Bolton:

> *just as a patent affords protection only to the means of reducing an inventive idea to practice, so the copyright law protects the means of expressing an idea; and it is as near the whole truth as generalization can usually reach that, if the same idea can be expressed in a plurality of totally different manners, a plurality of copyrights may result, and no infringement will exist (714 F.2d at 122-124, citations omitted).*

After the Franklin case, the intellectual property protection afforded software momentarily was expanded, apparently in the belief that non-literal elements of software can be identified with an accounting of the "structure, sequence, and organization" (SSO) of computer software. In *Whelan Associates v. Jaslow Dental Laboratory* (1986), the Third Circuit Court of Appeals adopted the reasoning of the lower district court in suggesting a way to protect non-literal parts of software. The District Court held that:

The mere idea or concept of a computerized program for operating a dental laboratory would not in and of itself be subject to copyright ... The "expression of the idea" in a software computer program is the manner in which the program operates, controls, and regulates the computer in receiving, assembling, calculating, retaining, correlating, and producing information either on a screen, print-out or by audio communication.

The court went on in the *Whelan* decision to give an account of this new area of protection, SSO:

Although the economic implications of this rule are necessarily somewhat speculative, we nevertheless believe that the rule would advance the basic purpose underlying the idea/expression distinction, "the preservation of the balance between competition and protection reflected in the patent and copyright laws." As we stated above, among the more significant costs in computer programming are those attributable to developing the structure and logic of the program. The rule proposed here, which allows copyright protection beyond the literal computer code, would provide the proper incentive for programmers by protecting their most valuable efforts, while not giving them a stranglehold over the development of new computer devices that accomplish the same end. (797 F.2d at 1236-1237, 490-491, citations omitted)

SSO was one way of describing what non-literal components of a program could be protected under copyright law. But what is one person's "structure" is another's "organization." The phrases are extremely malleable, and so they capture too much. By placing SSO on the "expression" side of the distinction, the *Whelan* court seems to overpopulate a typical program with instantiations of universals. In indicating that structure is expressed, in the same sense in which a line of code is expressed, the court opens the door to the view that almost anything can be the expression of a universal.

Yet six years later, the Second Circuit Court of Appeals would reject the Third Circuit's hyper-protective doctrine in announcing the decision in *Computer Associates International v. Altai* (1992). The Second Circuit introduces a new rubric that comes to be known as the Abstraction-Filtration-Comparison (AFC) Test. Here the court describes the test:

As applied to computer programs, the abstractions test will comprise the first step in the examination for substantial similarity. Initially, in a manner that resembles reverse engineering on a theoretical plane, a court should dissect the allegedly copied program's structure and isolate each level of abstraction contained within it. This process begins with the code and ends with an articulation of the program's ultimate function. Along the way, it is necessary essentially to retrace and map each of the designer's steps — in the opposite order in which they were taken during the program's creation.

As an anatomical guide to this procedure, the following description is helpful: At the lowest level of abstraction, a computer program may be thought of in its entirety as a set of individual instructions organized into a hierarchy of modules. At a higher level of abstraction, the instructions in the lowest level modules may be replaced conceptually by the functions of those modules. At progressively higher levels of abstraction, the functions of higher level modules conceptually replace the implementations of those modules in terms of lower level modules and instructions, until finally, one is left with nothing but the ultimate function of the program ... A program has structure at every level of abstraction at which it is viewed. At low levels of abstraction, a program's structure may be quite complex; at the highest level it is trivial. (982 F.2d at 707)

When comparing two programs for the possibility of illegal copying, the AFC Test asks experts for both plaintiff and defendant to draw up abstractions of the programs. These abstractions may include data structure, control structure, data flow, information architecture, and textual organization of the code (Hollaar, 2002). Then the court filters out elements that are unprotected — processes (that may or may not be patentable), conventional programming methods, code required for interoperability, etc. — and compares what is left. Even experts who have worked closely with the courts agree that this is a process that requires many judgment calls at the filtration stage, and will likely place the decision in the hands of the experts who perform the AFC (Hollaar, 2002).

Concurrently, several cases and appeals involving Apple, Microsoft, Lotus, and Borland worked their way through the courts. From 1989 to 1996, these cases considered whether there were protections of the "look and feel" of the GUI (for Apple) and the menu structure (for Lotus). Apple eventually lost, and thereby ceded ground to Microsoft in the operating systems market. The Lotus case made it to the Supreme Court, and many commentators were optimistic that we would get a definitive opinion on an important non-literal protection of software. The court deadlocked at 4-4, with one judge having recused himself.

One wonders, given these meanderings, whether cases will be decided on grounds that are intrinsic or extrinsic to the actual code in the programs. Perhaps extrinsic considerations, such as whether the plaintiff has a monopoly on operating system software, or whether the defendant can afford the lengthy AFC process, might prove compelling in some cases. In light of these problems, it is not surprising that a judge who hears these cases has suggested abandoning the idea/expression distinction in software copyright law (Newman, 1999).

Finally, the AFC Test can be seen to join the universals debate between the two realist positions. If the defendant in a copying case can argue convincingly that the software idea can only be expressed in one way, then the expression and idea are said to have "merged." A plaintiff then loses the claim to protection, since this software expression would protect (simultaneously) an idea. Of course, it does so only on the assumption of immanent realism — that we can have ideas uniquely expressed by some particular.

CONCLUSIONS

By casting the idea/expression distinction as the universal/particular distinction, we can see that realists about universals will want to protect *some* of the non-literal parts of computer programs through copyright law. The key to having a clarifying and predictive doctrine of copyright, however, turns on agreement over *which* parts are to be protected. And that issue turns on one's view of programming "ideas" or universals: are they discovered, but in principle limitless, or are they only found in expressions, and hence created when the programming lines are written? Further, we might wonder whether nominalism is so indefensible concerning software as intellectual property. Does not the user change the software, at least in small ways, to incorporate it into the computing environment? Would not open-source software make every program a particular expression, in principle?

A suggestion in the works of the later Wittgenstein may help to dissolve, rather than solve, the special problem of universals for software. In his famous discussion of games in the *Philosophical Investigations* (1953/1967), Wittgenstein casts doubt on the view that all tokens of one type have some one thing in common, in virtue of which they are of that type. He brings in the simile with games to show that similarities in games are like family resemblances. Build, gait, eye color, and other features often serve to identify a person as a member of a family. But family members do not share *all* features, nor do they often have one particular feature in common (Bambrough, 1961). One brother has the father's eyes but lacks his nose; another has the nose but lacks the chin, and so on. Such characteristics may fallibly identify individuals with their families; the only certain method is, in effect, to evaluate reproduction.

Two computer programs might be much like family members. We might use them and remark on certain similarities; we might uncover their structure, or even perform the AFC Test, and find significant overlap in code. Is this like

DNA analysis? The inquiry seems to run in that direction. Here we seem not to be searching for clues to paternity, but something like illegitimacy.

Of course, computer programs, like people, do not have to be "related" in order to look and behave alike. And children do not "steal" the genes of parents, though they have them, in effect. Perhaps copyright law would profit by considering which of two issues is more important: what is the "genotype" of a suspect program, and what is its "phenotype"? Settling on which issue to pursue can only aid litigants and the software industry in being able to predict the judgment of the law concerning software copyright.

REFERENCES

A&M Records, Inc., v. Napster, Inc. (239 F. 3d 1004, 2001).

Apple v. Franklin. (714 F.2d 1240, 1983).

Baker v. Selden (101 U.S. 99, 1879).

Bambrough, R. (1961). Universals and family resemblance. *Proceedings of the Aristotelian Society,* 60. Reprinted in M. Loux, (Ed.) (1970) *Universals and particulars: Readings in ontology,* 109-127. New York: Anchor Books.

Computer Associates International v. Altai. (982 F.2d 693, 1992).

Copyright Act of 1976 (title 17 of the U.S. Code). Retrieved at http://www.copyright.gov/title17.

Hoehling v. Universal City Studios, Inc. (618 F. 2d 972, 1980).

Hollaar, L. (2002). *Legal protection of digital information.* Washington DC: BNA Books. Retrieved at: http://digital-law-online.info/.

Newman, J. (1999). New lyrics for an old melody: The idea/expression dichotomy in the computer age. *Cardozo Arts & Entertainment Law Journal,* 17(3). Also available online at: http://www.cardozo.yu.edu/news_events/papers/4.pdf.

Russell, B. (1997). *The problems of philosophy* (Rev.ed.). New York: Oxford University Press. (Originally published 1912).

Sony Corporation of America, Inc., v. Universal City Studios, Inc. (464 U.S. 417, 1984).

Whelan Associates v. Jaslow Dental Laboratory (797 F.2d 1222, 1986).

White-Smith Music Publishing Co. v. Apollo Co. (209 U.S. 1, 1908).

Wittgenstein, L. (1967). *Philosophical investigations* (Rev. ed.). Oxford, UK: Blackwell Publishers. (Originally published 1953).

Section III

Ethical and
Legal Perspectives

Chapter V

Exporting Trademark Confusion

Ann Bartow
University of South Carolina, USA

ABSTRACT

A judicial determination of "likelihood of confusion" is the linchpin of successful trademark infringement actions in the United States, and is often useful to prevail on a trademark dilution cause of action as well. Such determinations are exceedingly subjective, and often seem premised on a very low estimation of the intelligence and powers of discernment of the typical consumer. Many appear virtually pretextual, simply adopted as a necessary step in "protecting" trademarks and according trademark holders broad property-like rights that can impair competition and silence free speech. Though seemingly irrational and generally socially undesirable, U.S. "likelihood of confusion" jurisprudence has gained a foothold in cyberspace through dispute-resolution procedures addressing disputes about Internet domain names. In consequence, trademark holders generally prevail and are increasingly seen as holding inchoate rights in any domain name containing, alluding to, or similar to their trademarks across the globe, even though U.S. trademark law logically should not have extraterritorial application.

EXPORTING TRADEMARK CONFUSION

"Likelihood of confusion" among consumers is the evil that a large segment of U.S. trademark law and jurisprudence is intended to guard against. In addition to stopping and punishing activities by others that are objectionable to trademark holders, successful outcomes in trademark infringement and trademark dilution cases discourage third parties from using trademarks of their own in commerce that are even mildly similar, and dissuade others from making arguably legally permissible uses of the trademark itself. In the context of such litigation, trademark holders will generally assert that consumers are easily confused because judicial acceptance of this assumption always helps them prevail in trademark infringement suits. Assertions of consumer confusion are sometimes useful in winning trademark dilution actions as well. While dilution claims are generally understood not to require proof of actual or likely consumer confusion, raising the possibility of confusion or concepts very much like it (such as the "danger of false assumptions") is often analytically useful to trademark holders.

The meaning of "likelihood of confusion" has taken on surprising and alarming dimensions in cyberspace where it has become a rhetorical device used to grant trademark holders rights to domain names that incorporate or even vaguely insinuate vigorously protected trademarks. Domain name jurisprudence, like the Internet that spawned it, touches every corner of the earth, so the form and texture of the trademark rights it fabricates may spread internationally as well.

INFRINGEMENT AND DILUTION IN THE U.S.: POWERFUL LIKELIHOOD OF CONFUSION

In most applications of U.S. trademark law, context is everything. For example, whether a word can even function as a protectable trademark can only be determined in the context of the good or service with which it is used in conjunction. The trademark taxonomy is generally deemed to contain four categories: generic, descriptive, suggestive, and arbitrary or fanciful.[1]

Generic

Words that are generic with respect to the associated product or service can never be protected as trademarks because this would be unfair to competitors.[2] To allow one company a monopoly on the words "ice cream" when the product is ice cream would force another entity marketing the same substance to call its product something along the lines of "sweet frosty dairy confection." If that second company obtained an enforceable trademark on "sweet frosty dairy confection," a third competitor might have to resort to the somewhat unappealing appellation "frozen flavored high-fat milk solids" to communicate the nature of the goods it was selling to consumers. A fourth competitor, if sufficiently cowed by the threat of a trademark infringement suit, might forgo entering the ice cream marketplace altogether, freezing out the presumptive benefits in terms of quality, price, and selection that consumers might otherwise milk from commercial competition.

Descriptive

A descriptive term references a quality or characteristic of the underlying good or service, such as "Arthriticare," for a topical heat analgesic designed to provide arthritis relief;[3] "Pet Pals," for a program that promotes the well-being of pets;[4] and "Skinvisible," when applied to medical and surgical tapes through which the skin of the user is visible.[5] A descriptive term can only function as a valid trademark if it acquires "secondary meaning," which means the mark is recognized by the consuming public as referencing a particular product from a unitary source.[6] For example, all businesses in which eyeglasses and contact lenses are available for purchase may be referred to as "vision centers" but one specific enterprise cannot obtain a valid trademark in the descriptive words "Vision Center" unless it can demonstrate that the public distinctly associates the term "Vision Center" with its particular optical merchandise establishment.[7]

Suggestive

A suggestive term is one that suggests, rather than describes, an attribute of the marked good or service, and requires imagination to cognitively link the trademark to the exact nature of the product.[8] The term "Pizza Rolls" was held to be suggestive when "used in association with party snacks consisting of pillow-shaped egg batter crusts filled with various food products to obtain different flavors."[9] The court concluded:

The term PIZZA ROLLS could suggest a number of items, including small pizzas, pizza rolled up, pizza-flavored candy, or a bread dough roll filled with pizza flavoring. It takes imagination and thought to perceive the nature, quality, characteristics or ingredients of plaintiff's products based upon the mark PIZZA ROLLS, all of which clearly indicate that the term is suggestive.[10]

Other marks that have been deemed to be suggestive include "psychocalisthenics," for a combination of various yoga systems, dance, and calisthenics designed to produce specific mental, emotional, and spiritual results;[11] "brown-in-bag" for transparent plastic film bags in which foods could be cooked,[12] and "The Money Store" for money-lending services.[13]

Trademarks held to be suggestive are deemed "inherently distinctive" and therefore valid and enforceable without proof of secondary meaning.[14] This makes the distinction between "descriptive" and "suggestive" very important to the mark holder,[15] but where the taxonomic division between the two categories is situated can be difficult to ascertain. According to one court:

In the 1930s two courts split on the question of whether the trademark "Chicken of the Sea" for tuna was descriptive or suggestive. The indirectness of the association between "Chicken of the Sea" and tuna may thus be taken as a rough indicator of where the borderline between descriptive and suggestive marks lies.[16]

Another court observed:

The line between descriptive and suggestive terms is often blurred, and the categorization of a name as 'descriptive' or 'suggestive' is frequently 'made on intuitive basis' rather than as a result of a logical analysis susceptible of articulation.[17]

Arbitrary and Fanciful

"Arbitrary" trademarks are usually defined as those that adapt a common word to an unfamiliar circumstance, such as "automobile" as a mark for a brand of paper napkins, or for a line of plumbing supplies, or any other good or service not even remotely associated with motorized transportation.[18] The "fanciful" appellation is generally reserved for words and symbols that are "invented solely for their use as trademarks"[19] such as Kodak or Xerox, or "the word 'CHAMS' on the top side of a curved, inverted almost-equilateral triangle with a triple-bar wing-like design and a heavy letter 'C' superimposed in the center of the shield," embroidered on garments.[20]

CATEGORIZATION AND CONTEXT

The word "apple" is the generic word for a particular tree-growing fruit, so "apple" cannot be a valid trademark for apples. It is, however, an arbitrary or fanciful trademark for computers, or for musical sound recordings, hence Apple Computers[21] and Apple Records.[22] Similarly, "popcorn" is generic when it references eponymous kernels of snack food drenched in butter and salt, but was found suggestive when pertaining to a line of oddly shaped silver anodes.[23]

The word "ice" is generic for cubes of frozen water, but was held to be a suggestive and therefore protectable mark with respect to chewing gum.[24] "Ice" also has been used as a trademark for beer, and in one lawsuit was asserted to be generic by one litigant, while the mark holder claimed that the relationship between "ice" and beer was "either arbitrary, fanciful or suggestive."[25] The court held that the keys to correctly categorizing the mark are consumer understanding and common usage of the term at the time the issue is presented to a court.[26]

Legal protections for trademarks are doctrinally justified by the need to prevent consumer confusion, which potentially disadvantages both individuals who are tricked by confusing or deceptive trademarks into purchasing goods and services other than those they intended to procure, and the providers of goods and services who lose sales when consumers are so confused or deceived.[27] Alternatively phrased, trademark infringement occurs when one party adopts a trademark that is the same as or is so similar to an existing mark that, when it is applied to the second user's goods or services, the purchasing public is likely to be confused, mistaken, or deceived about the source goods or services themselves, or about the relationship between the parties that make the goods or provide the services.[28] This "likelihood of confusion" is the touchstone of trademark infringement liability.[29]

A trademark can be infringed by the unauthorized use of exact replicas of the mark on the same products (where the act might be characterized as counterfeiting), or on related goods.[30] Trademarks can also be infringed by the non-permissive use of "colorable imitations" of the mark.[31] Whether a mark accused of infringing another mark is similar enough to constitute an actionable "colorable imitation" is a subjective decision that courts make, and is usually articulated as a judgment about whether the contemporaneous co-existence of the marks underlying the dispute is likely to cause consumer confusion.[32]

When trademark holders attempt to convince a court that the trademark-related activities of another entity should be enjoined, they argue overtly or by implication that consumers are easily confused, because this helps them prevail in both infringement and dilution actions, which in turn broadens the scope of, and increases the strength of, their trademarks. Strong, broadly enforceable trademarks are desirable because they may discourage competitors from using otherwise attractive and advantageous trademarks of their own that are even mildly similar, and simultaneously frighten away those who might otherwise make non-competing or even arguably noncommercial uses of the mark.

TRADEMARK INFRINGEMENT AND CONFUSION

Accusations of trademark infringement are generally raised when one entity makes use of a mark that is the same or similar to a mark that is "owned" by another. In this context the term "ownership" connotes the holding of trademark rights, often (but not always) by virtue of use of the mark in commerce,[33] and by federal registration of the mark obtained through the U.S. Patent & Trademark Office. If a competitor makes unauthorized use of another's exact trademark in a clearly deceptive manner, that rival may be accused of criminal counterfeiting[34] and trademark infringement.[35]

While there is a fairly universal agreement that unauthorized uses of confusingly similar trademarks by competitors is unfair and should be prevented, a meaningful explanation of what "confusingly similar" means eludes even a careful reader of the *Lanham Trademark Act of 1946,* the federal statute underpinning trademark law. The *Lanham Trademark Act of 1946* defines infringement as the "use in commerce of any reproduction, counterfeit, copy or colorable imitation of a registered mark" in commerce in a manner "likely to cause confusion, or to cause mistake, or to deceive,"[36] and then rather circularly and unhelpfully defines "colorable imitation" as a term that "includes any mark which so resembles a registered mark as to be likely to cause confusion or mistake or to deceive."[37] This means that for all practical purposes a confusingly similar mark is statutorily defined as: a mark likely to cause confusion or mistake or to deceive that is used in a manner likely to cause confusion, or to cause mistake, or to deceive. This certainly provides a powerful conceptual illustration of the word "confusing," but gives little guidance to courts about when a competing mark accused of being infringing is "confusingly similar." As a result, federal judges give meaning to the term on a case-by-case basis as they issue verdicts and opinions in the context of trademark litigation.

Actual confusion of consumers need not be demonstrated to prevail in an infringement action, merely the likelihood thereof.[38] If the judges assume the average shopper is rather guileless and simpleminded, than anything that is even arguably mildly perplexing can supportably be presumed to meet this low threshold. Once it is met, the jurist's task is essentially complete, because likelihood of confusion connotes likelihood of success on a trademark infringement claim, and irreparable injury to the mark holder is then presumed.[39] Judges who enjoin infringers conveniently escape the difficult task of precisely articulating how likely confusion has to be before "likelihood of confusion" is found. They typically elucidate any theory of causation, neither explaining how likelihood of confusion in a given context leads to harm, nor specifying how to measure the amount of confusion that is likely to be generated by a particular usage or substantiality of similarity.

Even the very nature of the inquiry is ambiguous. *The Restatement (Third) of Unfair Competition* (American Law Institute, 1995) characterizes the conclusion that "likelihood of confusion [is] a question of fact subject to the clearly erroneous rule" as "the better view, adopted by the majority of courts."[40] The Court of Appeals for the Federal Circuit, however, views likelihood of confusion as a question of law,[41] while the Second and Sixth Circuits assert that it is a mixed question of law and fact.[42] The authors of one of the leading trademark law textbooks have written:

Predictably, the diverging viewpoints in this area have produced a muddled body of case law, characterized by such inconsistency among and within the circuits that it has become difficult to predict how a court will deal with a particular case.[43]

Trademark holders of textual trademarks do not "own" the words comprising their trademarks for all communicative purposes.[44] They don't even hold a monopoly over all uses of these words for trademark purposes.[45] If two products or markets are sufficiently unrelated, two entities can use the same words as trademarks without triggering legally actionable consumer confusion. As one court stated:

Two marks that serve to identify products in two unrelated markets may very well coexist without confusion in the public's eye. Thus Notre Dame brand imported French cheese has been permitted to coexist with Notre Dame University; Bulova watches with Bulova shoes; Alligator raincoats with Alligator cigarettes; "This Bud's for you" in beer commercials with the same phrase used by a florist; White House tea and coffee with White House milk; Blue Shield medical care plan with Blue Shield mattresses; Family Circle magazine with Family Circle department store; Ole' cigars with Ole' tequila; and Sunkist fruits with Sunkist bakery products.[46]

Two parties may have legitimate, discrete national trademark rights that conflict only when they operate conterminously in a specific marketplace using the same or similar trademarks on the same or similar products or services. This is what might be described as a classic "innocent" trademark dispute in the sense that there is no indication either party has chosen their mark with any nefarious "free-riding" or "palming-off" motivation, but cognizable numbers of consumers could plausibly be confused, to the detriment of both mark holders. The mark holders would not fully reap the benefits of their "good reputations" and "desirable product features" and might be forced to invest in communicative advertising simply to distinguish their goods or services from those offered by competitors. They may alternatively feel compelled to change their trademarks or to use whatever legal mechanisms are available to try to get a competitor to stop using a mark, or both. These cases can arise when companies expand into new geographic regions;[47] when two companies begin using the same or similar marks contemporaneously;[48] when an entity adopts a mark unaware that another business has been using it; or when a mark is adopted with knowledge of prior use, but with the assumption that either the pre-existing marks or the underlying goods and services are sufficiently dissimilar such that the adoption and use of a particular mark will not be viewed as a problem.[49]

JUDICIAL SUBJECTIVITY AND CONFUSION

A federal court will consider both allegedly conflicting trademarks in the contexts in which they are used and make a determination about whether the dual usages create a "likelihood of confusion." If so, the mark holder with inferior rights to the disputed mark (usually because usage commenced later in time) may be restricted to using the mark in a limited geographic area, or may be ordered to stop using it in commerce altogether.

As a general policy matter when the goods produced by the alleged infringer compete for sales with those of the trademark owner, infringement usually will be found if the marks are deemed sufficiently similar that confusion can be expected.[50] For example, an attempt to launch a line of "Levy" denim jeans would almost certainly be met with a trademark suit and would likely be found to infringe upon the "Levi's" trademark even if "Levy" was the surname of the individual behind this doomed entrepreneurial effort.

When the goods are related but not competitive, several other factors are added to the calculus including strength of the plaintiff mark, proximity of the goods or services, similarity of the marks, evidence of actual confusion, marketing channels used, type of goods or services and the degree of care likely to be exercised by the purchaser, defendant's intent in selecting the mark, and the likelihood of expansion of the product lines.[51] The mark "Ben's Bread" was deemed confusingly similar to the Uncle Ben's mark for rice products, premised in part on the observation that: "While there are some obvious differences between the marks UNCLE BEN'S and BEN'S BREAD, they both contain the possessive form of the name 'BEN'."[52] That both products were sold in grocery stores, and that Uncle Ben's also used its mark on stuffing mix, were also deemed important.[53] In a similar vein, the Trademark Trial and Appeal Board held that artificial sweetener and salt are "closely related, complimentary products,"[54] and concluded:

We think it quite likely that purchasers familiar with the NUTRASWEET product, either as an ingredient in EQUAL artificial sweetener or as an ingredient in various other food products, would, upon viewing NUTRA SALT salt with trace minerals, be likely to believe that this was a new product line put out by the same producer as the NUTRASWEET producer or that the salt product was somehow associated with or sponsored by the people producing the NUTRASWEET product.[55]

If the goods are totally unrelated, as a doctrinal matter an infringement action should not be supportable because confusion is unlikely.[56] For this reason, Smith Brothers Auto Repairs and Smith Brothers Cough Drops can independently co-exist without unleashing trademark infringement litigation. (Trademark dilution, however, is another matter, as is discussed below.)

In assessing whether confusion is likely, judges are relatively free to base their findings on purely subjective reactions. As one judicial opinion proclaimed: "The determinative test cannot focus on how close or related the industries or products are, but rather by whether confusion is created so that an appreciable number of typical consumers will likely be confused."[57] Note that the test is not premised on proof that appreciable consumers have been confused, only that in the court's estimation, they are likely to be confused. Though evidence of actual confusion is helpful to trademark holders, the absence of any actual confusion does not usually affect them at all, as courts embrace the idea that a showing of actual confusion would be very difficult to demonstrate with reliable proof.[58] In consequence, mark holders do not have to prove much of anything to prevail, they simply have to persuade a judge that some consumers could be confused some of the time.

Where a large corporation uses the same mark on a diverse variety of products, some courts perceive a presumptive right on the part of the entity to be the only user of the mark in any commercial context on the grounds that multiple users of a mark will cause consumer confusion.[59] For example, the fact that Virgin Enterprises Limited and its related companies (collectively, the "Virgin Group") operated various worldwide businesses, which included an airline; a travel-related company; a limousine service; a soft drink bottler and distributor; and a chain of retail stores selling CDs, books, and clothing all using the Virgin trademark and service mark, gave it the right to prevent an unrelated retail gasoline establishment from calling itself "Virgin Petroleum."[60] This, despite the fact that the Virgin Group was not in the fuel business at all, nor were gasoline stations within the corporation's planned or likely zones of expansion.

Similarly, the use of the name PHONES-R-U.S. by a business that sold retail phones, accessories, and answering machines was found both infringing and dilutive, "likely 'to cause confusion, or to cause mistake or to deceive' consumers into believing some sponsorship, association, affiliation, connection, or endorsement exists" between the toy store chain Toys "R" Us and the defendant.[61] The court explicitly noted that: "the category of a buyer protected by trademark law against this confusion includes not only the careful or discriminating buyer, but also the ignorant, the inexperienced, and the gullible."[62]

Confusion can be found sufficient to result in a finding of trademark infringement even when it is anticipated that consumers will resolve or overcome any actual confusion well before reaching the "point of sale." Mark holders can win infringement suits simply by proving "initial interest" confusion, which is what piano consumers were deemed likely to experience when they were drawn to Grotrian-Steinweg pianos, though it was clear to the court that no one would actually purchase a Grotrian-Steinweg piano believing it to be a product of the Steinway & Sons company.[63] One somewhat stunning articulation of the adequacy of initial interest confusion to support an infringement finding occurred in a dispute between the Blockbuster chain and an upstart competitor that called itself Video Busters. That even stupid consumers would quickly figure out that Video Busters was a different entity, was deemed "unimportant" and "irrelevant" by a court that held:

[T]he issue in this case is the degree of likelihood that the name "Video Busters" would attract potential customers based on the reputation built by Blockbuster. That a customer would recognize that Video Busters is not connected to Blockbuster after entry into a Video Busters store and viewing the Video Busters membership application, brochure, videocassette jacket, and store layout is unimportant. The critical issue is the degree to which Video Busters might attract potential customers based on the similarity to the Blockbuster name. The court finds that Video Busters might attract some potential customers based on the similarity to the Blockbuster name. Because the names are so similar and the products sold are identical, some unwitting customers might enter a Video Busters store thinking it is somehow connected to Blockbuster. Those customers probably will realize shortly that Video Busters is not related to Blockbuster, but . . . that is irrelevant.[64]

The implication that a mark holder only has to convince a court that consumers are likely to be confused momentarily suggests the burden of proof on this issue can be feather-light indeed.

TRADEMARK DILUTION AND MORE CONFUSION

In the United States, holders of "famous" trademarks[65] can assert a statutory right to prevent others from "diluting" their marks.[66] Dilution, as defined by the *Lanham Trademark Act of 1946* as amended by the *Federal Trademark Dilution Act of 1995* means:

... the lessening of the capacity of a famous mark to identify and distinguish goods and services, regardless of the presence or absence of competition between the owner of the famous mark and other parties, or the likelihood of confusion, mistake or deception.[67]

Trademark dilution is thus the use of a mark (or similar mark) by an unauthorized entity that does not fit traditional notions of infringing conduct because there is little risk that consumers will be confused or mislead by the use.[68] A mark holder could argue that unauthorized use of a trademark on a dissimilar, non-competing good or service diluted the mark, undermining the mark's uniqueness and unfairly usurping the goodwill associated with the mark that the mark holder had worked hard to generate. The nationwide right to enjoin trademark dilution is a fairly recent development, as it was codified in the federal trademark statute in 1996, though many states had antidilution laws previously.[69]

By giving famous mark owners the ability to prevent "dilution" in addition to infringement, these mark holders are given improperly expansive property rights (sometimes called "trademarks in gross") in words and symbols.[70] Customarily, a mark could not be registered unless it was in use or the registration applicant asserted an intention to begin using the mark in commerce shortly. Warehousing of trademarks for future uses is discouraged.[71] Under antidilution principles, however, famous mark owners gain the ability to "reserve" pre-existing marks for a wide variety of future uses, even if they have no intention of ever utilizing the marks in alternative ways. For example, the General Motors Corporation may have no interest in making or marketing Chevroletâ ice cream, but can bring a trademark dilution suit against any dairy company that attempts it. As one commentator explained:

Trademark dilution is based not on the notion of protecting consumers from deception, but on protecting mark owners from a possible diminution in the value of their marks. The theory of dilution ... is that a second use of a well-known mark, even where the second use does not confuse consumers, gradually erodes the unique symbolism of that mark. Over time, many such uses erode the unique connection between a well-known mark and goods produced by the mark's owner. Once that connection is partially severed by the presence of other (usually non-competing or non-similar) goods with the same brand name, the value of the trademark as a marketing device is eroded. Dilution proponents have cited these as potential examples of diluting uses of a mark: Buick candy bars, Kodak laundry detergent, and the like. In contrast to ordinary trademark infringement, dilution is not predicated on any showing of likelihood of confusion. The injury is the reduced marketing value of the mark, rather than confusion in the marketplace.[72]

Thus, dilution was intended to be a cause of action for famous mark holders who objected to uses of the same or similar marks in commerce that did not confuse consumers, such as on unrelated goods or services. Consumer confusion plays no overt role in dilution analysis where the interloper uses the exact same mark as the famous one. Judicial confusion is often apparent when U.S. courts attempt to articulate what it means to "lessen distinctiveness,"[73] but whether consumers are perplexed or deceived by the use of a pre-existing mark on unrelated goods is, at least according to some courts, doctrinally irrelevant.[74] However, dilution claims are not limited to exact copying. Famous marks are also protected from dilution by similar marks, and deciding whether an accused mark is similar enough to trigger dilution concerns requires a determination of whether or not it is similar enough to be confused with the famous mark. In the context of claims of dilution by similar marks, some courts have even required proof of consumer confusion.[75] Though consumer confusion in the dilution context is theoretically a somewhat different construct, the reasoning used by many courts in making this subjective determination often substantially parallels the analyses applied when ascertaining whether consumer confusion is likely in trademark infringement disputes. For example, one of the first dilution cases was brought by a company that owned the mark WAWA for convenience stores, against an entity that began using the mark HAHA for its own convenience stores.[76] WAWA submitted a marketing survey in support of its dilution claim, and the court found the survey persuasive, writing: "Plaintiff buttresses its position by introducing evidence of a marketing survey which concludes that persons in HAHA's neighborhood who were interviewed about Defendant's market tended, in 29% of the cases, to associate Defendant's market with a WAWA market."[77] How this "tendency to associate" differed from a likelihood of confusion was not articulated and is difficult to distill from the wildly varying case law that has developed subsequent to this decision.[78] Several courts have overtly adopted aspects from trademark infringement analysis pertaining to consumer confusion for use in deciding trademark dilution cases.[79]

One observer wrote:

[T]he harm that dilution seeks to address might best be described as a loss of consumer attention due to the proliferation of similar or identical symbols of trade.[80]

What causes consumers to lose attention and how to quantify attendant damages are issues generally not addressed by judges. The Supreme Court has recently held that:

[A]t least where the marks at issue are not identical, the mere fact that consumers mentally associate the junior user's mark with a famous mark is not sufficient to establish actionable dilution.[81]

How a mark holder might adequately demonstrate a reduction in the capacity of a famous mark to identify the goods of its owners was not spelled out, though the opinion suggested that establishing that the defendant's mark caused consumers to "form a different impression" of the plaintiff's mark was necessary.[82] The Court did not appear to explicate the concept of trademark dilution in a manner that is straightforward enough to allow for consistent application across a broad range of factual situations.

MULTILATERAL TRADEMARK TREATIES DO NOT DEFINE THE SCOPE OF MARK HOLDER RIGHTS

A United States trademark registration does not currently have extraterritorial effect, and if the owner of a mark wants to protect the mark abroad, available protection must be sought separately under the relevant laws of each nation in which trademark protection is sought.[83] The United States is in the process of becoming part of the Madrid system,[84] which will enable U.S. trademark holders to efficiently obtain and maintain trademark registrations that will be recognized by all other participating countries.[85] Madrid ascension is intended to reduce the costs and paperwork associated with developing and administering trademarks that functionally become multinational in nature[86] (just as they do now when they are registered country by country), but will not effectuate any sort of uniformity with respect to the privileges or obligations that adhere to them.[87]

The trademark treaties to which the U.S. is a current or likely signatory are concerned almost entirely with standardization and mutuality of registration. For example, the Agreement on Trade-Related Aspects of Intellectual Property Rights (known as the TRIPS Agreement) provides a definition of trademarks and expressly requires the protection of service marks.[88] TRIPS requires members of the World Trade Organization (WTO) to adopt the minimum standards of protection set out in the Paris Convention[89] and grants the owner of a registered mark the right to prevent confusing uses of similar or identical marks on similar or identical goods,[90] but provides no guidance as to what a "confusing use" might be or how alike marks or goods must be to reach the threshold of objectionable similarity. Though treaties create trademarks that are effectively transnational in nature, the breadth and texture of the rights that accompany these multinational trademarks are not defined by treaties.[91] Further, there is no expectation that any future treaty will lead to the harmonization of trademark rights or make the scope of the rights predictable much beyond straightforward protection from counterfeiters, which is the one unambiguously articulated goal of every national trademark system.[92] Foreign trademarks simply receive levels of protection that are coextensive with whatever protections domestic trademarks receive in the "host" nation if the country is a trademark treaty signatory.[93]

TRADEMARKS AND DOMAIN NAMES: CONFUSION GOES GLOBAL

The World Intellectual Property Organization (WIPO) defines a trademark as "a distinctive sign that identifies certain goods or services as those produced or provided by a specific person or enterprise."[94] It does not articulate in any meaningful way the rights that flow from holding a trademark with respect to domain names, but this should not be perceived as an indication of neutrality on the subject. Evidencing a clear commitment to meeting trademark owners' perceived needs, WIPO issued a report recommending that easy ouster and the preemptive blocking mechanism be incorporated into the domain name system when conflicts between trademark holders and domain name registrants began to emerge,[95] despite objections that this proposal was tilted to give commercial trademark owners unfair advantages over anyone using the Internet for political or personal speech.[96]

As a consequence of its accessibility to the world, trademark conflicts can arise on the Internet in several ways,[97] but the most contentious has been in the context of domain names. While registering an Internet domain name does not confer trademark rights on the registrant,[98] trademark rights seem to include the right to domain names that use or incorporate a mark, at least as against registrants who do not hold recognized trademark rights in the domain names they register.[99]

Domain names that are identical or similar to well-known marks have at times been registered by "cybersquatters" who tried to sell the domain to the mark owner for large sums of money. Entities that own "cybersquatted" trademarks have in response had a great deal of success arguing that their trademark rights extend to domain names on the Internet in the United States. Even before the Anticybersquatting Consumer Protection Act (ACPA) was enacted, courts found non-permissive registration of text-based trademarks as domain names to be actionable. For example, Panavision, a movie industry company, was deemed to have trademark-based rights in the "panavision.com" domain name, even though the domain name had been purchased by someone else.[100]

The trend both nationally and internationally is for adjudicators to award trademark owners rights to domain names that comprise or incorporate their marks.[101] Though "[I]nternational and U.S. trademark law both proceed from the premise that it is possible for a multiplicity of entities to own the same or similar trademarks for different products and in different geographic areas,"[102] the act of registering a domain name that uses or incorporates a pre-existing trademark has been treated as though it intrinsically implicates the existing rights of those mark holders, rather than as a new, independent and prospectively legitimate use of the mark in a novel and potentially non-confusing context. While registering the trademarked text of another as a domain name and then offering to sell it to the mark holder has been held adequately commercial to constitute a trademark infringement,[103] registering a word as a domain name is inadequately commercial to support a claim to trademark rights in that word.[104]

Domain name conflicts are not addressed by any negotiated international treaty. Instead, they are either resolved in U.S. courts under U.S. trademark law, via the ACPA *in rem* jurisdiction provisions,[105] or through the Internet Corporation for Assigned Names and Numbers' (ICANN) Uniform Domain Name Dispute Resolution Policy (UDRP),[106] which while putatively an international forum, is not grounded or governed by any actual substantive law. This void is largely filled by tacit adoption and application of certain U.S. trademark law principles by UDRP arbitrators. The legal principles most enthusiastically globalized by UDRP include the presumption that web-surfing potential consumers are pathetically easy to confuse, and the assumption that any use of a trademark, or even something that somewhat resembles a trademark, is made in bad faith if it is not authorized by the trademark holder.

Domain names do function in some sense as source identifiers, but whether and to what degree the public views them as trademarks, rather than "locations," is uncertain.[107] Even more questionable is how strong the perception of domain-name-as-trademark would have been if the legal system had not stepped in to sanction and even encourage this connection. Domain names have been deemed to intersect with trademarks, a substantive area of law in which context is critical to assessing what rights are at issue and whether conflicts exist, but on a stand-alone basis they are often devoid of context. Unless they explicitly connote or reference specific goods or services, they are unlikely to evoke any unified source, especially not on a globally recognized basis.

Domain names must be unique in order to function properly, because obviously if more than one Internet site had the same domain name, one couldn't be confident of accessing the desired web page. This would be "confusing" to individuals in the sense that they might not immediately understand why they wound up at the wrong URL or how to maneuver to the correct one, but it is reasonable to assume that they could still tell the difference between a Ford.com that pertained to the Ford Motor Company[108] and a Ford.com that pertained to Ford Models,[109] the Ford Foundation,[110] or one of the almost seven thousand Ford-related trademarks registered with the U.S. Patent and Trademark Office alone.[111] While a URL may be ambiguous, once it is placed in the context of the web page it brings up, unless there actually is deceptive intent at play, any confusion about its associative source is quickly cured if one is willing to assume even slight amounts of intellect and common sense on the part of the ordinary observer. Once domain name disputes encounter fact-finders, however, it is clear that such assumptions do not serve the trademark protectionist agenda.

ACPA

Verisign (formerly NSI) uses a first-come, first-served registration system, which allows parties with no rights in a trademark to register it as a domain name. If this is done to sell competing products or services, it is arguably likely to cause consumer confusion and falls within the prohibitions of infringement law under traditional *Lanham Trademark Act of 1946* analysis by the U.S. courts. The *Lanham Trademark Act of 1946* as amended by the *Anticybersquatting Consumer Protection Act of 1999* provides (with enumerated exceptions):[112]

Any person who registers a domain name that consists of the name of another living person, or a name substantially and confusingly similar thereto, without that person's consent, with the specific intent to profit from such name by selling the domain name for financial gain to that person or any third party, shall be liable in a civil action by such person.[113]

In cases such as *Caesars World, Inc. v. Caesars-Palace.com* (2000),[114] U.S. courts have confirmed that ACPA claims regarding domain names that were registered with Verisign (and its precursor, Network Solutions, Inc.) are subject to *in rem* jurisdiction in the judicial district in which the domain name registrar, registry, or other domain-name authority that registered or assigned the disputed domain name, is located.[115] The overall implication of this holding is that, since the majority of existing .com, .gov, and .net domain names were registered with Verisign (or NSI, its precursor), most cybersquatting claims can be brought in the U.S., regardless of the citizenship or location of the registrant.

U.S. courts decide domain name disputes pursuant to the mandates of ACPA. One of the factors that ACPA directs courts to consider in determining whether a domain name that uses, contains, or is similar to a trademark owned by another has been registered in bad faith is:

... the person's intent to divert consumers from the mark owner's online location to a site accessible under the domain name that could harm the goodwill represented by the mark, either for commercial gain or with the intent to tarnish or disparage the mark, by creating a likelihood of confusion as to the source, sponsorship, affiliation or endorsement of the site.[116]

One observer has noted that this factor "is a summary of all of the trademark and unfair competition law-related rights a trademark owner possessed prior to the enactment" of ACPA.[117] As a consequence, all foreign domiciliaries who are haled into U.S. courts to defend domain name registrations by virtue of ACPA's *in rem* jurisdiction provisions appear to be subject to the full gamut of *Lanham Trademark Act of 1946* trademark provisions. Courts have been willing to find trademark infringement where they determine that consumers are likely to experience "initial interest confusion" due to the use of a trademark in a domain name.

Courts are also willing to make surprising leaps of logic to find trademark dilution in the domain name context.[118] Consider the improbable but true story of a man given the name Uzi Nissan at birth. His father's last name was Nissan, his grandfather's last name was Nissan, and so on.[119] Nissan is a biblical term identifying the seventh month in the Hebrew calendar and the Arabic term for the month of April. It is also the trademark used by a car company previously known as "Datsun."

In 1991, Uzi Nissan incorporated Nissan Computer Corporation, and in 1994, he registered the domain name "nissan.com" and created a website to promote computer-related products and services business on the Internet.[120] In August 1999, nissan.com began hosting third-party banner advertisements, and links for automobile merchandisers were displayed on the site. In response, Nissan Motor Company filed suit, claiming trademark infringement, trademark dilution, domain-name piracy, false designation of origin, and violation of state unfair competition law.[121] In 2000, a court issued a preliminary injunction that prohibited Nissan Computer Corporation from displaying any automobile advertising or links on its site and directed the company to post a disclaimer at nissan.com stating that the site was not affiliated with Nissan Motors and setting forth the URL of Nissan Motor's website.

Ironically, in a 1992 lawsuit, Nissan Motor was the defendant in a trademark lawsuit after the automaker introduced its Altima line of cars and an identically denominated computer firm claimed infringement.[122] The car company's likely defense in 1992 was that Altima as a computer product and Altima as a brand of cars do not overlap, and therefore consumers were not likely to be confused, so the car company's use of the mark was not infringing. This cannot be confirmed, however, because Nissan asked the court to keep that file under seal after the case was settled.[123]

Nissan Computers posted the requisite disclaimers, removed the enjoined advertisements, and vented its frustration over the dispute by posting negative commentary about its litigation adversary on its website. In response, the district court ruled that criticism of Nissan Motor posted by Nissan Computers at nissan.com was enjoinable commercial speech by virtue of the following analysis:

... the instant case presents a situation in which the mark itself is also the domain name. The goodwill that Nissan Motor has built up in the "Nissan" mark ensures a steady stream of visitors expecting to find Nissan Motor at nissan.com and nissan.net. Critical commentary at nissan.com and nissan.net would exploit this goodwill in order to injure Nissan Motor. Under these circumstances, the critical speech becomes commercial and is subject to the proscriptions of the FTDA.[124]

Once reconstituted as commercial speech, the posted criticism, seemingly an exercise of free speech (and arguably political speech at that), was judicially transmogrified into actionable trademark dilution and was therefore subject to injunctive silencing, and was ordered removed from the nissan.com home page. In fact, the court even enjoined "[p]lacing, on nissan.com or nissan.net, links to other websites containing disparaging remarks or negative commentary regarding Nissan Motor Co., Ltd. or Nissan North America, Inc."[125]

UDPR

ICANN implemented its UDRP in response to concerns about emerging conflicts between geographically rooted trademark systems and "global" domain-name disputes. The UDRP is a set of contractual provisions that are incorporated by reference into registration agreements between domain-name registrants and ICANN-approved registrars. It requires domain-name registrants to submit to mandatory arbitration if in the future a third party asserts that the domain name is "identical or confusingly similar to a trademark or service mark in which the complainant has rights," that the registrant has no "rights or legitimate interest" in the domain name, and that the registrant has acted in bad faith. The policy lists factors that demonstrate bad faith, as well as defenses by which a registrant can show that it has a legitimate interest in a domain name.

The UDRP arbitration proceeding determines whether the contested domain name will be transferred to the complainant or remain with the entity that registered it. Arbitrators have little guidance and broad discretion. The Rules promulgated by ICANN to accompany the UDRP instruct dispute-resolution panels to "decide a complaint on the basis of the statements and documents submitted and in accordance with the Policy, these Rules, and any rules and principles of law that it deems applicable." The Policy and the Rules themselves are vague. Language in the *travaux preparatoires* to the UDRP suggests that in certain cases where a particular national interest predominates, national sources may be the appropriate basis for finding interpretive guidance, but nothing appears to preclude the development and application of autonomous standards drawn from any appropriate source.[126] The UDRP functions much like a judicial system; domain-name registrants are categorically subject to its jurisdiction as a condition of registration, and every decision is published, creating an archive of precedent.[127] Most of the precedent that has accumulated so far has aggregated to the benefit of complaining trademark holders.[128]

Like U.S. courts, UDRP arbitrators can easily and consistently spot dubious uses of trademarks in domain names that are clearly intended to fool consumers into making incorrect assumptions about the source of the associative web pages. However, to reach the level of trademark strength that many mark holders desire, UDRP arbitrators are required and have been quite willing to assume that the people who use the Internet are stupid, easily confused, and often evil. These assumptions, whether sincerely held or merely pretextual, are then used to justify the construction and enforcement of powerful trademark rights that are duly given the international scope of the Internet.

In one notable UDRP decision, *Wal-Mart Stores v. Walsucks* (2000),[129] a WIPO panel transferred several domain names, including wal-martcanadasucks.com and walmartpuertoricosucks.com, to the Wal-Mart company based on the panel's conclusion that the registrations were confusingly similar to the Wal-Mart mark and were registered with bad faith intent.

The decision found confusing similarity, despite the extreme unlikelihood that a reasonable consumer would conclude that Wal-Mart was the source of a website disparaging Wal-Mart.

In a subsequent Wal-Mart case, however, *Wal-Mart Stores v. wal-martcanadasucks*[130] (2000) a differently constituted WIPO panel explicitly disagreed with the previous decision, stating that it could "not see how a domain name including "sucks' can ever be confusingly similar to a trademark." Although this common sense and otherwise convincing finding alone would have been grounds for denial of transfer, the panel went on to suggest that a "sucks" domain name may qualify as a legitimate vehicle of free expression under the First Amendment to the United States Constitution, despite the fact that neither the arbitrators nor the Canadian registrant was even putatively constrained or protected by the United States Bill of Rights.

U.S. federal courts have held that "sucks.com" domain names may not infringe trademark rights. In *Lucent Technologies, Inc. v. Lucentsucks.com*,[131] the federal court stated that "a showing that lucentsucks.com is effective parody and/or a [site] for critical commentary would seriously undermine the requisite elements" of trademark infringement, including the element of a likelihood of confusion. The legislative history of the Anticybersquatting Consumer Protection Act lends support to this position in the House Report,[132] which notes: "comment, criticism, [or] parody...may be an appropriate indication that the person's registration or use of the domain name lack[s] 'bad faith'," and that the "sucks" registration should therefore not be transferred or canceled.

In the "Bally sucks" case a disgruntled former health club member was held to have a First Amendment right to post negative consumer commentary about Bally Total Fitness, Inc. on a website posted at www.ballysucks.com because it was a completely noncommercial venture.[133] The court stated that "[n]o reasonable consumer comparing Bally's official website with [the "sucks.com"] site would assume [the "sucks.com"] site 'to come from the same source, or thought to be affiliated with, connected with, or sponsored by, the trademark owner." Had the defendant attempted to sell posters or T-shirts proclaiming that Bally sucked, there is some suggestion in the opinion that the court might have been more protective of the Bally trademark.[134]

Not surprisingly, several commentators have suggested that the problem with these sorts of grossly disparate outcomes in factually similar cases is the egregious lack of consistency.[135] In fact, the problem is much broader: The UDRP was not designed to deal with complicated trademark law nuances,[136] and it is largely adopting certain facets of U.S.-style high protectionist trademark analysis as its default jurisprudence. As under ACPA, winning control of a domain name under UDRP is almost automatic for entities that can plausibly assert trademark rights in some aspect of the domain-name text. This is regarded as highly advantageous to trademark holders, and at least two commentators have suggested that a coordinated multinational approach such as UDRP may be more beneficial to U.S. trademark holders in the long run than expansive use of ACPA's *in rem* jurisdiction provisions.[137]

This is starkly illustrated by the sequential UDRP panel decisions arising out of a dispute over ownership of the domain name greglloydsmith.com. In the first instance, the complainant's demand for transfer of the domain name was denied because no trademark rights in "greglloydsmith" were asserted.[138] After this adverse UDRP arbitrator's decision was issued in February 2002, the complainant registered "Greg Lloyd Smith" as a trademark in the United Kingdom and filed for trademark registration on the name in the United States.[139] The complainant next filed a second complaint in September 2002, and this time prevailed on the basis of his shiny new trademark rights. With little apparent effort he managed to convince the WIPO arbitrator of the registrant's bad faith, even though it is clear from the recitation of facts that at the time the domain name was registered the complainant did not hold the asserted trademark rights, and that the true dispute between the complainant and the registrant has to do with the content of the website at the disputed domain name, which the panel acknowledged was the subject of separate legal proceedings pertaining to allegations of defamation.[140]

A survey of UDRP decisions suggests that too many of the arbitrators are unwilling to consider the context in which the use of a trademark in a domain name arises, preferring bright line distinctions that often isolate domain names from the actual websites with which they are connected. This is a radical deviation from the "context is everything" starting point that infuses real-space trademark infringement and dilution analysis and threatens what little coherence trademark law and jurisprudence maintains.

JURISPRUDENCE OF CONFUSION WILL SPREAD

The U.S. has greatly influenced the substance and texture of international treaties pertaining to trademarks. TRIPS in particular required little internal alteration of U.S. trademark regulation, while mandating substantial changes in trademark protection by other countries.[141]

For the countries that are wrestling with defining the scope of trademark rights,[142] domain name jurisprudence offers an example of the seeming attractiveness and efficiency of trademark rights in gross. Domain-name dispute resolution is in the process of establishing new trademark norms, embracing norms that favor trademark-holder rights above speech principles[143] and ascertain bad faith in relatively innocuous behavior. Once established, largely United-States-centric trademark precepts will enter real space through the domain-name system window. Those that promulgate trademark rights as broad and property-like are likely to be applied to all trademark-related conflicts, while the limiting principles rarely in evidence in the domain-name context may be completely left behind. The precedent of easily confused consumers will concurrently find its way into the domestic trademark laws of wired nations, and it is inevitable that biases will manifest themselves as well.

CONCLUSIONS

Both free speech rights and efficient commerce would be best served if courts entertained trademark infringement claims only where either identical or exceedingly similar marks are used on directly competing or closely related goods and services, and dilution claims only where dilution protections were limited to very famous marks that are arbitrary and fanciful and invented by the mark holder. Rather than adopting troubling, and at times seemingly indefensible, theories about confusion and dilution, U.S. courts applying ACPA and the UDRP could abstain from applying trademark law altogether to any dispute beyond straightforward counterfeiting, appropriation, and deception. Domain-name disputes could then be resolved by alternative means rooted in common sense, such as requiring the use of disclaimers,[144] and then monitoring in use, or using certain URLs as directories.[145] Otherwise, the world will continue to incrementally and largely involuntarily embrace certain trademark law precepts without treaties, consensus, or even coherence in the domain-name context. This same interpretive framework can be expected to spread to trademark rights in real space as well, "harmonizing" some very discordant trademark law constructs.

ENDNOTES

[1]   These are often referred to as the "Abercrombie & Fitch" categories because they were first specifically enunciated in Abercrombie & Fitch Co. v. Hunting World, Inc., 537 F.2d 4, 9-11 (2d Cir. 1976).

2   E.g., Soweco, Inc. v. Shell Oil Co., 617 F.2d 1178, 1183 (5th Cir. 1980). Trademarks can also become unprotectable over time if they "commit genericide" — that is, become used as the generic term for a product or service. See, e.g., International Trademark Association (2001). Aspirin brand or aspirin tablets? Retrieved December 5, 2003, from http://www.inta.org/library/stories/01/jan/INTA.htm and Erakat, S. (2003). Losing trademark rights. Retrieved December 8, 2003, from: http://www.iplg.com/resources/articles/losing_trademark_rights.shtml or Legal-Definitions.com (2003). Genericide. Retrieved December 8, 2003, from: http://legal-definitions.com/IP/genericide.htm.

3   Bernard v. Commerce Drug Co., 964 F.2d 1338 (2d Cir. 1992).

4   P.A.W. Safety Charities v. Petco Animal Supplies, Inc., 2000 U.S. Dist. LEXIS 3110 (N.D. Tex. 2000) ("The concept of descriptiveness is broadly construed. A mark need not convey every relevant piece of information about the nature of a product to be characterized as descriptive. Rather, it must only "immediately convey an important attribute of plaintiffs' products." The noun "pet" commonly refers to "a domesticated animal kept for pleasure rather than utility." *Merriam-Webster's Collegiate Dictionary* (10th ed.). (1993). Springfield, MA: Merriam-Webster. The dictionary defines "pal" as "a close friend." *Merriam-Webster's Collegiate Dictionary* (10th ed.). (1993). Springfield, MA.: Merriam-Webster. Thus, the literal interpretation of "pet pal" is one who is a friend to his or her pet. It is a common and distinctive quality of friendship to care for and seek the well-being of one's friend. Thus, it takes no imagination or perception to conclude that a program called "Pet Pals" is one that promotes the well-being of pets. The mark describes the essence of plaintiff's program, even though it does not specifically spell out all the associated services.").

5   Minnesota Mining & Mfg. Co. v. Johnson & Johnson, *454 F.2d 1179 (C.C.P.A. 1972).*

6   Lanham Act, § 2(e)(1), 15 U.S.C. § 1052 (2003); *see also, e.g.*, Bernard v. Commerce Drug Co., 774 F. Supp. 103 (E.D.N.Y. 1991) (Holding that where the issue in a trademark infringement action becomes one of establishing secondary meaning, the relevant inquiry focuses upon whether the mark, although not inherently distinctive, comes through use to be uniquely associated with a single source, that is, whether the public is moved in any degree to buy an article because of its source. Moreover, the burden of proof rests upon the party claiming rights in the mark, and entails vigorous evidentiary requirements. Direct or circumstantial evi-

dence may establish secondary meaning, including the use of survey evidence by a representative sample of consumers. The extent of public exposure to the mark as determined by the sales volume, length of time of use, and promotional efforts may also be utilized to establish secondary meaning.).

[7]   See Vision Center v. Opticks, Inc. 596 F.2d 111 (5th Cir. 1980).

[8]   Soweco, Inc. v. Shell Oil Co., 617 F.2d 1178, 1184 (5th Cir. 1980).

[9]   Jeno's Inc. v. Comm. of Patents & Trademarks of the U.S., *227 U.S.P.Q. (BNA) 227, 231* (D. Minn. 1985).

[10] *Id.*

[11] West & Co. v. Arica Institute, Inc., 557 F.2d 338, 343 (2d Cir. 1977) ("While 'psychocalisthenics,' as noted, bears some relationship to the physical exercises conducted by Arica, this would be expected of any suggestive mark, and, in fact, would be one of the purposes of the mark. But we cannot say that 'psychocalisthenics' merely describes 'a combination of various yoga systems, dance and calisthenics' which require continual motion and are designed to produce specific mental, emotional and spiritual results. We think the term does 'require imagination, thought and perception to reach a conclusion as to the nature of [the services].'").

[12] Application of Reynolds Metals Co., 480 F.2d 902 (C.C.P.A. 1973).

[13] The Money Store v. Harriscorp Finance, Inc., 689 F.2d 666 (7th Cir. 1982).

[14] E.g., Zatarain's, Inc. v. Oak Grove Smokehouse, Inc., 698 F.2d 786 (5th Cir. 1983).

[15] E.g., West & Co. v. Arica Institute, Inc., 557 F.2d 338 (2d Cir. 1977) ("In the broad middle ground where most of the trademark battles are fought are the terms which are primarily descriptive and those which are only suggestive. The distinction, while not always readily apparent, is important, because those which are descriptive may obtain registration only if they have acquired secondary meaning, while suggestive terms are entitled to registration without such proof."); *see also* Abercrombie & Fitch Co. v. Hunting World, Inc, 537 F.2d 4, 9 (2d Cir. 1976); W.E. Bassett Co. v. Revlon, 435 F.2d 656, 661 (2d Cir. 1970).

[16] Lewis Management Co. v. Corel Corp., 1995 U.S. Dist. LEXIS 18704 (S.D.N.Y. 1995).

[17] Calamari Fisheries Inc. v. The Village Catch. Inc., 698 F. Supp. 994, 1008 (D. Mass. 1988).

[18] Abercromie & Fitch Co. v. Hunting World, Inc, 537 F.2d 4, at 4 n.12 (2d Cir. 1976); *see also* McKee Baking Co. v. Interstate Brands Corp., 738

F. Supp. 1272, 1274 (E.D. Mo. 1990) ("Fanciful marks are coined terms with no dictionary meaning. Arbitrary marks are common words applied in an unfamiliar way, in a way that is non-descriptive.").

[19]   Abercromie & Fitch Co. v. Hunting World, Inc, 537 F.2d 4, at 4 n.12 (2d Cir. 1976).

[20]   Chams De Baron Ltd. v. H. Cotler Co., 1984 U.S. Dist. LEXIS 18993 (S.D.N.Y. 1984).

[21]   U.S. Trademark No. 78170383, Apple Computer, Inc. 2003. Available: http://www.apple.com/.

[22]   U.S. Trademark No. 74693839, *see, e.g.*, J.V. Schomakers, Holland. July 6, 2002. The Complete Apple Records [On-line] Available: http://www.schomakers.com/.

[23]   RFE Indus. v. SPM Corp., 105 F.3d 923 (4th Cir. 1997).

[24]   Nabisco v. Warner-Lambert, 32 F. Supp.2d 690 (S.D.N.Y. 1999) (trademark "ice" for mint flavored chewing gum was suggestive).

[25]   Anheuser-Busch, Inc. v. John LaBatt Ltd., 1995 U.S. Dist. LEXIS 5341 (E.D. Mo. 1995) ("A-B argues that the "ice" marks are generic while Labatt argues that they are either arbitrary, fanciful or suggestive.").

[26]   Anheuser-Busch, Inc. v. John LaBatt Ltd., 1995 U.S. Dist. LEXIS 5341 (E.D. Mo. 1995).

[27]   Leaffer, M.A. (1998). The new world of international trademark law. *Marquette Intellectual Property Law Review, 2,* 1-31, pp. 5-6 ("A reliable, stable, and efficiently structured trademark system benefits consumer and business interests alike. Trademarks serve the interests of consumers because they reduce search costs and allow buyers to make rational purchasing and repurchasing decisions with speed and assurance. Just as important, a strong trademark system creates incentives for firms to create and market products of desirable qualities, particularly when these qualities are not observable before purchase.").

[28]   See 15 U.S.C. 1114(1).

[29]   See 15 U.S.C. 1114(1)(a).

[30]   Lanham Act, §32(1)(a), 15 USC §1114(1)(a) (2003).

[31]   Lanham Act, §32(1)(a), 15 USC §1114(1)(a) (2003).

[32]   E.g., Washington Speakers Bureau, Inc. v. Leading Authorities, Inc., 33 F. Supp. 2d 488 (E.D. Va., Feb. 2, 1999).

[33]   See Lanham Act, §45, 15 USC §1127 (2003).

[34]   See, e.g., U.S. Department of Justice (October, 1997) Trademark counterfeiting – Introduction. Retrieved December 4, 2003, from: http:/

/www.usdoj.gov/usao/eousa/foia_reading_room/usam/title9/crm01701.
htm.

The Trademark Counterfeiting Act of 1984, Pub. L. No. 98-473, Tit. II,
§ 1502(a), 98 Stat. 2178 (1984), and the Anticounterfeiting Consumer
Protection Act of 1996, Pub. L. No. 104-153, 110 Stat. 1386 (1996),
address the growing problem of trafficking in counterfeit trademark
goods, which has primarily involved the clandestine manufacture and
distribution of imitations of well-known trademarked merchandise. The
1984 Act created an offense, codified at 18 U.S.C. § 2320, which
provides that "whoever intentionally traffics or attempts to traffic in goods
and services and knowingly uses a counterfeit mark on or in connection
with such goods or services" shall be guilty of a felony. 18 U.S.C. §
2320(a). Section 2320(b) enables the United States to obtain an order for
the destruction of articles in the possession of a defendant in a prosecution
under this section upon a determination by the preponderance of the
evidence that such articles bear counterfeit marks. These Acts also amend
the Lanham Act, 15 U.S.C. § 1501 *et seq.*, to create stronger remedies
in civil cases involving the intentional use of a counterfeit trademark. They
provide mechanisms for obtaining statutory damages, treble damages and
attorney's fees. 15 U.S.C. § 1117. The Lanham Act also provides for ex
parte application by a trademark owner for a court order to seize
counterfeit materials and instrumentalities where it can be shown that the
defendant is likely to conceal or transfer the materials. *Id.* § 1116(d). New
amendments permit the seizure order to be served and executed either by
federal law enforcement officers or by state or local law enforcement
officers. *Id.* § 1116(d)(9). The Lanham Act also requires applicants to file
a notice of application for an ex parte seizure order with the United States
Attorney, who may participate in such proceedings if they appear to affect
evidence of a federal crime.

[35]   "Counterfeit" is defined in Section 1127 of the Lanham Act as "a spurious
mark which is identical with, or substantially indistinguishable from, a
registered mark."

[36]   Lanham Act, §32, 15 USC §1114.

[37]   Lanham Act, §45, 15 USC §1127.

[38]   E.g., Lois Sportswear, USA, Inc. v. Levi Strauss & Co., 799 F.2d 867,
875 (2d Cir. 1986) ("Of course, it is black letter law that actual confusion
need not be shown to prevail under the Lanham Act, since actual
confusion is very difficult to prove and the Act requires only a likelihood

of confusion as to source."); *see also*, *e.g.*, Scarves by Vera, Inc. v. Todo Imports Ltd., Inc., 544 F.2d 1167, 1175 (2d Cir. 1976) ("a showing of actual confusion is not necessary and is very difficult to demonstrate with reliable proof."); Kobialka, L. (1997, Winter). Not likely, but possible: a lesser standard for trademark infringement in V*ersa Products Co. v. Bifold Co. University of San Francisco Law Review, 31,* 477-503 The "likelihood of confusion" standard is a happy medium between a "possibility of confusion" standard and an "actual confusion" standard. Demonstrating a possibility of confusion is quite easy. On the other hand, proof of actual confusion is difficult, if not impossible, to establish. However, evidence of actual confusion is only one of several factors employed to make a likelihood of confusion determination. Any proof of actual confusion is persuasive evidence that there is a likelihood of confusion, but a lack of actual confusion is not dispositive. (citations omitted).

[39]   E.g., id.

[40]   American Law Institute (1995). *The Restatement (Third) of Unfair Competition.* (3rd ed.). St. Paul, Minn.: American Law Institute (comment to section 21, "Proof of Likelihood of Confusion – Market Factors).

[41]   See, e.g., Giant Foods, Inc. v. Nation's Foodservice, Inc. 710 F.2d 1565, 1569 (Fed. Cir. 1983)

Some circuit courts hold that the question of likelihood of confusion is one of fact and is subject to the "clearly erroneous" standard of Fed. R. Civ. P. 52(a). However, other courts hold that it is a conclusion of law. Our predecessor court, the Court of Customs and Patent Appeals, recognized in DuPont that the question of likelihood of confusion "has been termed a question of fact" by other courts, but did It went on to say that "if labeled a mixed question or one of law, it is necessarily drawn from the probative facts in evidence." Id. Subsequently in the case of Interstate Brands v. Celestial Seasonings, 576 F.2d 926 (CCPA 1978), Chief Judge Markey stated for the majority that the question of likelihood of confusion "is a legal conclusion" and cannot be "admitted" as a fact. However the ultimate issue of likelihood of confusion is characterized, it is clear that our predecessor court did not apply the "clearly erroneous" standard of review to the issue. In DuPont, Chief Judge Markey wrote that "... it is the duty of the examiner, the board, and this court (emphasis added) ..." to determine the ultimate issue of likelihood of confusion. A review of cases in which the CCPA reversed the decision of the TTAB on this issue will demonstrate that our predecessor court did not consider itself bound by a narrow standard of review of the question. We have held that the decisions of the Court of Customs and Patent Appeals are binding upon us. Therefore, we hold that the issue of likelihood of confusion is the ultimate conclusion of law to be decided by the court, and that the clearly erroneous rule is not applicable.

[42]   See, e.g., Bristol-Myers Squibb Co. v. McNeil-P.P.C., Inc., 973 F.2d 1033, 1043 (2d Cir. 1992) ("In this Circuit, a district court's determination of the individual Polaroid factors are subject to review as findings of fact, subject to reversal only if clearly erroneous, while the ultimate balancing of all the Polaroid factors to determine the likelihood of confusion in any given case is done de novo by this Court."); Wynn Oil Co. v. Thomas, 839 F.2d 1183, 1186 (6th Cir. 1988) ("This Circuit considers the question of whether there is a likelihood of confusion a mixed question of fact and law. When reviewing a lower court's decision in these cases, we apply a clearly erroneous standard to findings of fact supporting the likelihood of confusion factors, but review de novo the legal question whether, given the foundational facts as found by the lower court, those facts constitute a 'likelihood of confusion.'").

[43]   Ginsburg, J.C., Litman, J., & Kelvin, M. (2001). *Trademark and unfair competition law.* (3rd ed. P. 419). New York, NY: Foundation Press.

[44]   See, e.g., Carter, S.L. (1993). *Does it matter whether intellectual property is property? Chicago-Kent Law Review, 68*, 715-723, 720 ("Certainly, one may conceptualize trademarks as property in the Lockean sense.... In American law, of course, it is axiomatic that trademarks are not property in this sense."); Gray, M.E. (1996, Winter). Defending against a dilution claim: A practitioner's guide. *Texas Intellectual Property Law Journal, 4*, 205-208, 209-10.
The trademark right is an exclusionary right, not a property right in the word itself. To be more specific, trademark owners do not actually own the underlying mark at issue — they only possess a right to exclude others from using the mark in a manner that would harm consumers. A pure ownership right in a mark has not been granted, nor is it likely to be granted, because of the potential monopolization of language to which this could lead. Dilution statutes obviously grant broader protection than traditional trademark law since a dilution cause of action allows a trademark owner to exclude those who use the mark in a non-confusing manner. However, dilution statutes only grant a quasi-property right in a mark.

cf. Alexandri, M. (2000, Winter). The international news quasi-property paradigm and trademark incontestability: A call for rewriting the Lanham act, *Harvard Journal of Law & Technology, 13,* 303 ("Trademarks are not — or at least, were not — property prior to the passage of the Lanham Act; incontestability... raises a serious question, descriptively speaking, as to whether trademarks now are property.).

[45]   Trademarks deemed "famous" receive very broad protections under the Lanham Act, 15 USC Sections 1125(c) and 1127. The statute lists 8 factors for determining whether a mark is famous, but application of these factors by the courts has been varied. *See, e.g.*, Nguyen X-T. N. (1999, Fall). A circus among the circuits: Would the truly famous and diluted performer please stand up? The federal trademark dilution act and its challenges. *Journal of Intellectual Property, 1,* 158-190.

[46]   Quality Inn International v. McDonald's Corp., 695 F.Supp. 198, 210 (D.Md. 1988).

[47]   E.g., United Drug Co. v. Theodore Rectanus Co., 248 U.S. 90 (1918); Dawn Donut Co. v. Hart's Food Stores, Inc., 267 F.2d 358 (2d Cir. 1959); Thrifty Rent-A-Car System v. Thrift Cars, Inc. 831 F.2d 1177 (1ˢᵗ Cir. 1987).

[48]   E.g., Blue Bell, Inc. v. Farah Mfg. Co., 508 F.2d 1260 (5ᵗʰ Cir. 1975); Shalom Children's Wear, Inc. v. In-Wear A/S, 26 U.S.P.Q.2d 1516 (T.T.A.B. 1993); Lucent Information Management, Inc. v. Lucent Technologies, Inc., 986 F. Supp. 253 (D. Del. 1997).

[49]   E.g., Int'l Kennel Club of Chicago, Inc. v. Mighty Star, Inc., 846 F.2d 1079 (7ᵗʰ Cir. 1988); Procter & Gamble Co. v. Johnson & Johnson, Inc., 485 F. Supp. 1185 (S.D.N.Y.), *aff'd* 636 F.2d 1203 (2d Cir. 1980).

[50]   AMF Inc. v. Sleekcraft Boats, 599 F.2d 341, 348 (9ᵗʰ Cir. 1979).

[51]   Id.

[52]   Uncle Ben's, Inc. v. Stubenberg International, Inc., *1998 TTAB LEXIS 118, 47 U.S.P.Q.2D (BNA) 1310.*

[53]   Id.

[54]   The NutraSweet Company by change of name from G.D. Searle & Co. v. K & S Foods, Inc., 1987 TTAB LEXIS 19; 4 U.S.P.Q.2D (BNA) 1964:

While artificial sweeteners and salt with trace minerals are obviously different products, we think it likely that they would be sold in the same sections of grocery stores and supermarkets and would appear side by side in restaurants and on kitchen tabletops of ordinary consumers. We further note that the respective products are low-cost impulse type items where the purchasing decision is not likely to be as careful as it would be with a higher-priced product. In short, we conclude that the artificial sweetener and salt products are closely related, complementary products and that the use of the same or of a similar mark in connection with these products would likely result in confusion as to source or sponsorship.

55   The NutraSweet Company by change of name from G.D. Searle & Co. v. K & S Foods, Inc., 1987 TTAB LEXIS 19; 4 U.S.P.Q.2D (BNA) 1964.

56   AMF Inc. v. Sleekcraft Boats, 599 F.2d 341, 348 (9th Cir. 1979).

57   Quality Inn International v. McDonald's Corp., 695 F.Supp. 198, 210 (D. Md. 1988).

58   E.g., Lois Sportswear, U.S.A., Inc. v. Levi Strauss & Co., 799 F.2d 867 (2d Cir. 1986); *see also, e.g.*, Scarves by Vera, Inc. v. Todo Imports Ltd., Inc., 544 F.2d 1167, 1175 (2d Cir. 1976; and American Home Products v. Chattem, *1986 U.S. Dist. LEXIS 25051 (S.D.N.Y. 1986)*.

59   This right is doctrinally available only to famous marks under dilution principles, see "Trademark Dilution and More Confusion" *supra*.

60   Virgin Enterprises, Ltd. v. Virgin Petroleum, Inc., 2000 U.S. Dist. LEXIS 8100 (C.D. Calif. 2000).

61   Geoffrey, Inc. v. Stratton, 1990 U.S. Dist. LEXIS 19504, *16 U.S.P.Q.2D (BNA) 1691 (C.D. Calif. 1990)*.

62   *Id.*

63   Grotrian, Helfferich, Schulz, Th. Steinweg Nachf. v. Steinway & Sons, *523 F.2d 1331 (2d Cir. 1975)*.
       The issue here is not the possibility that a purchaser would buy a Grotrian-Steinweg thinking it was actually a Steinway or that Grotrian had some connection with Steinway and Sons. The harm to Steinway, rather, is the likelihood that a consumer, hearing the "Grotrian-Steinweg" name and thinking it had some connection with "Steinway", would consider it on that basis. The "Grotrian-Steinweg" name therefore would attract potential customers based on the reputation built up by Steinway in this country for many years. The harm to Steinway in short is the likelihood that potential piano purchasers will think that there is some connection between the Grotrian-Steinweg and Steinway pianos.

64   Blockbuster Entertainment Group v. Laylco, Inc., 869 F. Supp. 505 (E.D. Mich. 1994).

65   Definition of "famous" in Lanham Act and in case law, *e.g.*, TCPIP
      Holding Co. v. Haar Communications, Inc. 244 F.3d 88 (2d Cir. 2001);
      Avery Dennison Corp. v. Sumpton, 52 USPQ 2d 1920 (9th Cir. 1999);
      Star Markets, Ltd v. Texaco, Inc., 950 F. Supp. 1030 (D. Hawaii 1996);
      Gazette Newspapers v. New Paper, Inc. 934 F. Supp. 688 (D. Md.
      1996); Times Mirror Magazines Inc. v. Las Vegas Sports News LLC,
      212 F.3d 157 (3d Cir. 2000); *see also e.g.* Vassallo, E.E. & Dickey, M.
      (1999, Winter). Protection in the United States for "Famous Marks": The
      Federal Trademark Dilution Act Revisited, *Fordham Intellectual Prop-
      erty, Media & Entertainment Law Journal, 9,* 503-527.

66   15 U.S.C. § 1125.

67   15 U.S.C. § 1127 (definition of the term dilution).

68   See Federal Trademark Dilution Act of 1995, Pub. L. 104-98, 109 Stat.
      985 (1996); *but see* Nabisco Inc. v. PF Brands, Inc. 191 F.3d 208 (2d
      Cir. 1999) (Goldfish cracker case).

69   See, e.g., Gray, M.E. (1996, Winter). Defending against a dilution claim:
      A practitioner's guide. *Texas Intellectual Property Law Journal, 4,*
      205-228, 207-08.
      Dilution statutes are a relatively new phenomenon in the trademark
      protection field. The first dilution law was passed in Massachusetts in
      1947. Since then, approximately twenty-five states have adopted dilution
      laws of their own. Three states include dilution as part of their common
      law. In fact, one court has recently noted that a dilution claim is practically
      boilerplate in trademark actions. The vast majority of states with dilution
      laws have adopted statutes that are much the same as section 12 of the
      Model State Trademark Bill. Despite this similarity in language, courts
      have been wildly inconsistent in their interpretations of dilution statutes.

70   But see Heald, P.J. (1996). Trademarks and geographical indications:
      exploring the contours of the TRIPS agreement. *Vanderbilt Journal of
      Transnational Law, 29,* 635-660, 642-43. ("Article 16 of TRIPS
      requires that a dissimilar use 'indicate a connection between [the infring-
      ing] goods or services and the owner of the registered trademark.' The
      requirement of a mistaken belief in a 'connection between those goods'
      seems much closer to the traditional Lanham Act false sponsorship cause
      of action than to a cause of action for dilution.").

71   E.g., Procter & Gamble Co. v. Johnson & Johnson, Inc., 485 F. Supp.
      1185 (S.D.N.Y.), *aff'd* 636 F.2d 1203 (2d Cir. 1980); *see also* Buti v.
      Impressa Perosa, S.A., 139 F.3d 98 (2d Cir.), *cert. denied* 525 U.S.
      826 (1998); Landau, M.B. (1997). Problems arising out of the use of

"WWW.TRADEMARK.COM": The application of principles of trademark law to internet domain name disputes. *Georgia State University Law Review, 13,* 455-515, 467 ("One cannot simply create "catchy" marks, not use them and then assert them against the users. In order to maintain rights in a mark, the trademark owner must maintain the mark's usage in connection with goods and/or services.").

[72] Welkowitz, D.S. (2000, Fall). Protection against trademark dilution in the U.K. and Canada: Inexorable trend or will tradition triumph? *Hastings International & Comparative Law Review, 24,* 63-124, 67-68.

[73] E.g., Port, K.L. (2000, Winter). The congressional expansion of American Trademark Law: A civil law system in the making. *Wake Forest Law Review, 35,* 831-913 ("Part IV of this Article analyzes section 43(c) of the Lanham Act and concludes that this congressional expansion of the trademark right in the United States has created a state where circuit courts have no real idea of what a likelihood of dilution means and therefore, conclude, in most instances, that a famous mark is a diluted mark without any real justification for this conclusion."); *see also* Magliocca, G.N. (2001). One and inseparable: Dilution and infringement in trademark law. *Minnesota Law Review, 85,* 949-1036 ("Courts repeatedly throw up their hands in frustration when asked "to identify the legal interest sought to be protected from "dilution,' [and] hence the legal harm sought to be prevented." Since any concurrent use of a mark diminishes that mark's distinctiveness in some sense, separating unauthorized uses that dilute from those that do not has proven quite difficult. Unless dilution is read to prohibit virtually all unauthorized uses of a given mark, the doctrine can begin "to lose its coherence as a legally enforceable norm.").

[74] Panavision Int'l v. Toeppen, 141 F.3d 1316 (9th Cir. 1998) ("trademark dilution laws protect 'distinctive' or 'famous' trademarks from certain unauthorized uses of the marks regardless of a showing of competition or likelihood of confusion.").

[75] E.g., Mead Data Cent., Inc. v. Toyota Motor Sales, Inc., 875 F.2d 1026 (2d Cir. 1989) ("Indeed, some courts have gone so far as to hold that, although violation of an antidilution statute does not require confusion of product or source, the marks in question must be sufficiently similar that confusion may be created as between the marks themselves. We need not go that far. We hold only that the marks must be "very" or "substantially" similar and that, absent such similarity, there can be no viable claim of dilution.") (citations omitted).

[76] Wawa, Inc. v. Haaf, *40 U.S.P.Q.2D (BNA) 1629 (E.D. Pa. 1996).*

[77] Id.

[78] Criticism of the inconsistent ways in which courts apply antidilution laws come from a variety of normative viewpoints. *See, e.g.*, Rayner, R.R. (1999, Fall). In search of a dilution solution: Implementation of the federal trademark dilution act, *Mississippi College Law Review, 20,* 93-105, 94 ("… federal courts have struggled with the development of a body of case law interpreting the FTDA. As more fully described below, the various circuits have, on occasion, reached diametrically opposed conclusions as to the interpretation of certain provisions of the FTDA."); Ahearn, T. (2001). Comments: Dilution by blurring under the federal trademark dilution act of 1995: What is it and how is it shown? *Santa Clara Law Review, 41,* 893-919, 893-94 ("The FTDA was designed to provide uniform national protection to the value of trademarks and replace the "patch quilt system" of state laws that had produced inconsistent and unenforceable results. However, dilution theory has never been unanimously accepted as a viable extension of traditional trademark protection, and as previous failed legislation and state court experience has shown, the application of dilution theory is intensely debated and begrudgingly applied."); Nguyen, X-T. N. (1999, Fall). A circus among the circuits: Would the truly famous and diluted performer please stand up? The federal trademark dilution act and its challenges. *Journal of Intellectual Property, 1,* 158-190, 158. ("Each of the circuit courts that has had the opportunity to address the Act has its own idea about dilution and fame, the meaning of dilution, how to establish fame, and how to prove dilution. With the conflicting rulings from these circuits, there is a circus among the circuits. Each performer at the circus is carrying its own act leaving trademark owners a federal anti-dilution system that is almost as chaotic as the original patchwork system of more than twenty-five state statutes.").

[79] E.g., Mead Data Central, Inc. v. Toyota Motor Sales USA, Inc., 875 F.2d 1026 (2d Cir. 1989); Nabisco Inc. v. PF Brands, Inc., 191 F.3d 208 (2d Cir. 1999); Eli Lilly & Co. v. Natural Answers Inc., 233 F.3d 456 (7 Cir. 2000); Times Mirroe Magazines v. Los Vegas Sports News, 212 F.3d 157 (3d Cir. 2001); V Secret Catalogue, Inc. v. Moseley, 259 F.3d 464 (6 Cir. 2001), *cert. granted,* 122 S. Ct. 1536 (2002).

[80] Merges, R., Menell, P., & Lemley, M. (2001). *Intellectual property in the new technological age.* (2d ed., p. 713). New York, NY: Aspen Publishers.

81   Moseley v. V Secret Catalogue, Inc., 537 U.S. 418 (2003).

82   Id.

83   See, e.g., Sacoff, R.W. (2001, Spring). Trademark law in the technology-driven global marketplace. *Yale Symposium of Law & Technology, 4,* 8-83.

84   See, e.g., USPTO. (October 3, 2002) . *Congress expands protection for American intellectual property* (Press Release). Retrieved December 4, 2003, from http://www.uspto.gov/web/offices/com/speeches/02-64.htm (proclaiming in pertinent part, "Congress enacted today, as part of the Justice Department Reauthorization Act, a bill that will simplify international trademark registration ... Permitting the U.S. to join the Madrid Protocol, a procedural agreement allowing U.S. trademark owners to file for registration in any number of over 56 member countries by filing a single standardized application at the USPTO, in English, with a single set of fees. American businesses—large and small—seeking to market their products in new countries can gain valuable protection for their trademarks, faster and less expensively than is presently possible."). *See* Dinwoodie, G. (2001). International agreements on registration of trademarks. In Ginsburg J.C., Litman J., & Kevlin M. (2001). *Trademark and unfair competition law* (3d. ed., pp. 1001-02). New York: Foundation Press.; *see also* U.S. Department of State (May 31, 2000). U.S. – E.U. Madrid protocol on trademark registration. Retrieved December 4, 2003, from http://usinfo.state.gov/topical/econ/ipr/ipr-madrid protocol.htm; *see also* Hines, P.J. & Weinstein, J.S. (2003). Using the Madrid Protocol after U.S. accession. Retrieved December 4, 2003, from: http://www.inta.org/downloads/tmr_HinesWeinstein.pdf ("On November 2, 2002, President Bush signed into law legislation to implement the Madrid Protocol, a treaty to facilitate international registration and maintenance of trademarks.").

85   See Dinwoodie, G. (2001). International agreements on registration of trademarks. In Ginsburg, J.C., Litman, J., & Kevlin, M. (2001). *Trademark and unfair competition law* (3d. ed., pp. 1000-1002). New York: Foundation Press.

86   E.g., WIPO (2003). What does a trademark do? Retrieved December 4, 2003, from: http://www.wipo.org/about-ip/en/about_trademarks.html In order to avoid the need to register separately with each national or regional office, WIPO administers a system of international registration of marks. This system is governed by two treaties, the Madrid Agreement Concerning the International Registration of Marks and the Madrid Protocol. A person who has a link (through nationality, domicile or

establishment) with a country party to one or both of these treaties may, on the basis of a registration or application with the trademark office of that country, obtain an international registration having effect in some or all of the other countries of the Madrid Union. At present, more than 60 countries are party to one or both of the agreements.

[87]   See, e.g., Sacoff, R.W. (2001, Spring). Trademark law in the technology-driven global marketplace. *Yale Symposium of Law & Technology, 4,* 8-83; *see also, e.g.,* International Trademark Association (2003). Madrid protocol. Retrieved December 4, 2003, from: http://www.inta.org/madrid/

[88]   Trade Related Aspects of Intellectual Property Rights, signed December 15, 1993, art. 15, (1994). *International Legal Materials, 33,* 81-111, 89 [hereinafter TRIPS].

[89]   Id.

[90]   Id.

[91]   Port, K.L. (1998). Trademark harmonization: Norms, names & non-sense. *Marquette Intellectual Property Law Review, 2,* 33-49, 44. ("Each of the recent efforts at trademark harmonization curiously side-steps the definition of trademark rights. This has been done intentionally so that progress on non-substantive areas can be recognized.").

[92]   E.g., Cabinet Chaillot (2003) Industrial property law. Retrieved December 8, 2003, from http://www.frenchlaw.com/pages/intelec3.htm and Embassy of France (2003) Information for private individuals: Counterfeit goods. Retrieved December 8, 2003, from http://www.info-france-usa.org/intheus/customs/9000.asp (Trademark infringement can, and frequently does, give rise to both civil and criminal action in France. French courts generally take a very strong position against knock-offs and brand infringement.).

[93]   E.g., WIPO (2003). About intellectual property. Retrieved December 4, 2003, from: http://www.wipo.org/about-ip/en/about_trademarks.html ("Almost all countries in the world register and protect trademarks. Each national or regional office maintains a Register of Trademarks which contains full application information on all registrations and renewals, facilitating examination, search, and potential opposition by third parties. The effects of such a registration are, however, limited to the country (or, in the case of a regional registration, countries) concerned.").

[94]   See WIPO (2003). Trademarks. Retrieved December 4, 2003 from: http://www.wipo.org/about-ip/en/trademarks.html.

[95]   See Litman, J. (Spring 2000). The DNS wars: Trademarks and the internet domain name system. *Journal of Small & Emerging Business*

Law, 4, 149-165, 160 (citing an interim report on WIPO Internet Domain Name Process, The Management of Internet Names and Addresses: Intellectual Property Issues. The final report is available at http://wipo2.wipo.int/process1/report/index.html.) and Froomkin, A.M. (May 19, 1999). A Commentary on WIPO's "The Management of Internet Names and Addresses: Intellectual Property Issues." Retrieved December 4, 2003, from http://personal.law.miami.edu/~amf/commentary.htm/

[96]   Id.

[97]   E.g., concerning use of trademarks in metatags, and within the text of web pages.

[98]   See, e.*g.*, Brookfield Communications v. West Coast Entertainment Corp., 174 F.3d 1036 (9th Cir. 1999); Metaphor Name Consultants (2001). What kinds of trademarks are most protectable? Least protectable? Retrieved December 5, 2003, from http://www.metaphor name.com/verb_set.html?/primer_3.html ("Domain names in themselves do not hold a lot of weight as a way to establish a trademark, especially outside the United States. However, the existence of a similar trademark can block your use of a domain name.").

[99]   See, e.g., Geist, M. (2002). International telecommunications governance?: Fair.com?: An examination of the allegations of systemic unfairness in the ICANN UDRP. *Brooklyn Journal of International Law, 27,* 903-937.; Froomkin, A.M. (2002). *ICANN's "uniform dispute resolution policy" — causes and (partial) cures. Brooklyn Law Review, 67,* 605-717; *see also* ICANN   (February 20, 2002). *Statistical summary of proceedings under uniform domain name dispute resolution policy. Retrieved December 4, 2003, from* http://www.icann.org/udrp/proceedings-stat.htm.

[100]   *See* Panavision Int'l v. Toeppen, 141 F.3d 1316 (9th Cir. 1998).

[101]   In some situations, the names of individuals (generally celebrities) have been accorded trademark like protection in the domain name context. Names of people (living, dead or fictitious) can actually function like, and be registered as, trademarks, if they are used to identify goods and services in commerce. This creates a cause of action when entities register the names of living people as domain names and then either post material at these sights that might be objectionable, or try to sell the "cybersquatted" domain names to the named individuals.

[102]   Ginsburg, J.C., Litman, J., & Kevlin, M. (2001). *Trademark and unfair competition law,* (3d ed., p. 768). New York: Foundation Press.

[103]   E.g., Panavision Int'l v. Toeppen, 141 F.3d 1316 (9th Cir. 1998).

[104]   E.g., Brookfield Communications v. West Coast Entertainment Corp., 174 F.3d 1036 (9th Cir. 1999).

[105]   Forrest, H.A. (2001). Note: drawing a line in the constitutional sand between congress and the foreign citizen "cybersquatter". *William & Mary Bill of Rights Journal, 9,* 461-489 (arguing that "under traditional Commerce Clause analysis, foreign citizens' registration of domain names with intent to sell those registered domain names does not substantially affect interstate commerce, and that applying the Lanham Act to this activity is an improper application of Congress' Commerce Clause power.").

[106]   See ICANN (1999). Uniform domain name dispute resolution policy. Retrieved December 4, 2003, from http://www.icann.org/dndr/udrp/policy.htm.

[107]   But see Leaffer, M. (1998, Fall). Domain names, globalization, and internet governance. *Indiana Journal of Global Legal Studies, 6,* 139-165, 145.

[108]   See Ford Motor Company website, http://www.ford.com/en/default.htm

[109]   E.g., U.S. Trademark No. 78080795, "Ford Models" — trademark of Ford Models, Inc.

[110]   E.g., U.S. Trademark No. 76257452, "Ford Foundation International Fellowships Program" — service mark of International Fellowships Fund, Inc.

[111]   See results of TESS search performed at the U.S. Patent & Trademark Office, http://www.uspto.gov (Boolean search of word "Ford" on 10/15/02 found 6612 records).

[112]   See 15 U.S.C. Section 1125(d)(1)(B), Cyberpiracy Protections for Individuals.

[113]   See 15 U.S.C. Section 1125(d)(1)(A), Cyberpiracy Protections for Individuals.

[114]   Caesars World, Inc. v. Caesars-Palace.Com, 112 F. Supp. 2d 502 (E.D.Va. 2000) (holding that the provisions of the Anticybersquatting Consumer Protection Act (the "Act") that permit a trademark holder to proceed with an *in rem* action against a domain name do not violate the Due Process clause of the United States Constitution. The Act permits a trademark holder to prosecute certain designated claims in an *in rem* action against domain names "in the judicial district in which the domain name register, domain name registry or other domain name authority that registered or assigned the domain name is located" if "the court finds that the owner either (1) is not able to obtain *in personam* jurisdiction over an

allowed defendant, or (2) through due diligence was not able to find a person who would have been an allowed defendant after meeting certain notice requirements set out in the Act." The court determined that, for the purpose of the Act, Congress mandated that a domain name is property located in the forum in which the domain name register that registered the domain in question is located. Because the domain name is the subject of the suit, the Due Process clause does not require that the defendant have minimum contacts with the forum state sufficient to permit the assertion of personal jurisdiction. Even if such minimum contacts with the Virginia forum in which the suit is pending were required, they are supplied by the registration of the domain name with Virginia-based Network Solutions, Inc., given the limited nature of relief that can be granted under the statute in an *in rem* proceeding — namely forfeiture, cancellation or transfer of the domain name.)

115 Mattel, Inc. v. Barbie-Club.Com, No. 01-7680 (2d Cir., November 7, 2002) Subsection (d)(2)(A) of the Anticybersquatting Consumer Protection Act of 1999 provides for in rem jurisdiction only in the judicial district in which the registrar, registry, or other domain-name authority that registered or assigned the disputed domain name is located. Full text of this opinion available at http://laws.lp.findlaw.com/2nd/017680.html.

116   Lanham Act, 15 USC §1125(d)(1)(B)(V).

117   Port, K.L. (Winter 2000). The Congressional expansion of American trademark law: A Civil law system in the making. *Wake Forest Law Review, 35,* 827-883.

118   See e.g. Grotrian, Helfferich, Schulz, Th. Steinweg Nachf. v. Steinway & Sons, 523 F.2d 1331, 1342 (2d Cir. 1975). "The issue here is not the possibility that a purchaser would buy a Grotrian-Steinweg thinking it was actually a Steinway or that Grotrian had some connection with Steinway and Sons. The harm to Steinway, rather, is the likelihood that a consumer, hearing the 'Grotrian-Steinweg' name and thinking it had some connection with 'Steinway', would consider it on that basis. The 'Grotrian-Steinweg' name therefore would attract potential customers based on the reputation built up by Steinway in this country for many years. The harm to Steinway in short is the likelihood that potential piano purchasers will think that there is some connection between the Grotrian-Steinweg and Steinway pianos." *Id.;* Blockbuster Entm't Group v. Laylco, Inc., 869 F. Supp. 505, 513 (E.D. Mich. 1994) ("[T]he issue in this case is the degree of likelihood that the name "Video Busters" would attract potential customers based on the reputation built by Blockbuster. That a customer

would recognize that Video Busters is not connected to Blockbuster after entry into a Video Busters store and viewing the Video Busters membership application, brochure, video cassette jacket, and store layout is unimportant. The critical issue is the degree to which Video Busters might attract potential customers based on the similarity to the Blockbuster name. The court finds that Video Busters might attract some potential customers based on the similarity to the Blockbuster name. Because the names are so similar and the products sold are identical, some unwitting customers might enter a Video Busters store thinking it is somehow connected to Blockbuster. Those customers probably will realize shortly that Video Busters is not related to Blockbuster, but ... that is irrelevant.").

[119]   Nissan, U. (April 9, 2003). The Story. Retrieved December 4, 2003, from http://www.ncchelp.org/The_Story/the_story.htm; Anderson, M.K. (January 3, 2001). Who gets to drive Nissan.com? Retrieved December 4, 2003, from: http://www.wired.com/news/politics/0,1283,40939 ,00.html.

[120]   Nissan, U. (April 9, 2003). The Story. Retrieved December 4, 2003, from: http://www.ncchelp.org/The_Story/the_story.htm.

[121]   Nissan Motor Co., Ltd. v. Nissan Computer Corporation, 89 F. Supp. 2d 1154 (C.D.Cal. 2000), *aff'd. without opinion*, 246 F.3rd 675 (9th Cir. 2000).

[122]   Anderson, M..K. (January 3, 2001). Who gets to drive Nissan.com? Retrieved December 4, 2003, from: http://www.wired.com/news/politics/0,1283,40939-2,00.html.

[123]   Anderson, M..K. (January 3, 2001). Who gets to drive Nissan.com? Retrieved December 4, 2003, from: http://www.wired.com/news/politics/0,1283,40939,00.html.

[124]   Nissan Motor Co. v. Nissan Computer Corp., 2002 U.S. Dist. LEXIS 22212 (C.D. Cal. 2002).

[125]   Id.

[126]   Dinwoodie, G.B. (2001, Summer). International intellectual property litigation: A vehicle for resurgent comparativist thought? *American Journal of Comparative Law, 49,* 429-453.

[127]   Id.

[128]   See ICANN (November 15, 2002). Statistical summary of proceedings under uniform domain name dispute resolution policy. *Retrieved December 4, 2003, from* http://www.icann.org/udrp/proceedings-stat.htm (providing a numerical breakdown of the results of all UDRP disputes filed in the last two years). As of November 15, 2002, UDRP proceedings have

led to the resolution of 6,179 disputes involving 10,185 domain names.
The Respondent prevailed in 1267 disputes, about twenty percent of the
decided cases.

[129] Wal-Mart Stores, Inc. v. Walsucks and Walmarket Puerto Rico, Case
No. D2000-0477 (2000) (WIPO Arb.), available at: http://arbiter.wipo.int/
domains/decisions/html/2000/d2000-0477.html.

[130] Wal-Mart Stores, Inc. v. Walmartcanadasucks.com and Kenneth J.
Harvey, Case No. D2000-1104 (2000) (WIPO Arb.), available at: http://
/arbiter.wipo.int/domains/decisions/html/2000/d2000-1104.html.

[131] Lucent Technologies, Inc. v. Lucentsucks.com, Civil Action No. 99-
1916-A, U.S. District Court, Eastern District of Virginia (May 3, 2000).
Retrieved December 4, 2003, from: http://www.haledorr.com/pdf/
Lucentsucks.com.pdf.

[132] U.S. House of Representatives (October 25, 1999). Trademark
Cyberpiracy Prevention Act, House Rept. 106-412. Retrieved December 4, 2003, from: http://www.haledorr.com/pdf/106-412.pdf.

[133] Bally Total Fitness Holding Corp. v. Faber, 29 F. Supp. 2d 1161 (C.D.
Calif. 1998).

[134] Bally Total Fitness Holding Corp. v. Faber, 29 F. Supp. 2d 1161, 1167
(C.D. Calif. 1998).
None of the cases that Bally cites involve consumer commentary. In
Coca-Cola, the court enjoined the defendant's publication of a poster
stating "Enjoy Cocaine" in the same script as Coca-Cola's trademark.
Likewise, in Mutual of Omaha, the court prohibited the use of the words
"Mutant of Omaha" with a picture of an emaciated human head resembling
the Mutual of Omaha's logo on a variety of products as a means of
protesting the arms race. Here, however, Faber is using Bally's mark in
the context of a consumer commentary to say that Bally engages in
business practices which Faber finds distasteful or unsatisfactory. This is
speech protected by the First Amendment.

[135] Sharrock. L.M. (2001). Note: the future of domain name dispute resolution: Crafting practical international legal solutions from within the UDRP
framework, *Duke Law Journal, 51,* 817-849, 836.

[136] E.g., Dinwoodie G.B. (2000, Fall). Essay: (national) trademark laws and
the (non-national) domain name system. *University of Pennsylvania
Journal of International Economic Law, 21,* 495-521.
The UDRP, however, was intended only to put in place quick and cheap
administrative procedures for the easy cases - those concerning obviously
abusive registrations of trademarks as domain names (loosely,

cybersquatting). Some more difficult problems have been presented (although not always recognized) by fact patterns already brought before panels. But as soon as the facts go beyond the easy cases and begin to embrace contentious issues of trademark law, the UDRP may be severely tested. For example, trademark protection, especially for words, collides with free speech concerns. Although there exists a broad-based international commitment to the core principles of free speech, different countries deal with the collision in different ways, reflecting the wide range of free speech notions that exist around the world once we move beyond those core principles. And the UDRP system does not presently require us to venture into the murky waters of enforcement because the remedies (transfer of domain name) are limited to those that can be effectuated by the registrars without the aid of national courts. Finally, expansion of the system would also make any procedural inequities of the current system more significant; complaints about these inequities have been largely ignored given the system's preoccupation with easy cases.

[137]   Struve, C.T. & Wagner, R.P. (2002, Summer). Realspace sovereigns in cyberspace: Problems with the anticybersquatting consumer protection act, *Berkeley Technology Law Journal, 17,* 989-1041, 1038-39. ("In particular, our analysis here establishes the strong interests that realspace sovereigns, and especially the United States, have to coordinate their regulatory behavior with an eye to avoiding segmentation. Such coordination will invariably require greater deference to nonterritorial domain name regulatory bodies.").

[138]   See Greg Lloyd Smith v. Lucky Allan Short, File Number: CPR 0207, Date of Commencement: February 28, 2002, Domain Name(s): greglloydsmith.com, Registrar: directNIC.com, Arbitrator: Sandra A. Sellers. Retrieved December 5, 2003, from: http://www.cpradr.org/. Complainant alleges that the domain name, greglloydsmith.com, is identical or confusingly similar to Complainant's actual name, Greg Lloyd Smith. However, Complainant makes no attempt to prove that "Respondent's domain name is identical or confusingly similar to a trademark or service mark in which complainant has rights," as required by UDRP Rule 3(b)(viii). Indeed, in the complaint, Complainant states that this requirement is "not applicable" (Complaint outline, Paragraph 5). The threshold question, therefore, is whether this claim — based solely on a personal name, without attempt to show that the name constitutes a trademark or service mark in which complainant has rights — is cognizable under the UDRP. To support a claim under the UDRP, a personal

name must constitute a trademark or service mark in which the complainant has rights; a personal name, without more, does not qualify. See Report of the Second WIPO Internet Domain Name Process, "the Recognition of Rights and the Use of Names in the Internet Domain Name System", September 3, 2001 ("the 2nd WIPO Report"), at ¶¶ 181-204. Here, the Complainant has made no effort to prove that the name is a trademark or service mark in which the complainant has rights, despite bearing the burden of proof on each element. Complainant has dismissed UDRP Rule 3(b)(viii) as "not applicable." None of the exhibits to the complaint shows Complainant's use of the name. Accordingly, I find that Complainant has not proven that the name is a trademark or service mark in which complainant has rights. Since Complainant has not proven the first of the required elements, I need not reach a decision with respect to the second and third elements.

[139] See WIPO Arbitration and Mediation Center, ADMINISTRATIVE PANEL DECISION, Greg Lloyd Smith v. None, Harry Carr a.k.a. Raymond McDonald and/or Gerald McDonald, Case No. D2002-0844. Retrieved December 4, 2003, from: http://arbiter.wipo.int/domains/decisions/html/2002/d2002-0844.html.

Complainant contends that it is the owner of the trademark "Greg Lloyd Smith" registered in the United Kingdom in Class 35 under No 2296692 and has filed an application for registration under Serial number 78117117 in the United States of the same trademark and with priority as from the United Kingdom registration. The Panel notes in this context that Complainant has submitted an extract from the United Kingdom Patent Office Trade Marks Database which indicates that the filing date for the application for registration was April 2, 2002, and the registration date was September 6, 2002. The list of goods and/or services for the trademark is indicated as "Business acquisition and merger consultation." The Panel furthermore notes that, according to a copy of an extract from the Trade mark Electronic Search System (TESS) of the United States Patent and Trademark Office, the application for registration of the word mark "Greg Lloyd Smith" was filed on March 24, 2002, and was given the serial number 78117117. On the basis of the evidence submitted the Panel considers it established that Complainant has a right under trademark law at least in the United Kingdom — where also Respondents are domiciled — in respect of the trademark "Greg Lloyd Smith." The domain names and the trademark differ in some respects both as regards the spelling and as regards the way of combining the words which form part of the trademark. Furthermore, the domain names contain the addition of ".com." The overall impression is however, in the view of the Panel, that there is a clear similarity between the domain names and Complainant´s distinctive trademark. The addition of ".com" is an insignificant distinction that does not remove the likelihood for confusion. On the basis of these findings the Panel considers it established that there exists a confusing similarity between the domain names at issue and Complainant´s protected trademark rights.

[140] Id.

In this respect, Complainant has, according to Paragraph 4.a(iii) of the Policy, to prove that the domain names have been registered and are being used in bad faith. Furthermore, Paragraph 4.b sets out some circumstances which, in particular but without limitation, shall, if found by the Panel to be present, be considered as evidence of registration and use in bad faith. In this respect Complainant has basically contended that the domain names were in fact registered and used in bad faith until June 25, 2002, when the Registrar deactivated them as a consequence of Complainant´s lawsuit in the United States. Complainant alleges that Respondents registered the domain names in order to prevent Complainant from reflecting its trademark in corresponding domain names and to use them in a campaign of defamation which is now the subject of two separate sets of legal proceedings in the United Kingdom and the United States.

[141] E.g., Heald, P.J. (1996, May). Trademarks and geographical indications: Exploring the contours of the TRIPS agreement. *Vanderbilt Journal of Transnational Law, 29,* 635-660.

[142] The U.S. is not the only country in which trademark law poses interpretive challenges. In France, for example, statutory law establishes that protectable trademarks cannot be comprised of words or images that are "immoral or contrary to public order" or of words or images "likely to confuse or deceive third parties," or of "a word or image already having been taken or protected by others," and must be clearly distinctive and enable the identification of a particular product or service compared to like articles. French Law Publications Ltd. (2002). French trade marks. Retrieved December 4, 2003, from: http://www.frenchlaw.com/ trade_marks.htm. One commentator giving an overview of French trademark law reported: "Trademarks constitute a particularly complex area of French Law and the greatest care should be exercised in this field." French Law Publications Ltd. (2002). French trade marks. Retrieved

December 4, 2003, from http://www.frenchlaw.com/trade_marks.htm
In the United Kingdom, the pertinent law states that a trademark "may be
infringed by the use of an identical or confusingly similar mark not only in
relation to the goods or services specifically covered in the registration,
but also in relation to similar goods or services." Ladas & Parry (1994).
United Kingdom — New trademark law. Retrieved December 5, 2003,
from: http://www.ladas.com/BULLETINS/1994/1194Bulletin/
UK_NewTMAct.html Prior to 1994 changes to the governing Act, UK
Trade Marks Act 1994, infringement could arise only with respect to the
good and services covered in the trademark registration. Id. In 2000, the
country of Brunei enacted new trademark laws patterned after this Act,
and similarly "widen[ed] the definition of infringement to include the use of
an identical or similar mark in relation to similar goods and/or services."
Ella Cheong & G. Mirandah (2002). Brunei new trade marks law.
Retrieved December 5, 2003, from http://www.ecgm.com.sg/
BruneiTMA.htm An infringement cause of action is triggered by "a
likelihood of confusion or association." *Id.*
In Australia, prior to legislative amendments in 1995, "it had been clear
that the exclusive rights of the owner of a registered trademark did not
extend beyond the mark itself." *See* Honey, R. & Sinden, P. (December,
2000). The Interface between trademark, designs, and passing off under
Australian law: The Philips case. Retrieved December 4, 2003, from http:/
/www.murdoch.edu.au/elaw/issues/v7n4/sinden74.html Section 120(1)
of that country's Trade Marks Act of 1995 stipulated that a person would
infringe a trademark if she "uses as a trade mark a sign that is substantially
identical with, or deceptively similar to, the trade mark." Australasian
Legal Information Institute (2003). Definition of "deceptively similar."
Retrieved December 5, 2003, from: http://www.austlii.edu.au/au/legis/
cth/consol_act/tma1995121/ Section 10 of the Australian Trade Marks
Act of 1995 provides this rather vague and unhelpful definition of
deceptively similar: "For the purposes of this Act, a trade mark is taken
to be *deceptively similar* to another trade mark if it so nearly resembles
that other trade mark that it is likely to deceive or cause confusion." *Id.*
Section 14, which addresses the concept of sameness or similarity in good
and services, is comparably obtuse and pithy, stating:
1. For the purposes of this Act, goods are *similar* to other goods:
(a) if they are the same as the other goods; or
(b) if they are of the same description as that of the other goods.
2. For the purposes of this Act, services are *similar* to other services:

(a) if they are the same as the other services; or

(b) if they are of the same description as that of the other services. Australasian Legal Information Institute (2003). Definition of similar goods and similar services. Retrieved December 4, 2003, from: http://www.austlii.edu.au/au/legis/cth/consol_act/tma1995121/s14.html (emphasis in original). Many other nations provide similarly sparse definitions of confusion and similarity in their trademark laws, including (to pick a few examples) Czechoslovakia (Industrial Property Office of the Czech Republic (2001) Law on trademarks. Retrieved December 5, 2003, from: http://www.upv.cz/english/z137-95.htm *E.g.*, Article 14 of the Law on Trademarks, No. 137 of June 21, 1995, states: "No one may use a trademark without the authorization of its owner or use a sign that is identical or confusingly similar to the mark for identical or similar goods and services as those for which the trademark is registered, or use it in relation to such goods and services, especially to affix it on the goods and their packaging, offer or place goods on the market under the sign, or store for that purpose, import or export goods under the sign, or use such sign in a trade name, in correspondence or in advertisements."); India (The Trade and merchandise marks act, 1958. Retrieved December 4, 2003, from http://www.naukri.com/lls/tm/tmactc2.htm#s9. Chapter II Section 12 (1) of the Trade and Merchandise Marks Act, 1958 provides that "no trade mark shall be registered in respect of any goods or description of goods which is identical with or deceptively similar to a trade mark which is already registered in the name of a different proprietor in respect of the same goods or description of goods" after Chapter I Section 2(d), accessed at http://www.naukri.com/lls/tm/tmactc1.htm#s9, explains that "a mark shall be deemed to be deceptively similar to another mark if it so nearly resembles that other mark as to be likely to deceive or cause confusion."); Germany (Vossius and Partner (2001). Hermann, G. Germany. Retrieved December 4, 2003, from http://www.vossiusand partner.com/eng/publication/pub-cyberspace.html . "Under Section 14 [of the German Trademark Act], any trademarks protected under Section 4 confer to their proprietor exclusive rights against the use, in the course of trade, of identical marks for identical goods/services, and also against the use of identical or similar marks for identical or similar goods/services if there exists a likelihood of confusion on the part of the public, including a likelihood of association in the mind of the public."); and China (Chinatoday.com (2003). Trademark law of the People's Republic of China. Retrieved December 5, 2003, from http://www.chinatoday.com/

law/a02.htm . (Adopted at the 24th Session of the Standing Committee of the Fifth National People's Congress, on August 23, 1982), Chapter VII, Article 38 states it shall be an infringement of the exclusive right to use a registered trademark: "(1) to use a trademark which is identical with or similar to the registered trademark in respect of the same or similar to the registered trademark in respect of the same or similar goods without the authorization of the proprietor of the registered trademark.").
By contrast, the Canadian Trade-marks Act appears to do a valiant job of defining confusion, stating in Section 6:
...
2. The use of a trade-mark causes confusion with another trade-mark if the use of both trade-marks in the same area would be likely to lead to the inference that the wares or services associated with those trade-marks are manufactured, sold, leased, hired or performed by the same person, whether or not the wares or services are of the same general class.
3. The use of a trade-mark causes confusion with a trade-name if the use of both the trade-mark and trade-name in the same area would be likely to lead to the inference that the wares or services associated with the trade-mark and those associated with the business carried on under the trade-name are manufactured, sold, leased, hired or performed by the same person, whether or not the wares or services are of the same general class.
....
5. In determining whether trade-marks or trade-names are confusing, the court or the Registrar, as the case may be, shall have regard to all the surrounding circumstances including
(*a*) the inherent distinctiveness of the trade-marks or trade-names and the extent to which they have become known;
(*b*) the length of time the trade-marks or trade-names have been in use;
(*c*) the nature of the wares, services or business;
(*d*) the nature of the trade; and
(*e*) the degree of resemblance between the trade-marks or trade-names in appearance or sound or in the ideas suggested by them.
R.S., c. T-10, s. 6. April 30, 2003. Canadian Department of Justice (2003). Trademarks Act. Retrieved December 5, 2003, from http://laws.justice.gc.ca/en/t-13/102791.html.
[143]   E.g., Olsson, H. (January 23, 2002). WIPO arbitration and mediation center: Administrative panel decision Bundesrepublik Deutschland (Federal Republic of Germany) v. RJG Engineering Inc., Case No. D2001-

1401. Retrieved December 5, 2003, from http://arbiter.wipo.int/do-mains/decisions/html/2001/d2001-1401.html; *See also* ICANNwatch (January 29, 2002). WIPO arbitration on neo-nazi use of domain names. Retrieved December 4, 2003, from http://www.icannwatch.org/article.pl?sid=02/01/29/181708.
The issue is political extremely thorny as these names were used by a convicted neo-nazi party leader for promoting their Nazi-Devotionalien-Shops under the domain names (a practice that is forbidden in Germany). The issue was decided on an interpretation by WIPO on "Trademark-rights" on these names. This road was taken by the German government as seizure of the U.S.-based websites was not possible under the U.S. laws regarding freedom of speech. ... The rub in this case, however, is on 'legitimate' use. The use of the name to spread Nazi messages was illegal in Germany, but legal in the USA, where the respondent was located. Respondent defaulted, but even so this decision seems — on the rather sketchy facts in the decision — to be an example of the UDRP being used in a way at odds with the First Amendment rights, however disgusting, of the Respondent; from what one can tell the site at issue was non-commercial propaganda, which would not be a trademark infringement in the U.S.

[144]   *E.g.*, Cerruti 1881, S.A. v. Cerruti Inc., No. 95 Civ. 7782 (MBM), 1997 U.S. Dist. LEXIS 20860 (S.D.N.Y. Jan. 5, 1998) (Court required defendant to add disclaimer to website rather than restrain him from using his own surname in domain name.)

[145]   Krieger, T.W. (1998). Note: internet domain names and trademarks: strategies for protecting brand names in cyberspace. *Suffolk University Law Review, 32,* 47-79, 67-68 ("One domain has developed its own solution: multiple registrants in the Indian Ocean's top level domain ".io" may register the same name. If identical domain names are registered, visitors to the site will go to a directory page describing the companies to whom they can link.")

Chapter VI

Feminism and Copyright in Digital Media

Dan Burk
University of Minnesota, USA

ABSTRACT

This chapter examines the relationship between hypermedia and feminist discourse, critiquing the role of copyright in controlling or suppressing such discourses. Hypertext and related media may lend themselves to relational webs of meaning rather than linear progressions of meaning. Given the importance of non-hierarchical, associative webs to feminist discourse, digital media may lend themselves to feminist modes of thinking or, at a minimum, challenge dominant textual constructions. However, current copyright doctrine assumes that works remain linear, hierarchical, and controlled. The exclusive rights conferred by copyright and, most especially, the right of adaptation lend themselves to authorial control over not only the text, but to a reader's use of the text. This deterrent characteristic of copyright has appeared in several recent legal disputes involving hypertext linking and annotation. Thus, copyright remains hostile to non-traditional collaborative or relational user engagement. This hostility may ultimately frustrate copyright's purpose of promoting the "progress" of knowledge.

INTRODUCTION

The confluence of feminism and hypertext, and its implications for copyright, is perhaps best illustrated by a short vignette, drawn from the first day of my first job as a tenure-track assistant professor. Accompanied by my spouse, I went to find the associate dean in order to procure the keys to my new office.

We found him in his own office, discussing with his research assistants the transfer of a textbook he had authored, from print media to an electronic version. The platform to which the textbook was being ported included full-text search capability, hyperlinking, and pop-up annotations. As we entered, he was in the process of instructing his assistants on adding pagination to the electronic version.

Being the technologically savvy brand-new assistant professor that I was, I pointed out that pagination was really unnecessary in a text that had so many other options for user navigation. He responded by articulating with some vigor his views on the need for page numbers, which led to a fairly animated discussion about the propriety of pagination in a hypertext document. Realizing that my view was unlikely to prevail and that provoking an argument with a senior colleague before I had even begun my new job was perhaps risky, I exercised the better part of valor, obtained the keys, and my spouse and I excused ourselves.

"He thinks like a man," my spouse observed after we were a distance down the hall.

I admitted that this observation was likely correct, but queried as to what precisely she might have meant.

"He wants everything to be all linear — sequentially numbered," she said. "As a woman, I actually feel much more comfortable making my own web of associations among the subjects in a casebook. Not adopting the order that someone else imposed."

Surprised, because neither her professional training nor her taste in reading was likely to have prompted the feminist terminology entailed in that particular observation, I asked if the name "Carol Gilligan" meant anything to her. She replied that it did not, and we spent a pleasant hour discussing Gilligan's metaphors of masculine "ladders" and feminine "webs" of meaning. But my spouse's immediate association of hypertext, relational meaning, and linear thinking illustrates the associations that have similarly developed in the academic literature at the intersection of these topics.

TEXT AND AUTHORITY

Discussions of hypertext theory typically begin with some definition of the medium in question, and previous commentators have striven, often without success, to capture the essential character of the medium in a formal classification. For my purposes here, I am content to avoid that exercise, leaving the definition generally vague and sketching only illustrative examples of the sort of media in question. The Folio platform to which my former colleague's textbook was being transferred is one such example, but other species of hypertext are varied. These electronic media typically present automated textual associations, which when activated by the user call up linked blocks of text (dubbed by hypertext theorists "lexia"), thus allowing the user to choose more than a single path through the interconnected sequences of material. The medium will frequently also allow the user personally to create or generate new automated associations, linking the portions of text either to other portions of the work itself or to other works. In many, although by no means all such applications, the user is also able to make additional alterations to the work, such as by attaching or overlaying annotations on the text, creating "highlighted" or emphasized portions of text, and generating customized indices or navigational aids.

The apparent interactivity and heightened user engagement of such media captured the imagination of early hypertext theorists, to whom such digital media appeared to present a practical instantiation of postmodern literary theory (Landow, 1992). These commentators have argued that the characteristics of hypertext make explicit the "recoding" of texts theorized by Barthes (1974), Derrida (1981), and others. Although postmodern literary theorists were primarily concerned with the interaction of the reader with standard print-based texts, their views on meaning, authorship, and interpretation of texts seemed readily extensible to hypertext. In particular, the distinction drawn by Barthes between "writerly" texts and "readerly" texts seemed directly applicable to hypertext.

These terms were intended to designate certain textual qualities that resulted in certain types of reader interaction. The terminology is perhaps unfortunate, as these commonly employed translations of Barthes' neologisms "lisable" and "scriptable" might at first glance seem to refer to textual characteristics afforded by the classic roles of the author and reader. But this was a distinction that Barthes rejected and sought to eliminate. In fact, the distinction is rather more subtle, referring to modes of interaction that the reader might assume. Barthes was concerned with the origination of meaning in texts, and with textual characteristics that invited new meanings.

Barthes (1974) defined writerly or scriptable texts as those that gain meaning from the reader, and which invite the reader to in essence become a writer by engaging in the "writerly" act of interpretation. Thus, writerly texts will tend toward openness or even incompleteness, and so may appear rough or unfinished or disorderly. Making sense of such a text requires the reader to participate in the creation of meaning, reinscribing the text to fill in interpretive gaps.

This type of text, with its conspicuous gaps and lacunae and multiple points of entry, exemplifies the incomplete quality of texts generally. Barthes maintained that any text consists ultimately of fragments drawn from multiple named and unnamed precursor sources, linked together in a matrix of conceptual relations, some of which might be intended by the author assembling them, others which might be perceived by later readers. Thus the rough texture of the writerly text merely exposes the characteristics of any text. Its unfinished quality differs from other texts in degree more than in kind.

In contrast to the explicit writerly text, readerly or lisable texts resist reinterpretation, adhering to an interpretation dictated by the initial author. These texts distance themselves from the reader's reinterpretation by facilitating only a single, linear progression of meaning. They leave the reader in the classic role of the reader, merely absorbing or accepting the meaning that seems most obvious on the face of the text. Because such classic texts lull the reader into passivity, they characterize for Barthes (1974) "the pitiless divorce which the literary institution maintains between the producer of the text and its user, between its owner and its customer, between its author and its reader."

Consequently, unlike the incomplete surface of the writerly text, readerly texts will tend to appear seamless and unified, and so convey the illusion of a predetermined and fixed reading. Even if the reader is in fact supplying a good deal of the textual meaning, she is not doing so consciously or purposefully as an act of writing or of rewriting. The reader thus falls into the role of a passive recipient of meaning, engaged only in the act of reading or accepting the "authorized" text — that is, the text originating from the author.

This sort of passivity Derrida (1981) equates with a "dead" text, which is static, inert, and never conveys more than a single authorized message. By contrast, when the text invites readers to imbue text with new meaning, it becomes dynamic, evolutionary, and alive. The difference in textual quality can thus dramatically shift the reader's role from mere consumption of text to production, making every reader in essence an "author." And paradoxically, on this view, the text termed "writerly" may seem least inviting to the reader, as its incomplete nature forces the reader to engage in consciously interpretive work, whereas the "readerly" text may seem the most satisfactory to the initial author, as it appears the more complete or polished product.

AUTHORITY AND HYPERTEXT

Many forms of digital media lend themselves to writerly manipulation, allowing the reader to reorder or link elements of the text, or to annotate and alter the content of the text. Readers have always mentally interpreted or recoded texts, but the malleability of digital texts makes this process manifest. By reconfiguring the elements of the text, readers may establish relationships within or between texts not contemplated by the initial author or authors. Hypertext thus tends toward the "writerly" appearance, and facilitates deconstruction of the text by displaying the text's cognitive skeleton, uncovering the relational structure of the constituent lexia.

Hypertext similarly foregrounds the relational linkages that postmodern theorists focus upon as creating meaning within a text. As the reader moves from node to node in a hypertext document, the work takes its meaning not so much from the words of the particular text, but from the relationship between lexia, not from what an initial author intended the text to mean, but from the rewriting that occurs as the text is being read. Thus, Bolter (1991) argues that readers of hypertext are no longer subject to authorial domination or control, they are able to choose their own paths and hence their own meanings.

Hypertext can thus be seen to work against authorial authority as the final arbiter of textual meaning. The characteristics of hypertext work against the illusion of textual unity and, in turn, against the assumption that the initial author constitutes the source of textual meaning. Hypertext allows the reader to more easily disintegrate the text and determine which textual relationships should be accorded meaning and which should not. The assumption that writing originates from a single fixed source of meaning is challenged by the possibility of collective authorship created when each reader has the ability to augment, alter, or edit the initial text. By reconfiguring digital texts, readers become collaborators with the initial creator in generating a new work that reflects the thought processes or learning style of the reader.

But more recent commentators have cautioned that these purported deconstructive features of hypertext, upon which early postmodern paeans are based, may be less revolutionary than they might seem. Rather, it may be that there is nothing particularly new or unprecedented in these features hypertext. Thus, Espen Aarseth (1997) locates hypertext within the broader and long-established category of "ergodic" literature, which requires active reader participation, is non-linear, and lacks the familiar sequence of beginning, middle, and end. She offers the ancient Chinese *I Ching*, certain postmodern novels, and even James Joyce as examples of such works prior to the advent of electronic digital media. Similarly, the venerable institution of scholarly footnoting constitutes a form of "linking" or referencing other texts and invites disruption in the linear progress of footnoted texts as readers peruse the footnotes.

Indeed, as the examples of footnotes demonstrates, random access to texts can, to some extent, be performed with more traditional textual embodiments by ignoring the linear invitation of a folio arrangement and accessing its pages out of order — for example, reading the end of a mystery novel early. Certainly many of the hypertextual operations that I describe above, such as annotation, cross-referencing, and highlighting, are mimetic of actions performed with hardcopy paper texts.

Other commentators have noted that far from consummating the "death of the author," hypertext may simply perpetuate authorial control. Hypertext is not altogether chaotic and does not lack imposition of authorial form; readers may proceed along more than one textual sequence, but they are still typically sequences chosen and enabled by an author. Just as classic print text channels reading in certain ways, so too does hypertext. Although readers of a hypertext document may have some ability to shape the reading by choosing and recombining the sequence of lexia, many documents will prescribe the availability of linkages or entry points, where those linkages will lead, and the choice of links available in each lexia. And in some ways, hypertext may be even more constraining than traditional print texts; to the casual reader, the mechanics of a digital document, such as the mark-up code, will be largely inaccessible, allowing the reader relatively little autonomy beyond the prescribed autonomy afforded by the initial author.

To some extent these arguments rest upon the unwarranted conflation of hypertext with the World Wide Web; the Web allows ordinary readers only relatively sparse opportunities to interact with the text, and creation of permanent Web links or annotation requires a degree of technical sophistication beyond that possessed by most users. Admittedly, the Web is the most prominent and ubiquitous example of digital hypermedia, having become so familiar online as to be in many instances mistaken for or conflated with the Internet itself. Because following Web links is the most common hypertext experience for most users of digital media, it may seem synonymous with hypertext use in general.

But just as the Web is not synonymous with the Internet, the Web is not synonymous with the hypertext. But many other hypertext systems exist or can be imagined that allow users a full range of easily accessible linking and revisioning tools, and such systems are the hypertext environment that Landow (1992) and other early theorists had in mind. Such systems would be far less constricted by the choices of initial authors than more recent critics have realized.

Such systems would also to some extent answer the criticism that hypertext is nothing new, as they would unquestionably offer far greater opportunity for "writerly" reinscription than other form of "ergodic" literature. While it may be possible to read a book out of linear order or to follow its footnotes, paper media simply do not lend themselves to quick and easy reordering in a comprehensive manner. One can certainly cut the book apart and rearrange it, even doing so multiple times, but the activity is not quick or convenient.

Thus, Landow (1992) argues that fully fledged hypertext systems afford readers the opportunity to write against the initial text, participating in the production of meaning by creating notes or linked lexia that may support or contradict the initial author's meaning. Even in less robust systems, the reader is confronted with choices regarding which links to follow or skip, and consequently which lexia to foreground and which to discount. While digital media may be configured so as to constrain use of a digitized text, it may also be applied to permit unforeseen use of texts or novel navigation of texts.

Still, even if the initial assessments of user empowerment were somewhat exaggerated, and the comparisons to postmodern theory somewhat over-blown, there is something more to the writerly character of this new media than there was to the old. Automation of ergodic features makes a decided difference, rendering comparisons to previous media incomplete. Hypertexts are clearly not paper texts, and footnotes are clearly not hyperlinks. Only so many reader annotations will fit in the physical margins of a paper text, as Fermat (Singh, 1997) demonstrated. Footnotes in paper texts do not call up and present the works referenced; physical retrieval is required. It is at least laborious, if not virtually impossible to perform a full-text search of a large printed text. The speed and extent of hypertext user engagement differs markedly from that of previous media in magnitude, if not in kind. And even if a given reader's pathway through the work does not permanently rearrange or alter the initial text, each new reading in some sense rewrites the text by reconsidering it, creating new orderings that subtly inflect the textual meaning.

FEMINISM AND HYPERTEXT

The potential congruence of these hypertext characteristics with feminist theory has not been lost on a number of commentators, who at their most enthusiastic depict hypertext as "a mode of thought and a language ripe with potential for speaking a new feminist critical voice" (Guertin, 1999). Admittedly, the feminist voice to which hypertext may lend itself might not be easily ascertainable. Feminism encompasses a diverse range of viewpoints and traditions, not all of which are compatible, and some of which are entirely contradictory (Bender, 1988). It would be difficult to summarize or distill a canonical perspective of what constitutes a "feminist voice" and probably counterproductive to try. Indeed, a central tenet of many if not most forms of feminist critique is the importance of alternative or neglected perspectives, making "feminism" by definition impossible to capture in a simple definition. But while feminist views do not lend themselves to bumper stickers or T-shirt slogans, it is possible for the present analysis to identify particular strands in the feminist tapestry, particularly those that have intersected with the literature on hypertext, and which may intersect with certain aspects of copyright.

A considerable body of feminist literature focuses on the themes of contextuality and responsibility that seem lacking in dominant cultural discourse, which feminist commentators characterize as emphasizing separation of self from others, adopting a linear or hierarchical approach to reasoning that defines the world in isolated terms and oppositional categories. Such categorical hierarchies tend to comprise strings of dichotomous pairs, one of which is either expressly or implicitly superior to the other. Feminist theory suggests that such evaluative structures both reflect and encourage habits of thought that lead to alienation and subordination of those categorized as "other."

A variety of feminist commentators have proposed that, in order to counteract patriarchal dominance, it is desirable to develop discursive approaches that emphasize interconnectedness or relational thinking. At least some commentators suggest that feminist thinking would entail understanding the self in relation to, rather than in opposition to, others and to the world. Under this approach, it is frequently suggested that the feminine biology of procreation, gestation, and childbearing gives rise to sense of self that is physically connected to others, and so mentally and emotionally connected as well. Thus, feminine experience may lend itself to collective and collaborative understanding, rather than to individual and confrontative understanding that characterize patriarchy.

The writings of Carol Gilligan, to which I alluded in my introductory vignette, have been highly influential in this regard. Based on responses to interview questions that appeared to show differing problem-solving approaches by gender, Gilligan (1982) proposed that women tend to approach reasoning in a distinctly "feminine" manner that is contextual, relational, and personal. By contrast, "masculine" reasoning appeared to emphasize objectivity, individuality, and abstraction. Gilligan metaphorically characterized the feminine approach in terms of "webs" of interconnectedness, and the masculine approach in terms of "ladders" of hierarchy. The feminine approach adopts a rhetoric of responsibility and caring, whereas the masculine approach adopts a rhetoric of rights and equality. The "different voice" of feminine discourse, she suggested, has historically been ignored or drowned out in favor of the more dominant masculine approach.

In the study of digital technologies, Gilligan's intellectual and empirical successors include researchers who have demonstrated that women tend to engage computer-mediated communication differently than their male counterparts (Herring, 1996, 2000). Studies conducted by these researchers find evidence that masculine and feminine styles of discourse occur in computer-mediated communication, particularly in listservs, Usenet groups, and other fora on the Internet. Men, they find prone to communicate in styles characterized by direct, terse, and even confrontative language, such as "flaming"; women tend to adhere to rhetoric of politeness, support, and personalization. The masculine style of discourse they find may be more compatible with, and even consonant with the relatively decontextualized design of the medium; absent the cues of gesture, facial expression, and vocal tonal quality, women may be hampered in their preferred contextual communicative mode.

Such studies suggest that computer technology is by no means gender-neutral and imply that women might be systematically disadvantaged by either the design of the computer technology or by the social customs attending its use, if indeed they tend to communicate differently. This line of reasoning further suggests that by privileging certain forms of communication over others, some digital technologies may be better adapted to different discursive modes and so may encourage or promote certain types of cultural assumptions.

It seems only fair to note that Gilligan's (1982) observations and analysis, although enormously influential, have also been controversial and often vigorously critiqued. As an initial matter, it is unclear whether Gilligan's empirical observations were robust enough to support her proposals. It is similarly unclear whether the "difference" Gilligan describes, if it indeed exists, arises as a matter of biology or as a matter of acculturation. Even among women, it is unclear whether variations in ethnicity, race, class, age, and sexual orientation might give voice to the same "difference" or to a chorus of differences. Which leads to yet another concern — that to the extent that such a difference exists, from whatever origins, injudicious emphasis on Gilligan's "different voice" might paradoxically tend to reinforce another of the false oppositions that so many feminists have critiqued in masculine or patriarchal discourse.

For purposes of this discussion, however, it is unnecessary to establish or defend any strong form of relational thesis, let alone of Gilligan's work; neither is it necessary to establish whether Gilligan's findings are statistically robust, or whether the "different voice" she identifies is biological or cultural, or even whether relational perception is gender-specific. The discussion here requires only a far more modest and, I hope, uncontroversial premise — i.e., that relational reasoning exists as an alternative to abstract hierarchical reasoning, and that it is the preferred form of learning by at least some people, of whatever gender, at least some of the time.

If, as Herring (1996, 2000) and others have suggested, such relational reasoning is stifled by the design characteristics of certain technologies, it may by the same token be that certain technologies are conducive to communication in Gilligan's "different voice." Hypertext may be an attractive candidate for possible congruence between such reasoning and media characteristics. Certainly this connection has been suggested by feminist commentators. Concerned as it is with themes of resisting hierarchy, resisting authoritarian dominance, reversing subordination, promoting relational reasoning, and exposing oppositional thinking, feminist theory seemed naturally consonant with the deconstructive attributes of hypertext. Because the linked and associative structure of hypertext appeared to reflect and embody the same relational motifs found in much feminist thought, feminist commentators reasoned that the medium might serve both the positive and critical agendas of feminist theory.

First, given the importance of associative, interconnected "webs" of meaning in much of feminist theory, it has been argued that digital media might naturally foster such feminist modes of thinking. In particular, the linked characteristics of hypertext and related media might lend themselves to relational webs of meaning rather than linear progressions of meaning, offering a conducive environment to the "different voice" that relational feminism argues has long been suppressed. By substituting a web of textual relationships for a linear, dialectic progression of concepts, hypertext appears to eschew old habits of textual dominance and subordination and to upend established conceptual hierarchies (Clark, 2001; Page, 1999). This in turn suggests that digital media might accommodate novel or subversive modes of learning and authorship.

This end might also be furthered by hypertext characteristics that collapse the false dichotomy of reader and writer. By placing the reader and the writer on an equal footing in a creative environment, hypertext seemed to merge the divided concepts of "author" and "reader" by which users and creators of text are defined as "other." This in turn seems to nullify the dominance of authorial control in favor of shared textual interpretation, tending toward the collaborative and collective modes of understanding so important to relational feminist theory.

In a more negative or critical vein, hypertext might, at a minimum, challenge textual constructions that have been characterized as masculine or dominating. The non-linear nature of hypertextual lexia appeared to disrupt hierarchies prevalent in classical texts much as feminism seeks to disrupt hierarchy in patriarchal society. Text embodies thought, and the form of text shapes the form of thought. If classic texts take the form of linearity and hierarchy, those reading such text might become accustomed to such forms — but by subverting those forms, hypertext might also subvert patriarchal habits of thought. Thus, attributes of hypertext might expose and ultimately help displace the patriarchal assumptions latent in the nature of classic linear texts. By foregrounding the reader and loosening the constraints of authorial sequencing, hypertext might well fulfill the feminist imperative to free readers from "constricting habits of mind, encouraging them to critically question authority and arrive at a vision of possibility radically different from the existing social construction" (Anderson, 1999).

Consequently, hypertext has been suggested as a medium uniquely suited to the embodiment of feminist discourse and equally suited to fostering the habit of feminist discourse. But certain cautions are also in order here — just as the more extravagant claims regarding the deconstructive virtues of hypertext required qualification, so too do the claims regarding hypertext's feminist virtues. Thoughtful commentators, while not abandoning the hope that hypertext might further feminist ends, caution that this medium may not inherently lend itself to that purpose. In particular, the argument that styles hypertextual conduct in terms of individual "empowerment" may tend to undermine the very purposes it intends to embrace. Power relations are a matter of concern in feminist discourse, and not all empowerment is beneficial. The claim that hypertext facilitates individual empowerment of the reader, overthrowing the hegemony of the author, is itself built upon the polarized concept of reader and author (Clark, 2002).

This is of course precisely the type of oppositional assumption that a feminist conception of hypertext would hope to avoid, and may define the point at which feminist and postmodernist conceptualization of the medium part company; feminist approaches are less likely to view "writerly" behavior as a struggle for interpretive control. But if the conceptual traps of power and control can be skirted, there remains ample room to regard hypertext as conducive to feminist thinking.

COPYRIGHT AND HYPERTEXT

The observations of feminist commentators suggest that the "writerly" characteristics of hypertext constitute a medium that may be conducive to learning, writing, and thinking outside the established linear and hierarchical structures of traditional media. However, feminist thinking also predicts that the dominant culture will resist such subversion of authority, and unsurprisingly, there is already evidence that this is the case. In particular, the current legal milieu may not be conducive to development of such feminist or other non-traditional readings of digital texts. Rather, the exclusive rights conferred by copyright and, most especially, the right of adaptation lend themselves to authorial control over not only the text, but over a reader's use of the text. The "writerly" approaches to text described above are not contemplated within the law of copyright, which governs the ownership and control of such works. Any explicit or tangible recoding of the material will likely constitute an infringing derivative work of the text, subject to legal sanction.

Copyright in the United States is typically justified under a utilitarian rationale that assumes more or better aesthetic works will be created if creators are offered an opportunity to make money from the works they create. The copyright statute, therefore, specifies a series of exclusive rights that allow the copyright holder to legally control certain uses of a work, ostensibly in order to exclude the public from using the work without paying for those uses. This constrains the availability of copyrighted works in the hope that more works will be produced in the first instance. This general rationale purports to follow from the Constitutional mandate that allows Congress the power to award copyright in order to "promote the progress of science"; that is, to benefit authors in the short term in order to benefit the public in the long term.

The rights specified under the statute include the exclusive right of reproduction – that is, the "copy" right — as well as exclusive rights to distribute, publicly perform, publicly display, and adapt protected works. The coercive power of the courts is available to copyright holders to prevent the specified uses from occurring without the copyright holder's permission. The subject matter covered by the statute includes: original literary works, including software; audiovisual works, including motion pictures; dramatic works; pictorial or graphic works; musical compositions; and sound recordings — all of which may be digitized to electronic form. To be eligible for protection under the statute, the work must be fixed in a tangible medium of expression long enough to be perceived by others, either unaided or with the aid of a machine, a requirement met essentially any time a digitized work is stored in computer memory, on magnetic or optical media, or in other electronic storage devices.

As a consequence, most digital texts, including hypertext, will meet the criteria for protection under the copyright statute and, because copyright arises spontaneously upon fixation of the work, will be subject to copyright. But even though most digital texts will fall under the copyright regime, the statute was neither drafted with such materials in mind nor with any allowance for reader manipulation or reinscription of texts. Whenever such manipulations occur in digital media, one or more of the exclusive rights of the original author will likely have been implicated, if not infringed. Almost certainly the exclusive right to prepare and authorize preparation of derivative works will be infringed by the alteration of the work, and other rights may be implicated as well, such as the right of reproduction if unauthorized copies are made in the process of reworking the initial work.

The long-standing assumptions in copyright law dictate that authorial rights will be triggered by user manipulation even when the work is instantiated in a medium that invites such manipulation. Copyright tends to assume that protected works are the product of a single guiding genius, and that the product of that mind remains static once fixed. The interplay of serial "writerly" revisions, predicted by postmodern literary theorists and facilitated by the malleability of hypermedia, is not contemplated within the nature of copyright.

Admittedly, the statute is not entirely devoid of provisions to address multiple or collaborative authorship, but the possibilities are discrete and sharply circumscribed. Under current United States copyright law, collaborative work can fall into one of six categories:

1. If one or more of the collaborators has failed to contribute the requisite quantum of "original expression" required for authorship under the Act, that contribution is not legally recognized. The contribution and its creator become invisible for legal purposes, and the result is considered the work of the author or authors who made recognized "original" contributions.

2. If the collaborators are employees of the same institution, working within the scope of their employment, then their product may be "work made for hire." In such a case the individuals contributing again disappear for legal purposes, becoming in essence extensions of the institution. The

employer, rather than the natural persons collaborating, will then be considered the author of the resulting work, effectively turning a collaborative work into the work of a single, albeit fictional, creator.

3. If the individual collaborators each contributed original expression, with the intent that the final product should constitute a unified and integrated whole, then the collaborators may be joint authors. As joint authors, each collaborator enjoys ownership of the entire product, such that any one of them can exercise any of the privileges of an author over the entire work, subject to an accounting to the other authors. Here each contributor is recognized as an author, but dual legal fictions treat each author as the author of the work in its entirety, and treat the work as if it were the work of a single guiding genius.

4. If the collaborators add authorized original expression sequentially to an existing work of original expression, the product may be a derivative work of the initial work. A derivative work is created whenever an existing work is recast, transformed, or adapted. In this case, each contributor is considered the author of his or her own original expression, holding copyright to the portions that he or she contributed to the final p r o d - uct. Here each contributor is treated as a separate author under the assumption that the individual contributions are distinct and conceptually separable from the whole.

5. In certain cases, the product of collaboration may comprise a collective work, such as an anthology, where each contributor holds a copyright to his or her particular contribution, and an editor or compiler holds the copyright to the selection and arrangement of the collection as a whole. Here again the assumption is that the contributions can be measured off in discrete packages, such that ownership can be delineated for the constituent embedded works as separate from ownership of the whole.

6. If the collaborators add original expression to an existing work *without* authorization, the result is considered an infringement of the initial work. The resulting work has no claim to copyright protection, as a penalty for altering the initial work without the author's permission — but because the infringing work contains original expression protected under the initial author's copyright, that author is able to dominate or control any use of the infringing work. Consequently, as in the case of the insubstantial alteration, the statute refuses to acknowledge the subsequent contribution, treating the   resulting work as in essence the property of the first author.

This regime of categories leaves unauthorized user manipulations of digital texts at best unrecognized and at worst illegal. In either case, whether unappreciated or impermissible, alterations will be subject to the control of the initial author. Authorization might move the manipulation into the category of derivative work, where the reader's contribution qualifies for its own authorial copyright. Such authorization might in some instances be inferred, for example where the work is made publicly available in a format that is commonly altered — such as openly accessible on the World Wide Web, available for hypertext linking. But such implication may be explicitly revoked, perhaps by posted terms of usage indicating the initial author's objection to such activity.

Thus, the threat of copyright infringement may be deployed to deter precisely the kind of collaborative and "writerly" activity lauded by hypertext commentators. This has already occurred in cases involving the unauthorized annotation of websites or unauthorized "deep linking" between web pages. An early example of such authorial saber-rattling occurred in conjunction with the development of the "Third Voice" web annotation system. The Third Voice system offered users of the World Wide Web a tool for annotating posted web pages, using a free web browser "plug-in" (Gartner, 1999). By highlighting any piece of text displayed on a web page, Third Voice users could create an accompanying annotation, much in appearance like a physical "Post-It" note. The annotations but not the referenced web page would be stored in the Third Voice server. When Third Voice users would access a web page, the "plug in" software would search for annotations related to the page and would display these in a layered fashion in the browser displaying the referenced text.

The service was never a great favorite with web users and eventually failed, like so many Internet start-ups, for lack of a viable financial plan. But in the interim it attracted the ire of website creators who claimed the service violated the integrity of their web documents. Copyright theories figured prominently in the arguments directed against the service's propriety. Although the Third Voice service did not copy web pages, which were served up from their usual hosts, detractors charged that the display of web page with annotations constituted the creation of an unauthorized derivative work (Knight, 1999).

Similar copyright claims have been raised in cases involving unwanted links between documents on the World Wide Web (Burk, 1998; Cavazos & Miles, 1997). In some cases, these disputes have involved so-called "deep links" that refer website users to pages out of the sequence intended by the website owner. In other cases, the disputes have involved "in line" linking, by which files from one server are called up to be displayed in frames generated by a different server. In such cases, no copy is ever made or distributed by the linking server;

in the case of "deep linking," the linking server supplies the user with only the information as to where the linked material can be found. In the case of "in line" linking, the linking server supplies the locational information and generates a "frame" within which the material will be displayed on the user's computer. But in each case, the linked material is served directly to the user's machine at the request of the user's computer.

Consequently, rights of reproduction or distribution cannot be at issue if the owner of the displayed material objects to the link — the site providing the link has neither reproduced nor distributed the linked files. Public performance and public display cannot seriously be at issue either, as long as it is the owner of the material who has done the displaying, serving the files up at the user's request. Rather, it is the right of adaptation that may be at issue, especially in the case of the "in line" link — the linked material is associated by link with other material not of the owner's choosing. Although the law relating to derivative works is unsettled, there is fairly strong support in cases involving traditional media that unauthorized presentation or rearrangement of a copyrighted work infringes the right of adaptation.

The result of such reasoning can be generalized to many or most hypertext applications by which the reader manipulates or alters the text as laid down by the author. Under the standard articulated in such decisions, the user-initiated reordering permitted by hypertext systems will essentially always result in unauthorized adaptation of the underlying material. Although these adaptations might arguably be excused in some case by implied permission or by a user privilege such as fair use, the activity remains largely subject to the whim of the initial author. This implies that "writerly" alterations of hypertext are unauthorized under current law, in every sense of that term; i.e., made without the copyright owner's explicit permission, by a user of the text who the law will not consider to be an author in the formal sense of the word, and who falls outside the canon of control implicit in the ideological development of that term.

COPYRIGHT AND FEMINISM

The upshot of such analysis, somewhat startling in its implications, is that copyright allows authors to control how readers read a text, particularly a digital text where Barthes' "writerly" manipulations become manifest. It is precisely the characteristics of hypertext that most appeal to feminists and hypertext theorists that violate the copyright owner's exclusive rights. Uses of a text that result in derivative works are not countenanced by the statute. Feminists may see within hypertext the potential for new relationships between writer and reader or for the flowering of interconnected, relational learning and thinking. But current copyright doctrine assumes that works remain linear rather than ergodic, static rather than dynamic, and fixed rather than fluid. The statute remains locked into a particular model of the relationship between author, reader, and text, and backs that relationship with the coercive power of the state.

That copyright displays an inherent hostility to such conjoint works should perhaps come as no surprise. Copyright scholars have over the past decade have amassed a sizeable body of critical and historical commentary identifying the concept of the "romantic author" as a key assumption underlying current legal doctrine (Jaszi, 1991; Woodmansee, 1992). Copyright law embraces a romanticized version of authorship, arising out of 18th and 19th Century notions of authorship, assuming that protectable works are the result of the creative efforts of a single heroic genius. This view tends to assume that collaborative work is a rare anomaly and to ignore or subordinate the predicate contributions of non-authors from whom an author may draw. It certainly makes no allowance for the "writerly" contribution that a reader or user of the work might make to the work's meaning.

This scholarly literature on copyright's latent assumptions regarding authors goes hand-in-hand with recent examination of the assumptions latent in the copyright statute regarding readers (Liu, 2003). Examining the various doctrines and statutory provisions regarding users or recipients of copyrighted works, Liu (2003) concludes that the copyright statute assumes that such users fall into one of two categories: either passive recipients of the work who simply absorb the work as delivered by the author, much like Barthe's passive consumer of readerly texts; or, occasionally, the statute may recognize the recipients of the work as follow-on authors themselves, who may be transforming old works into original new expression. Little or no provision is made for recipients who may be reinterpreting or revising the work without creating original new works. This statutory assumption reflects again the sharp division between author and reader, designating the reader as "other."

The gendered origin and character of these statutory assumptions has been identified in recent commentary. Historical analyses of institutionalized publication show that the milieu from which notions of authorship and copyright are drawn were rife with notions of paternity over texts that the masculine author had "begotten" (Rose, 1993). Texts were conceptualized as the feminized "other" against which the author was differentiated (Wall, 1993). Deborah Halbert (1999) thus notes that such discourses led inevitably from masculine notions of textual authorship to paternal conceptualizations of property and ownership; much as an man's child or wife were regarded as his chattel, so were his texts.

This quality of separation carries through to the present statute, shaping doctrines such as the right of adaptation in ways inimical to collaborative or hypertextual reformation of texts. Feminist critique of property notes that the separation between "owner" and "owned" sets the object of ownership apart, and that, in turn, engenders power over the thing so designated (Nedelsky, 1990). Power over a thing is effectively synonymous with property, especially private property (Clark, 2002). After all, the right to exclude others constitutes the canonical trope for defining property, meaning that canonical property, by definition, requires a boundary of separation from non-property. In the case of literary property, this necessitates clear separations between author and text, reader and text, author and reader. To the extent that hypertext dissolves or blurs such boundaries, its qualities are altogether alien to the copyright regime.

This characteristic of the statute should in some sense be expected. Copyright comprises a form of control or power over users, in part because the statute's stated purpose—at least under U.S. law—is to allow authors to extract payments in exchange for permission to use the protected work. That justification itself might be challenged under feminist theory, which might offer a differing view of the Constitutional mandate — an ambitious undertaking rather beyond the scope of this chapter. But even within the current justification of the copyright regime, copyright doctrine as it is presently formulated contemplates a specific canon of control that privileges some types of "progress" over others. The current assumptions embedded in the statute may in fact foreclose progress in the development of innovative, non-traditional works.

There is reason to believe that the term "Progress" as used by the framers of the Constitution may have meant something quite different than common usage of the term today, either colloquially or legally (Pollack, 2001). Under either definition, however, Margaret Chon (1993) points out that there is no reason to privilege a particular type of informational development at the expense of others. Yet the danger of suppressing alternative forms of knowledge, learning, and scholarship on the basis of the copyright law's unstated assumptions or hierarchy and linearity is real. The exclusive right of adaptation, suppressing as it does unauthorized uses of the text, implements a bias against collaborative or non-linear uses of text that forecloses certain modes of thought and discovery that might be termed "feminist." By doing so, the imposition of authorial control may again serve to impede copyright's stated goal of promoting the progress of science.

CONCLUSIONS

My goal in this chapter has been primarily critical, pointing out the disparity between what feminists have seen in hypertext media and what current conceptions of copyright will allow, suggesting that the legal constraint impoverishes the progress that copyright is nominally intended to promote. What may be required in order to accommodate such progress is not only revision, but perhaps revisioning of the statute, drawing on tenets of feminist theory. Although to date only a scant handful of commentators have applied any aspect of feminist theory to the analysis of copyright, those that have begun to do so have offered visions suggesting that feminism might constitute a different formulation of copyright and of the incentives that it might entail to foster "progress" (Halbert, 1999; Lunsford, 1999). While such exposition of a feminist approach to copyright remains tentative, these authors suggest a construct within which creativity is not so much something to be controlled and possessed as something to be reciprocated and shared; where progress is not so much driven by exclusion and separation, but by collaboration and connection. Such a revisioning of the statute would be ambitious and perhaps impractical, but may be necessary before digital media can fulfill the promise that feminist and hypertext theorists have seen within it.

REFERENCES

Aarseth, E. (1997). *Cybertext: Perspectives on ergodic literature.* Baltimore, MD: Johns Hopkins University Press.

Anderson, K. (1999). Some feminist predecessors of hypertext. University of Tromsø, *Women's World '99 International Interdisciplinary Congress on Women Proceedings and Report.* Retrieved online December 1, 2003, at: http://www.skk.uit.no/WW99/papers/Anderson_Kristine_J.pdf.

Barthes, R. (1974). *S/Z.* (R. Miller, Trans.). New York: Hill and Wang.

Bender, L. (1988). A lawyer's primer on feminist theory and tort. *Journal of Legal Education*, 38, 3-37.

Bolter, J.D. (1991). Writing space: The computer, hypertext, and the history of writing. Hillsdale, NJ: Lawrence.

Burk, D. (1998). Proprietary rights in hypertext linkages. *Journal of Information Law & Technology.* Retrieved online December 1, 2003, at: http://elj.warwick.ac.uk/jilt/intprop/98_2burk/default.htm.

Cavazos, E. & Miles, C. (1997). Copyright on the WWW: Linking, liability and license. *Richmond Journal of Law & Technology,* 4(2). Retrieved online December 1, 2003, at: http://law.richmond.edu/jolt/v4i2/cavazos.html.

Chon, M. (1993). Postmodern "progress": Reconsidering the copyright and patent power *DePaul Law Review,* 43, 97-147.

Chon, M. (1996). New wine bursting from old bottles: Collaborative Internet art, joint works, and entrepreneurship. *Oregon Law Review,* 75, 257-276.

Clark, C. (2001). Surely teaching hypertext in the composition classroom qualifies as a feminist Pedagogy? *Kairos,* 6(2). Retrieved online December 1, 2003, at: http://english.ttu.edu/kairos/6.2/binder2.html?coverweb/gender/clark/index.htm.

Clark, C. (2002). Hypertext theory and the rhetoric of empowerment: A feminist alternative. *Kairos,* 7(3). Retrieved online December 1, 2003, at: http://english.ttu.edu/kairos/7.3/binder2.html?coverweb/clark/page1.html.

Comte. A. (2000). Use of feminist literary theory in developing a critical language for hypertext. *The Journal of the Australian Association of Writing Programs,* 4(2). Retrieved online December 1, 2003, at: http://www.gu.edu.au/school/art/text/oct00/comte.htm.

Derrida, J. (1981). *Dissemination.* Chicago, IL: The University of Chicago Press.

Gartner, J. (1999). Readers speak with third voice. Wired News. May 17. Retrieved online at: http://www.wired.com/news/technology/0,1282,19722,00.html.

Gilligan, C. (1982). *In a different voice: Psychological theory and women's development.* Cambridge, MA: Harvard University Press.

Guertin, C. (1999). Gesturing toward the visual: Virtual reality, hypertext and embodied Feminist criticism. *Surfaces,* 8. Retrieved online December 1, 2003, at: http://www.pum.umontreal.ca/revues/surfaces/vol8/guertin.pdf.

Halbert, D. (1999). Poaching and plagiarizing: Property, plagiarism and feminist futures. In L. Buranen & A.M. Roy (Eds.), *Perspectives on plagiarism and intellectual property in a postmodern world.* Albany, NY: SUNY Press.

Herring, S. (1996). Posting in a different voice: Gender and ethics in computer-mediated communication. In C. Ess (Ed.), *Philosophical perspectives on computer-mediated communication,* (p. 115). Albany, NY: SUNY Press.

Herring, S. (2000). Gender differences in CMC: Findings and implications. *Computer Professionals for Social Responsibility Journal,* 18(1). Retrieved online December 31, 2003, at: http://www.cpsr.org/publications/newsletters/issues/2000/Winter2000/herring.html.

Jaszi, P. (1991). Toward a theory of copyright: The metamorphoses of "authorship." *Duke Law Journal,* 455-502.

Keller, C. (1986). *From a broken web: Separation, sexism, and self.* Boston, MA.

Knight, D. (1999). Third voice revisited. *Mac Musings.* June 29. Retrieved online at: http://www.lowendmac.com/musings/thirdvoice3.shtml.

Landow, G. (1992). Hypertext: The convergence of contemporary critical theory and technology. Baltimore, MD: Johns Hopkins University Press.

LeCourt, D. & Barnes, L. (1999). Writing multiplicity: Hypertext and feminist textual politics. *Computers and Composition,* 16.2, 55-77.

Liu, J. (2003). Copyright law's theory of the consumer. *Boston College Law Review, 44,* 397-431.

Lunsford, A. (1999). Rhetoric, feminism, and the politics of ownership. *College English,* 61, 529-544.

Nedelsky, J. (1990). Laws, boundaries, and the bounded self. *Representations, 30,* 162-189.

Page, B. (1999). Women writers and the restive text: Feminism, experimental writing, and hypertext. In M.-L. Ryan (Ed.), Cyberspace textuality. Bloomington IN: Indiana University Press.

Pollack, M. (2001). What is congress supposed to promote? Defining "Progress" in Article I, Section 8, Clause 8 of the United States Constitution, or introducing the progress clause. *Nebraska Law Review,* 80, 754-809.

Rose, M. (1993). *Authors and owners: The invention of copyright.* Cambridge, MA: Harvard University Press.

Singh, S. (1997). *Fermat's enigma: The epic quest to solve the world's greatest mathematical problem.* New York, NY: Anchor Books.

Wall, W. (1993). *The imprint of gender: Authorship and publication in the English Renaissance.* Ithaca, NY: Cornell University Press.

Woodman, M. (1992). On the author effect: Recovering collectivity. *Cardozo Arts & Entertainment Law Journal,* 10, 279.

Chapter VII

Recent Copyright Protection Schemes:
Implications for Sharing Digital Information

Herman T. Tavani
Rivier College, USA

ABSTRACT

*This chapter critically examines current copyright protection schemes that apply to digital information. We begin with a brief examination of the way in which copyright law has evolved in the United States, from its Anglo-American origins to the present, and then we examine three traditional philosophical theories of property that have been used to justify the granting of copyright protection. Arguing that each property theory is inadequate, we next consider and reject the view that intellectual property should not be protected at all (and thus should be completely free). We then critically analyze the notion of **information**, arguing that it should not be viewed as a commodity that deserves exclusive protection but rather as something that should be communicated and shared. Building on this view, we argue for a new presumptive principle for approaching the copyright debate — namely, the principle that **information wants to be shared**. Finally, we argue that presuming in favor of this* *principle would enable us to formulate a copyright policy that can avoid the extremes found in the two main competing contemporary positions, both of which are morally unacceptable: (1) the view that access to all digitized information should be totally free; and (2) the view that overreaching, and arguably oppressive, copyright legislation, such as the Digital Millennium Copyright Act and the Copyright Term Extension Act, is needed to protect digital information.*

INTRODUCTION

Whether, and to what extent, information in digital format should come under the realm of copyright protection is an issue that has been hotly contested in recent years. Deciding who should have ownership rights to, and thus control over, the information that resides in digital form will ultimately determine who will and will not have access to that information. Copyright law disputes involving digitized information have ranged from claims pertaining to ownership of proprietary software programs to arguments about whether digitized forms of proprietary information should be allowed to be freely exchanged over the Internet. Perhaps no copyright issue involving information residing in digital media has been more contentious during the past few years than the question of whether Internet users should be able to share proprietary MP3 files. Our principal concern in this chapter[1] is with recent copyright legislation in the United States and its implications for sharing digitized information.

COPYRIGHT LAW IN THE UNITED STATES

To understand the evolution of copyright law in the Anglo-American world, it is helpful to examine issues that emerged from the introduction of the printing press in England in 1476. As Halbert (1999) points out, with printing-press technology, the duplication of published material became easier and more accurate and mass distribution became viable. By the 18th Century, legal measures had been proposed to respond to two different kinds of concerns involving the widespread publishing of pamphlets made possible by the printing press. First, the British monarchy sought to more tightly control the spread of works it perceived to be subversive and heretical. Additionally, authors of literary works were interested in protecting their creative works from being reproduced without their permission. The English Statute of Anne, enacted in 1710, was the first law to give protection to authors for their literary works.

The American Colonies generally followed English law regarding copyright, and the framers of the U.S. Constitution included a specific provision in Article 1, Section 8, that gave Congress the power to "promote the Progress of Science and the useful Arts, by securing for limited Times to authors and inventors the exclusive Rights to their respective Writings and Discoveries." This passage is often cited by legal scholars as a justification for copyright law in the United States. In 1790, the first copyright law in the U.S. was enacted. Initially, this Act applied to books, maps, and charts; later, however, the law was extended to include newer forms of media. For example, photography, movies, and audio recordings were eventually covered under copyright law.

In 1909, the Copyright Act was amended to extend legal protection to any "form that could be seen and read visually" by humans. This qualification was prompted by a challenge to copyright law posed by advent of the player piano. The existing copyright law was challenged by a case in 1908 involving a song that was copied onto a perforated piano music roll. Since the musical copy could not be read visually (by humans) from the piano roll, the copy was not considered a violation of the song's copyright. The "machine-readable" versus "human-readable" distinction involving the player piano would later be used in the debate over whether software programs should be eligible for protection under copyright law. Even though a program's source code can be read by humans, its "executable code," which runs on a computer, cannot.

By the 1960s, arguments had been advanced for the view that computer programs, or at least parts of computer programs, should be eligible for copyright protection. When the copyright law was significantly modified in 1976, however, the crucial issue concerning the status of software programs as copyrightable entities still had not been resolved. The 1976 Copyright Act was amended in 1980, specifically to address this concern. That year, the concept of a literary work was expanded to include programs, as well as computer databases that "exhibit authorship." Under the amended Copyright Act, a computer program was defined as a "set of statements or instructions to be used directly in a computer in order to bring about certain results." However, the author of a computer program would be eligible for copyright protection only if he or she could show that the program contained an *original expression* (or original arrangement) of ideas and not merely the ideas themselves.

Because of rapid advances in the field of digital technology, the 1976 Copyright Act has since been amended on a number of occasions. In 1998, two important amendments were made to this Act, both of which are controversial: the Copyright Term Extension Act (CTEA) and the Digital Millennium Copyright Act (DMCA). Each is worth describing, if only briefly, because of the kinds of controversies it has generated. First, the CTEA extended the length of copyright protection from the life of the author plus 50 years to the life of the author plus 70 years. Also increased under this Act was the protection given to "works of hire," which often are commissioned by corporations. Protection for works of hire produced before 1978 was extended from 75 years to 95 years. Many of CTEA's critics noted that the law was passed just in time to keep Mickey Mouse from entering the public domain. These critics also pointed out that the Disney Corporation lobbied very hard for the passage of the CTEA.

The DMCA has also generated considerable controversy. Unlike CTEA, the DMCA does not increase the amount of time that a copyrighted work is protected; rather, it extends the kinds of *rights* that had previously been protected under copyright law. And because of the manner in which the DMCA has expanded these rights, many worry that the development and use of digital technology will be severely restricted. At the heart of the DMCA is a highly controversial "anti-circumvention clause," which forbids the development of any software or hardware technology that *circumvents* (or devises a technological workaround) to copyrighted digital media. This clause is controversial because of its implications for the principle of *fair use*, which is an important element of copyright law in that it provides a "balancing scheme."

The principle of fair use was incorporated into copyright law to balance the exclusive controls given to copyright holders against the broader interests of society. Because of the fair-use provision, every author or publisher may make limited use of another person's copyrighted work for purposes such as criticism, comment, news, reporting, teaching, scholarship, and research. Without the restrictions provided by the fair-use provision, the copyright holder of a work would enjoy total control over that work.

CHALLENGES TO "FAIR USE" POSED BY CTEA AND DMCA

How exactly is the principle of fair use challenged by recent amendments to copyright law? Let us consider two recent cases that illustrate some ways in which this principle is now challenged: one demonstrating how CTEA threatens the communication and sharing of information that once had been in the public domain but is now protected by copyright law; and another illustrating how the DMCA threatens our ability to use and exchange electronic books in the manner we have become accustom to with physical (or "paper and glue") books.

Regarding the challenge posed by CTEA, consider a recent case involving Eric Eldred of Derry, NH. Eldred set up a personal (nonprofit) website dedicated to electronic versions of older books. For example, on his site (www.eldritchpress.org), he included the complete works of Nathaniel Hawthorne. Many of the books on Eldred's site were either difficult to get (as physical books) or were out of print.

When Eldred constructed his website, it was perfectly legal for him to include electronic versions of these books; many were already in the public domain, and some had copyrights that had recently expired. With the passage of CTEA, however, some of the books on his site had come under the newly expanded scheme of copyright protection. Eldred elected not to remove any of the books from his site; instead, he decided to challenge the legality of the amended Copyright Act, which he argued is incompatible with the fair use provision and thus in violation of Article 1, Section 8, Clause 8, of the United States Constitution (see above). Although his court challenge (*Eldred vs. Attorney General John Ashcroft*) was turned down by a United States circuit court, many believed that the lower court's decision had a very good chance of being overturned. However, in January 2003, the U.S. Supreme Court upheld the earlier decision in a 7-2 ruling. The implications of the Eldred case in particular, and the CTEA in general, are considered in detail in a later section of this chapter.

A different kind of challenge to the principle of fair use is illustrated in a case involving Dimitri Sklyarov and the DMCA. Sklyarov had written a program, while he was a graduate student in Russia, that was able to decrypt the code for an electronic book reader developed by Adobe, a U.S.-based software company. Adobe's "e-book reader" is a software product that enables computer users to read digital books. Adobe worried that with Sklyarov's program, computer users would be able to read e-books for free. The software company also believed that Sklyarov's program was illegal under the DMCA, and it decided to press charges against Sklyarov. The United States government was eager to prosecute this case because it wanted to test the "anti-circumvention" provision of the DMCA; even though the Act was officially passed in 1998, it was not enforceable as a law until 2000. Federal authorities arrested Sklyarov in the summer of 2001, while he was attending a conference in Nevada, and confiscated Sklyarov's brief case which contained a copy of his controversial program. This case never went to trial, however, because Adobe soon dropped its charges against Sklyarov.

Sklyarov's arrest generated considerably controversy and protest in the summer of 2001, especially among many software engineers who realized the implications of the DMCA for the process of reverse engineering. (This process, which has been protected under the fair use provision in copyright law, is now also threatened by the DMCA; unfortunately, we are not able to examine DMCA-related issues affecting the practice of reverse engineering in this chapter.) While many of Sklyarov's sympathizers believed that Adobe had a legitimate concern, they were also concerned about the manner in which the principle of fair use was being technologically undermined by Adobe and legally undermined by the DMCA. Even some conservatives, who tend to support strong copyright property protection schemes, believe that the DMCA, and its anti-circumvention clause, may have gone too far.

Other "balancing" issues at stake in the DMCA-related controversy surrounding Adobe's e-book reader involve the principle of *first sale*, as well as the informal policy of being able to lend and borrow books. Consider that in the case of a physical book, an individual has the legal right to transfer the book once she has purchased or otherwise legally acquired it. For example, she can resell the book to a third party, lend it to a friend, or give it away free. Under the provisions stated in the DMCA, however, she would not have the right to transfer an electronic version of that book because of the increased protection granted to copyright holders of digital media. We revisit some of the implications of the DMCA in a later section of this chapter.

PHILOSOPHICAL THEORIES USED TO JUSTIFY COPYRIGHT LAWS

Thus far we have described some ways in which intellectual property in the form of digitized information is currently protected by copyright law in the United States. But why should we grant copyright protection or, for that matter, any kind of normative protection to intellectual property? One could respond to this question by noting that our current legal system has decided that intellectual property deserves protection. However, we could then further ask: On what philosophical grounds are our intellectual property right laws, including copyright law, based? Defenders of intellectual property rights generally appeal to one or more philosophical theories that have been used to justify property rights in the physical realm, arguing that these theories can be applied either directly or in modified form in justifying the protection of intellectual property.

Perhaps we should first note that some philosophers and political theorists have staunchly opposed the notion of private property rights in any form.

(Recall, for example, the arguments presented by Karl Marx that are described in Chapter I of this book.) However, we will not examine arguments for that position here. Instead, we will operate on the presumption that property ownership of some sort can be justified. We should also note that some philosophers and legal theorists who believe that claims involving property rights make sense in the case of tangible property or objects in the physical realm are, nevertheless, skeptical that property rights should apply to non-tangible property in the form of intellectual objects (defined in Chapter I). In a later section of this chapter, we will briefly examine some arguments for this position. First, however, we examine three distinct philosophical theories that have been used to justify the ownership of property.

Locke's Labor Theory of Property and the Notion of Property as a Natural Right

As noted in this book's introductory chapter, the labor theory of property traces its origins to 17th Century philosopher John Locke. Essentially, Locke's property theory is based on the notion of "just deserts" for one's physical labor. In the fifth chapter of his *Second Treatise of Government* (1690), Locke argues that when a person "mixes" her labor with the environment, she is entitled to the fruit of her labor. So, for example, if she tills the land and plants crops on land that is not already owned by another, she has a right to claim ownership of the crops. Similarly, if a person goes into the forest, cuts down a tree and saws it into several pieces of firewood, then he is entitled to ownership of the pieces of firewood that result from his labor. Locke also includes an important qualification — one that, following Nozick (1974), is frequently referred to as *Locke's Proviso* — which says that a person also must ensure that "enough and as good is left in common for others." According to this proviso, one does not have the right to cut down all of the trees in the forest; nor does that person have the right to take the last tree. Even with his proviso, however, critics have argued that Locke's theory falls short of providing an adequate account of property rights.

Locke's property theory can be attacked on at least two different kinds of grounds: (1) the claim that a property right is a natural right; and (2) the view that a justification for rights pertaining to physical property necessarily applies in the case of intellectual property. We briefly consider each criticism, beginning with (1). Although Locke asserts that a right to own property is a natural right, he fails to provide a convincing argument to demonstrate this claim. Furthermore, Locke seems to be inconsistent in his assertion about property being a natural right. For example, if the right to own property is indeed a natural right, then it would seem reasonable to infer that such a right (naturally) applies to all persons. However, Locke also suggests that property rights hold only for persons who "own their own bodies." Since slaves do not legally own their bodies, they would have no legal claim to the fruits of their labor. So it would seem that property rights, which according to Locke's labor theory are a type of natural right for humans, would not apply to all humans.

We can also consider the case of Native Americans, who were not slaves (and thus could be said to "own" their own bodies) and who mixed their labor with the soil. Should they have been granted property rights to the land in the various nations that currently make up North and South America? According to Locke's theory of property, it would seem to follow that they should. Historically, of course, they held no such rights. So it is not clear how Locke can claim that property ownership is a natural right, and yet at the same time allow that such a right could possibly be denied to some humans who happen to be slaves, Native Americans, or members of populations that Locke sometimes describes as "savages" (Tavani, 2004).

We next turn to our second criticism of Locke's labor theory of property, which can be formulated in the following way: Property theories that might justify a right to tangible property do not necessarily justify a right to intellectual property. Attempts to extend Locke's property theory to the intellectual realm can be challenged on two different fronts: (a) creating intellectual works does not necessarily require (physical) labor, and (b) intellectual objects, unlike tangible objects, are non-exclusionary and non-rivalrous. We begin with an analysis of (a). It would seem plausible for an author to claim that the production of an intellectual object required some labor on her part. For example, writing a book, a poem, or a software program can require a fair amount of toil, as it does the production of physical objects. The author might then go on to claim a right to own that creative work because of the labor she invested in it. Noting that Locke associated the justification of property rights with arduous physical labor, however, some critics argue that the production of intellectual objects does not necessarily demand the same kind of onerous toil (or "sweat of the brow") required in the production of many kinds of tangible goods. So the analogy involving an individual's physical labor and a corresponding claim to a right to some tangible property need not apply in the case of intellectual property.

Let us now turn to (b). Some critics of intellectual property rights point out that intellectual objects, unlike physical objects, are non-exclusionary and non-rivalrous in nature. Physical objects are exclusionary in the sense that if *A* possesses C (say a Mercedes-Benz automobile), then B cannot, and vice versa. But A and B can both possess copies of the same intellectual object (say a copy of an MS PowerPoint program); B's possession of a copy of that program does not preclude A from having it, and vice versa. Also consider that tangible property often is scarce and thus generates competition and rivalry. Intellectual objects, on the other hand, are potentially abundant in the sense that they can be reproduced easily, and are typically reproducible at a very low cost. Given these considerations, it would seem that intellectual objects are significantly different from tangible objects. How, if at all, should these (and other possible) differences affect the question of ownership rights for intellectual objects?

Because the characteristics of exclusivity and rivalry that apply in the case of competition for physical objects do not apply to intellectual objects, some question whether any kind of legal or normative protection should be granted to intellectual property. As Hughes (1997) asks: Why should one person have the exclusive right to use and possess something that all people could possess and use concurrently? Additionally, Hughes asks how Locke's theory can account for ownership of an expression of an idea "whose inception does not seem to have involved labor." So we can conclude our brief discussion of Locke's labor theory of property by noting that it must first respond to several key criticisms before it can be considered as an adequate justification for intellectual property rights, including copyright protection.

Utilitarian Theory of Property and Economic Incentives

As we have seen, there are good reasons to be skeptical of any claims that suggest that a property right is a natural right or that intellectual property right claims can be justified solely by virtue of one's labor. Some argue that a property right claim is better understood as an artificial or conventional right constructed by the state and then granted to individuals (and corporations) for the purpose of achieving greater overall *social utility*. Systematic formulations of utilitarian theory in general — the view that policies that maximize social utility are desirable — were introduced by Jeremy Bentham and John Stuart Mill in the 17th and 18th Centuries. Arguably, utilitarian theory underpins the rationale used by the framers of the U.S. Constitution for granting copyright and patent protection to individuals. The Founders reasoned that if incentives were given for individuals to bring out their creative products, including literary and artistic works, American society in general would benefit as a result.

What exactly is the relationship between intellectual property rights and social utility? Can the former be justified solely in terms of the latter? Are property rights justifiable only if they maximize the good for the greatest number of people in a given society? And what exactly is the *good* that ought to be maximized? For some utilitarians, the good is defined simply in terms of economic outcomes, and in this scheme, copyright law is justified because it promotes an efficient allocation of economic resources. This view is also sometimes associated with an economic theory of property, or what could be called the utilitarian/economic incentive model, which is similar to a position articulated by Landes and Posner (1989). According to this model, intellectual property law, like all law, is constructed to achieve desirable economic ends.

Although the utilitarian theory of property can avoid many of the criticisms leveled against the labor theory, utilitarians also have had their share of critics. The standard criticisms against utilitarian theory in general — such as the argument that individuals who happen to be members of groups not included within the scope of "the greatest number" in a given society tend to be treated unfairly — are well known, and there is no need to rehearse those critiques here. We should add to the standard criticisms, however, that when a utilitarian scheme for justifying property rights is tied too closely to economic incentives, it tends to view creative works merely as commodities in the marketplace and thus supports (indirectly, at least) the commodification of literary and artistic works. As we will see later in this chapter, thinking about intellectual objects in this way can have an adverse effect on society because it can result in significantly restricting the flow of information. So we can question whether a rationale for granting property rights that is based solely, or even primarily, on social utility and economic incentives would be adequate.

Personality Theory of Property and the Notion of Property as a Moral Right

Tracing its origins to the writings of G. W. F. Hegel, a 19th Century philosopher, the personality theory of property focuses on the role that the author's personality plays in producing creative works. A creative work is seen as a work of self-expression or self-realization of the author, and as such it is an extension of the author's or the creator's *personality*. Unlike Locke's theory, no analogy with labor is necessary to justify intellectual property rights; in fact, such an analogy may confuse and possibly even distort the status of the personality itself as well as the crucial role it plays in justifying intellectual property rights. In this scheme, an idea belongs to a creator for reasons that are totally independent of the labor she may have invested in producing it, or of any social utility/economic good that might result from bringing it into a public forum. Thus, the personality theory of property emphasizes the personal rights of the author/creator, as distinct from his or her economic rights. Personality theorists argue that because of the crucial role that the creator's personality plays, authors should be given protection for their artistic work, even if they have no legal claim to any monetary reward associated with that work. Moore (1997) aptly captures this point when he notes that, according to the personality theory, authors and inventors have the right to control the products of their intellectual efforts "independent of social and economic utility, and sometimes in conflict with it."

The personality theory lies at the foundation of various intellectual property laws enacted by nations in continental Europe. In France, this account of property is sometimes also referred to as the "moral rights" (*droits morals*) theory of property. The essence of the moral rights theory of property is embedded in Article 6 *bis* of the Berne Convention, which states that when an artist (that is, an author, painter, sculptor, architect, or musician) creates:

... he does more than bring into the world a unique object having only exploitative possibilities; he projects into the world part of his personality and subjects it to the ravages of public use. There are possibilities of injury to the creator other than merely economic ones; these the copyright statute does not protect.

In failing to consider the role that the author's *personality* plays in producing creative works, both the utilitarian and labor theories either grossly underestimate, or ignore altogether, the roles of self expression and autonomy in creating artistic works. For those subscribing to the personality/moral rights theory of property, what is paramount is the fact that a creative work is an extension of the creator's personality and thus is an expression of her "being" or soul. And it is because of this important relationship between the creative object and the author's personality that creative works deserve legal protection.

While the personality theory avoids many of the criticisms of the utilitarian and labor theories of property, it introduces others. For example, Hughes (1997) argues that such a theory is "inapplicable to valuable innovations that do not contain elements of what society might recognize as personal expression." Consider also the possibility that literary works created by some individuals might not express the "true" personality of the work's creator. This could be intentional on the part of an author who deliberately elects not to reveal her personality in one or more creative works (possibly even to deceive others about her true persona), or because through some unintentional means, she fails to do so. Thus it would seem that the personality theory, like the labor and utilitarian theories, falls short as an adequate justification for intellectual property rights.

AN ARGUMENT AGAINST GRANTING PROPERTY RIGHTS FOR SOFTWARE: *INFORMATION WANTS TO BE FREE*

We have seen that each of the traditional property theories is problematic in one or more respects. We have also seen that even if some of those theories can justify the granting of rights for physical property, they are not necessarily applicable to claims involving intellectual property rights. Some believe that there is no inconsistency in defending the protection of physical property while not granting ownership rights for intellectual property. Stallman (1995) has argued against copyright protection for computer software, even though he does not reject (at least not in his writing) that we should deny legal protection for physical property.

He has been a staunch advocate for the view that software should be freely available to users. Let us briefly examine some points in his argument. First, we should note that Stallman sees software ownership as a form of "hoarding," which he further claims disregards the welfare of society for personal gain and thus facilitates certain *social harms*. Among the social harms he identifies with proprietary software are: (1) a restricted use of software programs, (2) an inability to adapt or fix programs, (3) the loss of educational benefit for programmers, and (4) psychosocial harm (loss of social cohesion and altruistic spirit that would prevail if ownership were eliminated). To illustrate the fourth type of social harm, Stallman points to the fact that in the computer industry, software development has evolved from a pattern of cooperation and sharing to advance the state of the art for programs (in the early days of software development) to one in which cooperation is strictly forbidden. Stallman also believes that the ethical programmer is one who cooperates in the production of software, helping to make it freely available for humankind rather than supporting efforts to restrict its use.

Some who claim to be following Stallman subscribe to the mantra *information wants to be free* — a view that, according to Barlow (1997), can be credited to Stewart Brand. What exactly do people who hold this position mean? Do they literally want all information to be totally free? At first glance, this notion might seem ideal or perhaps even romantic. However, Spafford (1995) has cleverly pointed out some of the disturbing implications that could result if information were completely free. For example, he notes that, as individuals, we would have no privacy because any information about us could be freely exchanged without our knowledge and consent. Few people, if any, would find such a practice acceptable. However, we should not assume that this is what Stallman himself intends when he says that software should be free. In fact, he states quite explicitly that, in his scheme, "free" refers to "freedom not to price." Some interpret Stallman's distinction via the following analogy: software should be free in the sense of "free speech, not free beer." Unfortunately, we cannot pursue this distinction here, because doing so would take us beyond the scope of this chapter.

For our purposes, one point that Stallman makes is particularly useful in helping us to think about intellectual property issues from a radically different perspective. I believe that this particular insight of Stallman's also undergirds the claim of many who embrace the more extreme position that all information should be absolutely free. Fortunately, we do not need to accept that position to appreciate Stallman's insight that software is a form of *information*, and that information itself is something that humans desire to share with one another. In order to be shared, of course, information must be communicated. So elaborate intellectual-property structures and mechanisms, especially those that prohibit or even discourage the communication of information, would seem to undermine the very purpose of information as "something to be shared."

INFORMATION AS A FORM OF PROPERTY

What exactly is *information*? Is it a form of property, and if so, how does information differ from alternative forms of property? Barlow (1997) argues that information is "not a thing"; in fact, he believes that information is better understood "as a verb, not a noun." According to Barlow, information is "expressed not possessed," even when it is contained in a physical medium such as a book or a compact disk. Barlow also believes that information needs to *move*, and that the way that it moves is different from the way in which physical goods are distributed. For example, it can be transferred without ever leaving the possession of the original owner. De George (2003) points out that a great advantage of information is that it is "infinitely shareable," and that one can usually share information with others while retaining it oneself. Hence, we can share in its benefits without depriving others. Do any these factors, individually or collectively, entail (in a strict logical sense) or even lend support to the view that information should be free? More importantly for our purposes, however, is the question whether these factors support Stallman's insight that information is something that people desire to share.

Although only a few may agree with the notion that all information should be free, some philosophers have found Stallman's insight about the nature and purpose of information — that is, as something that humans naturally want to share and communicate — to be instructive. For example, they also point out that Stallman's insight dovetails with elements of virtue ethics (Carey, 1997) and natural law theory (McFarland, 2004). (Unfortunately, a discussion of how Stallman's insight fits into specific aspects of natural law theory and the theory of virtue ethics is beyond the scope of this chapter.) Neither Carey nor McFarland is willing to accept Stallman's claim that software should be totally free and thus be ineligible for legal protection. However, both authors believe that Stallman is correct in suggesting that the essential purpose of information is that it be communicated and shared. Hence, an adequate account of the purpose of information (as something to be communicated) must be taken into consideration in debates involving intellectual property.

McFarland (2004) points out that if we analyze intellectual objects simply in terms of the concept of property itself, then the central point of debate tends to be about issues of ownership and control of information. But according to McFarland, an adequate theory of information must take into account its *social nature*, which tends to get overlooked when we think of information exclusively, or even strictly, in terms of rights and property. We have already seen that traditional theories of property tend to do this. For example, the three property theories we considered focused either on: (1) an individual's (or a corporation's) labor, (2) the social utility (cost-benefits), or (3) the author's personality. But none considered that a primary function of information lies in its overall benefit to society, independent of any social utility/economic incentives that it may also provide. Although information pertaining to literary and creative works can certainly be understood as a form of self-expression (as the personality theory rightly suggests) and as something that can provide economic incentives to increase overall social utility (as utilitarians correctly suggest), it also has a social purpose or function that is even more fundamental than both personal expression and social/economic utility — namely, its ability to be shared.

A PRESUMPTIVE PRINCIPLE FOR GUIDING THE COPYRIGHT DEBATE: *INFORMATION WANTS TO BE SHARED*

We have defined "information" in a way that highlights its important social function as something that needs to be communicated and shared. Next, we consider how an understanding of information in those terms can be expressed in the form of a guiding principle that could inform the current debate involving copyright policy. Can we generate a *presumptive principle*, based on the conception of information that we have articulated, that could influence the policy debate involving copyright? First, we must define what we mean by a presumptive principle. One way that we can think about such a principle is to consider the various assumptions and biases, either tacitly or explicitly held, that we bring to a debate on a specific topic or issue. For example, we can ask what underlying assumptions or beliefs, or prima facie considerations, guide us in our deliberations about something by providing us with a default position as an entry point into a discussion of some topic or issue.

To illustrate how a presumptive principle can inform our position on a social policy, consider the current debate about privacy, especially in the context of computers and information technology. Should our default position — that is, our presumed approach — be to proceed on the side of personal privacy? Or should it be on the side of transparency for individuals? All things being equal, we might just as easily pick either side as a starting point. DeCew (1997) has argued that we should "presume in favor of privacy" and then let individuals decide, through a process of "dynamic negotiation," how much information about themselves they are willing to disclose. Following the tragic events of September 11, 2001, however, one might argue that we should presume in favor of security (and against privacy). Which of these two presumptive principles we happen to use will, of course, dramatically affect our stance in the negotiation process of formulating a privacy policy.

How is our brief discussion in the preceding paragraph about a presumptive principle involving the privacy debate relevant to our approach in this essay to disputes concerning intellectual property rights in general and copyright policy in particular? Consider some principles that could provide us with a starting point in the debate about intellectual property rights. Hettinger (1989) has suggested a "strong prima facie case against the wisdom of private and exclusive intellectual property rights." He has also suggested and that there be a "presumption against allowing restrictions on the free flow of ideas." And Boyle (2004) has argued for a "presumption in favor of informed democratic participation in the formation of entire property regimes." This view has also been intimated by Halbert (1999) who worries about "the ability of a world citizenry to participate in its own future" because of our current framework of intellectual property rights, which she describes as "detrimental to the free exchange of information." So there would seem to be some precedent for invoking a presumptive principle of the type that I envision for the copyright debate. I suggest that we presume in favor of the following principle: *information wants to be shared*. I believe that such a principle captures the essential aspects of the insights of Stallman (1995), Carey (1997), and McFarland (2004), and I have also argued elsewhere (Tavani, 2002, 2004) that such a view could be taken far more seriously by policy makers than the arguably radical notion that information should be totally free.

Applying our Presumptive Principle to a Specific Case

Consider at least one way in which the presumptive principle I suggest has already been anticipated. Tim Berners-Lee, who developed the code for HTTP (Hyper Text Transfer Protocol) that makes possible the exchange of information on the Web, never bothered to apply for a copyright for his code. As a physicist working at the CERN Laboratory in Switzerland, his desire to develop a common protocol for Internet communication was to provide a way that scientists could share information more easily with each other. So a contributing force to the development of the World Wide Web was Berners-Lee's belief that we should *share*, not hoard, information. As a scientist, his goal in writing the code for what was to become the standard protocol for the Web was to provide individuals with a forum in which they could freely share information with one another, and not so that he could become wealthy. Should we view Berners-Lee as someone who is eccentric and drastically out of touch with the economic rewards of capitalism? Or is it possible that he was motivated by factors other than financial incentives and monetary gain? Halbert (1999) points out that only rarely are authors, poets, musicians, artists, and academics motivated solely by economic incentives. To her list, we could also add many scientists like Berners-Lee, who like Thomas Jefferson and others who embraced the Enlightenment idea of the free flow of ideas, believe that the ability to exchange ideas should take precedence over the exclusive ownership of intellectual objects and any financial rewards that may accompany them.

Ironically, many entrepreneurs who now seek to control and thus restrict the flow of information in cyberspace have benefited in the past from the free exchange and sharing of information. For example, Microsoft benefited significantly from the work done by Apple Corporation on its graphical user interface

—that is, the system of icons that users can point to and click on to accomplish a task. And while Steve Jobs was an executive at Apple, he visited Xerox Park where he discovered that a graphical interface had already been designed by researchers there. Jobs then incorporated that design into Apple's MacIntosh computer. So it would appear that those who designed graphical interfaces for Microsoft's Windows operating system have clearly benefited from the *sharing* of information along the way. Would it be fair to credit any one company (say, Xerox Corporation) or single person (say, Doug Englebart who invented the mouse) with exclusive copyright protection for graphical-interface systems? And would it be fair to grant Microsoft exclusive control over the future development of graphical interfaces? If Hettinger (1989) is correct in his claim that every author stands on the shoulders of giants, then we can ask if it is moral to allow the last contributor either: (1) to reap the full reward or (2) to prevent some individuals from also building on the contributions of others.

The Concept of *Author* in the Copyright Debate

To what extent has our modern conception of *author* influenced copyright policy? According to Rose (1993), English copyright history illustrates how the notion of *authorship* has been used to enclose "new territories" under the rubric of private ownership (cited in Halbert 1999, p. 2). In focusing on the notion of author, many believe that our current intellectual property laws tend to overlook the social role both of the creator and of the work itself. For example, McFarland (2004) points out that because our conventional concept of property is highly individualistic, it focuses on the creator/developer of the work (that is, his or her labor, personality, or financial gain). Boyle (2004) makes a similar point when he notes that we have romanticized the notion of author, attributing to individuals a sense of originality that is not always warranted. As noted earlier, authors often borrow from one another, and in so doing make a greater overall contribution to society. Warwick (2004) believes that in the copyright debate, more weight is given to the interests of individual creators and she suggests that this extension of rights is based on economic rather than ethical considerations.

Halbert (1999) believes that the notion of *originality* stemming from a person's intellect, which underlies our contemporary notion of author, is an outgrowth of economic interests and legal definitions within a specific historical context—namely, the 18th Century struggle over copyright ownership and the development of the concept of *proprietary authorship*. She also believes that the concept of author that has evolved over the years has helped to "conceal the larger political and economic implications" of the intellectual property system with copyright laws that have been designed to benefit the publishers who hold copyrights, not the authors themselves. Consider that copyright usually belongs to the publisher who publishes the work, not the author. For example, major corporations such a Microsoft, who can own as well as control information systems and information itself, can claim to be an author. And this kind of control of information by large and powerful corporations tends to deter, rather than facilitate, the sharing of information. Thus our current trends in copyright law would seem to contradict the view that the essential purpose of information is that it should be shared.

Implications of Not Proceeding from our Presumptive Principle in the Copyright Debate

Historically, conflicts involving copyright can be seen as a tension between two competing interests: the ownership of ideas and the exchange of ideas. Shapiro (1993) describes this tension as one between *sovereignty systems* (ownership) and *exchange systems* (advocating the relaxation of control). Halbert (1999) expresses this tension involving copyright battles as "the mutually exclusive desires to maintain authority and control, and the necessity to relax control to facilitate circulation." Many critics now believe copyright has become a tool for securing property interests rather than a mode of encouraging new works. Consider that copyright laws originally intended to cover print media were designed to encourage the distribution of information (De George, 2003). Halbert (1999) believes that it is only through a process of commercialization that copyright has come to mean *protection for economic gain*. She believes that the *balance* between innovation as a social good vs. a private benefit codified in the Copyright Act in the United States Constitution is being replaced with the language of ownership that tilts in the favor of tightly controlled property rights. Earlier in this chapter we saw how recent copyright legislation in the United States pertaining to digital media, such as the DMCA, inhibits the distribution of electronic information. So Halbert's assertion seems quite plausible.

Even though digital technology has made information exchange easy and inexpensive, it would seem to follow that the exchange of digitized information is now also being discouraged by recent legislation. To illustrate this point, consider the case of interlibrary loan practices. Many individuals, including students, have benefited the interlibrary-loan policies found in most libraries. Such a practice not only benefits individuals, but arguably also contributes to the public good by expanding the notion of a learning community. If the books that we were so easily able to borrow in the past become available only in digitized form in the future, it might no longer be possible to access them through a interlibrary-loan system. By granting copyright holders of digital media the ability to prohibit the exchange of electronic versions of books, the DMCA discourages their sharing across libraries. As a result of this trend, many critics fear that digital information is now becoming less available and that the "intellectual commons" is beginning to disappear.

THE FUTURE OF "INTELLECTUAL COMMONS" AND THE DEMISE OF THE PUBLIC DOMAIN OF IDEAS

What exactly is meant by the expression "intellectual commons?" Perhaps we can better understand that concept by drawing an analogy with a "physical commons" or a common area that has been set aside and is open to an entire community. During the 18th Century, private property rapidly replaced the English commons. Rose (1993) points out that during this period, for example, laws were passed to prevent peasants from catching fish or shooting deer (cited in Halbert, 1999). So the physical commons has been shrinking, requiring significant effort on the part of conservationists to lobby on its behalf. One need only read the tale about "The Tragedy of the Commons" (Hardin, 1968) to understand the fragility of the commons and how easily it can erode and eventually disappear altogether. Are we also now in danger of losing our intellectual commons — that is, the public domain of ideas that has been freely available to us?

Lessig (2002), in a book subtitled *The Fate of the Commons in a Connected World*, raises some serious concerns about the "future of ideas" in a medium that is overly regulated and controlled by economic interests. Recall our earlier discussion of Eric Eldred's website that included classic books available in electronic form. We saw that books on Eldred's website had to be removed because of the retroactive provisions of the Copyright Term Extension Act (CTEA), which effectively took those books and others out of the public domain.

It is not difficult to imagine that more and more information that we have traditionally shared freely will eventually disappear from the public domain and enter the world of copyright protection. Suppose, for example, that at some point in the near future, all culinary recipes in digital format are copyrighted and are no longer able to be exchanged without the permission of the new rights-holder — that is, the legal "owner" of the recipes? In that case, we would not be permitted to use, exchange, or alter (with the intent to improve upon) a recipe without first getting permission from the copyright holder. Consider that up to this point in our history, internationally renowned chefs have been able to use freely and to improve upon earlier recipes to achieve their successful cuisine. Would it be fair if those chefs who had previously benefited from the sharing of recipes in the past were, all of a sudden, to be awarded exclusive rights to recipes just because they happened to be experimenting with food at a time when the legal system favored the privatizing of information for commercial interests? Recall Hettinger's analogy (1989) regarding "authors standing on the shoulders of giants." Also consider what effect this precedent would have for the public domain of ideas and for ordinary discourse and information exchange?

Responding to recent concerns about the disappearance of the public domain of intellectual objects, Boyle (2004) has argued for a need for a political movement similar, in key respects, to the environmental movement that emerged in the 1970s. He also believes that just as a political movement was necessary to save the environment from inevitable destruction, so too is an analogous movement needed to save the intellectual commons. To illustrate this point, Boyle notes that the environment almost disappeared under a presumption of highly individualistic property rights. In a similar way, the public domain of information is disappearing because of a system of intellectual property rights that are highly individualistic and entrepreneurial, where the stakeholders include individual entrepreneurs and corporations but not ordinary individuals. Boyle argues that just as the environmental movement "invented" the concept of the environment — so that farmers, consumers, hunters, and bird watchers could all "discover themselves as environmentalists" — we need to invent (or possibly reinvent) the concept of the public domain in order to create a coalition of vested stakeholders to protect it. I believe that if the presumptive principle defended in this chapter were adopted by lawmakers and policy experts, the public domain of ideas could be still be salvaged.

In making the case for the presumptive principle that information should be shared, and for why the intellectual commons should be preserved, we have not yet said much about the rights and interests of software manufacturers and of individual creators of literary and artistic works. Of course, their rights and interests also deserve serious consideration in any future debate regarding copyright protection for information residing in digital media. Like Carey (1997), I believe that manufacturers and individuals need to be compensated fairly for the costs they expend and for risks they undertake in developing and bringing to market creative products. The key phrase here, of course, is *fair compensation*. A fair copyright system is one that would enable us to achieve a proper balance. In reaching that state of equilibrium, however, we must presume in favor of sharing information and must not lose sight of the fact that information is more than merely a commodity that has commercial value.

CONCLUDING REMARKS

In this chapter, we have examined some intellectual property right disputes involving digitized information, particularly as it is affected by recent changes to copyright law in the United States. We critically analyzed three traditional philosophical theories of property that underpin many of the arguments currently used to defend current copyright protection laws and policies. In analyzing those theories, we also saw that an alternative framework for approaching issues surrounding the current copyright dispute suggests that we need to take into account the fact that an essential aspect of information is that it is something to be shared, and not merely a commodity of some sort whose value should be determined by forces in the marketplace. We have defended the view that the ultimate nature and purpose of information is something to be communicated and shared. It has been argued that in the copyright debate, we should presume in favor of the principle *information wants to be shared* (and that doing this does not commit us to the more radical view that information should be free). If we presume in favor of this principle, then we can begin to frame more equitable copyright policies that will both: (1) encourage the flow of information and its sharing, and (2) reward fairly the authors and creators of literary and artistic works, as well as software manufacturers.

ENDNOTES

[1]   An earlier version of this chapter was presented at the Sixth Annual Ethics and Technology Conference, Boston College, Chestnut Hill, MA, June 27, 2003. Portions of this chapter draw from, and expand upon, arguments introduced in two of my previously published works: Information Wants to Be Shared: An Alternative Framework for Approaching Intellectual Property Disputes in an Information Age, (2002). *Catholic Library World*, 73(2), 94-104; and *Ethics and Technology: Ethical Issues in an Age of Information and Communication Technology* (2004). Hoboken, NJ: John Wiley and Sons.

REFERENCES

Barlow, J.P. (1997). The economy of ideas: Everything you know about intellectual property is wrong. In A. E. Moore (Ed.), *Intellectual property: Moral, legal, and international dilemmas,* (pp. 349-372). Lanham, MD: Rowman and Littlefield.

Boyle, J. (2004). A politics of intellectual property: Environmentalism for the Net. In R.A. Spinello & H.T. Tavani (Eds.), *Readings in CyberEthics (2nd ed.),* pp. 273-293. Sudbury, MA: Jones and Bartlett Publishers.

Carey, D.H. (1997). The virtues of software ownership. In A. E. Moore (Ed.), *Intellectual property: Moral, legal, and international dilemmas,* (pp. 299-305). Lanham, MD: Rowman and Littlefield.

DeCew, J.W. (1997). *In pursuit of privacy: Law, ethics, and the rise of technology.* Ithaca, NY: Cornell University Press.

De George, R.T. (2003). *The ethics of information technology and business.* Malden, MA: Blackwell Publishers.

Halbert, D. (1999). *Intellectual property in the information age: The politics of expanding ownership rights.* Westport, CT: Quorum Books.

Hardin, G. (1968). The tragedy of the commons. *Science,* 162, 1243-1248.

Hegel, G.W.F. (1967). *The philosophy of right.* (T. Knox, Trans.) New York: Oxford University Press.

Hettinger, E.C. (1989). Justifying intellectual property. *Philosophy and Public Affairs,* 18, 31-52.

Hughes, J. (1997). The philosophy of intellectual property. In A. E. Moore (Ed.), *Intellectual property: Moral, legal, and international dilemmas,* (pp. 107-178). Lanham, MD: Rowman and Littlefield.

Landes, W.M. & Posner, R. (1989). An economic analysis of copyright law. *Journal of Legal Studies,* 18(2), 325-364.

Lessig, L. (2002). *The future of ideas: The fate of the commons in a connected world.* New York: Random House.

Locke, J. (1952). *The second treatise of civil government.* Indianapolis, IN: Bobbs-Merrill.

McFarland, M.C. (2004). Intellectual property, information, and the common good. In R.A. Spinello & H.T. Tavani (Eds.), *Readings in CyberEthics (2nd ed.),* pp. 294-304. Sudbury, MA: Jones and Bartlett Publishers.

Moore, A.E. (1997). Introduction. In A.E. Moore (Ed.), *Intellectual property: Moral, legal, and international dilemmas,* (pp. 1-14). Lanham, MD: Rowman and Littlefield.

Nozick, R. (1974). *Anarchy, state, and utopia.* New York: Basic Books.

Rose, M. (1993). *Authors and owners: The invention of copyright*. Cambridge, MA: Harvard University Press.

Shapiro, M.J. (1993). *Reading "Adam Smith": Desire, history, and value*. Newbury Park, CA: Sage Publications.

Stallman, R. (1995). Why software should be free. In D. G. Johnson & H. Nissenbaum (Eds.), *Computing, ethics and social values*, (pp. 191-200). Englewood Cliffs, NJ: Prentice Hall.

Tavani, H. (2002). Information wants to be shared: An alternative framework for approaching intellectual property disputes in an information age. *Catholic Library World*, 73(2), 94-104.

Tavani, H. (2004). *Ethics and technology: Ethical issues in an age of information and communication technology*. Hoboken, NJ: John Wiley and Sons.

Warwick, S. (2004). Is copyright ethical? In R.A. Spinello & H.T. Tavani (Eds), *Readings in CyberEthics (2nd ed.)*, pp. 305-321. Sudbury, MA: Jones and Bartlett Publishers.

Chapter VIII

Trespass and *Kyosei* in Cyberspace

Richard A. Spinello
Boston College, USA

ABSTRACT

This chapter considers the theme of trespass in cyberspace. In order to prevent unauthorized use of their data several U.S. companies have hastily filed lawsuits alleging trespass to chattels. But some of this data usage, especially for metasites, is socially valuable. Nonetheless, the courts are generally sympathetic with these trespass claims even if this means that activities like spidering or e-mail are constrained in certain contexts. Legal scholars have criticized this trend because it creates a novel property right in factual data which is not eligible for copyright protection. These legal concerns are justified, but what should moralists be saying about this matter? We argue here that both eastern and western philosophies recognize the need to respect the common good of a community or common venture. This awareness should temper a company's narrow focus on proprietary property rights. We attempt to define the Net's common good (or commonly shared values) and make the case that Internet users have a prima facie duty to support that common good. Thus, prudent and morally responsible companies operating on the Net will seek to balance their property entitlements with this affirmative duty to support the Internet's common good. There is no magic formula for achieving this precarious balance, but we offer some general criteria that will orient managers toward the right direction. Finally, we explain that a private settlement of trespass matters is clearly welfare-enhancing.

INTRODUCTION

Intellectual property issues in cyberspace have fascinated and preoccupied many legal scholars, but they have largely been ignored by philosophers and ethicists. Intellectual property laws involving copyright and patent protection seem clear-cut (at least to those trained as lawyers), and so the only issue is how they should be equitably applied in cyberspace. This is a matter for lawyers, but not for moralists.

Some issues, however, deserve our critical attention. Consider the problem of trespass in cyberspace. In the United States, the legal claim of "trespass to chattels" is being used as a pretext to prevent unwelcome speech and to stifle other socially beneficial activities that might be perceived as problematic for a particular website. In the case of *Intel v. Hamidi,* for example, Mr. Kenneth Hamidi was enjoined from sending any e-mail messages critical of the company's human resources policies to Intel employees. Although he sent only several messages over a two-year period, the court considered his electronic missives as the equivalent of spam and as a form of trespass. Similarly, in the case of *eBay v. Bidder's Edge,* a court sided with eBay in its quest for an injunction to prevent a Bidder's Edge spider from crawling the eBay website in order to extract data to be aggregated on the Bidder's Edge metasite.

There appears to be a problem, however, in labeling all unwelcome activity as the equivalent of trespass. Companies such as eBay and Intel reap the benefits of open connectivity but are unwilling to internalize the costs of that connectivity. Also, exclusionary laws such as trespass have the detrimental effect of fragmenting the network, "allowing sites that have been physically connected to segregate themselves...from the network" (Burk, 2000). But the more information that is accessible, hyperlinked, comparable, searchable, and indexed, the more valuable the whole Web becomes. Isn't there some obligation on the part of those who profit from the Internet to contribute to the good of the whole?

In this chapter we focus on this controversial debate about trespass from a distinctly moral perspective. What resources and insights can the moralist bring to this debate? Are companies like eBay and Intel, which zealously guard their property rights, doing anything that could be considered imprudent or even morally improper? If so, how do we ascertain the contours of responsible behavior in these situations?

Although we are sympathetic to the need to preserve intellectual property rights in the realm of cyberspace, we will argue that there is also a prima facie duty to support the common good of cyberspace. Companies should aspire to emulate the more collaborative approach to commercial activity found in the Eastern tradition and crystallized in the notion of *kyosei*. Followers of *kyosei* do not permit individual rights to overpower the collective good. In the spirit of that philosophy we contend that companies like eBay and Intel must strive to find harmony between the impulse to protect their rights and their moral duty to work on behalf of the collective good of the Internet. In the course of this discussion we will articulate the nature of this collective good and consider the arguments underlying the moral duty to support it.

SPIDERS AND SPAMMERS: RECENT TRESPASS CASES

In order to grasp the full import of the trespass issue, we will review three short case studies where the allegation of trespass is used to deter unwelcome extrinsic activities. As background for this discussion, it is instructive to briefly review the technology of spiders since it is relevant for a full understanding of two of the three cases. Most search engines rely on a software robot, often called a "spider," that automatically searches and retrieves information from websites. These robots recursively follow one hyperlink after another, indexing each web page that is found. The index of the search engine stores all of the Web pages found by the spider for future queries by users. While the work of some spiders is fairly benign, those that function as shopbots, "which comb through commercial websites, extracting pricing and product information" (Rosenfeld, 2002), generate some controversy. Shopbots are utilized to create metasites that contain prices of different vendors for the same item or other comparative information. These metasites "offer little original content, but rather aggregate and organize the content of other websites" (Rosenfeld, 2002).

We are now in a better position to consider three prominent trespass cases: *Intel v. Hamidi, Ticketmaster Corp. v. Tickets.com, Inc.* and *eBay v. Bidder's Edge*. All of these cases will shed light on the legal and moral issues that are part of the larger dispute about trespass. In each of these cases, the antiquated doctrine of *trespass to chattels* was invoked to prevent access by unwanted third parties. A chattel is simply an article of personal property. Unlike the more familiar *trespass to land* cause of action, this form of trespass "lies where an intentional interference with the possession of personal property has proximately caused injury" (*Thrifty-Tel v. Beznik,* 1996).

Intel v. Hamidi

The California semiconductor company had made it quite clear to Ken Hamidi that his e-mail messages were not welcome. But after repeated efforts to block these messages the company turned to the courts for injunctive relief.

On six occasions during a two-year period, Mr. Hamidi, an ex-employee of Intel, sent e-mail messages complaining about Intel's discriminatory employment practices to over 30,000 Intel employees at their e-mail addresses on Intel's system. Employees were provided with an opportunity to opt-out of future messages. One message accused Intel of grossly underestimating the size of an impending layoff. Intel regarded Hamidi's e-mails as intrusive, but Hamidi refused Intel's request to desist from sending the messages. Intel then attempted to filter out Hamidi's messages, but he was able to bypass Intel's blocking mechanism. Intel felt that it had little recourse, and in October, 1998, it sued Hamidi, requesting an immediate injunction to stop him from sending these e-mail messages to its employees. It accused Hamidi of trespass to chattels for the burden imposed on its servers by his unwanted e-mail. Hamidi lost the first round of this legal struggle when Judge John Lewis of the California Supreme Court issued a summary judgment in favor of Intel and enjoined Hamidi from sending unsolicited e-mail to any of the e-mail addresses on Intel's corporate system.

Hamidi's lawyers had argued that these e-mail messages did not disrupt or unduly burden Intel's system and that their client's free speech rights were being compromised. But according to Judge Lewis, "The evidence establishes (without dispute) that Intel has been injured by diminished employee productivity, and in devoting company resources to blocking efforts and to addressing employees about Hamidi's e-mail. These injuries, which impair the value to Intel of its e-mail system, are sufficient to support a cause of action for trespass to chattels" (*Intel Corp v. Hamidi,* 1999).

Ticketmaster Corp. v. Tickets.com, Inc.

Tickets.com is an online ticket distributor. It also operates as a data aggregator that offers information about other locations on the Web where a user can find tickets to entertainment or sporting events. Like other aggregators, it relies on spiders to do the work of extracting data from the websites of ticket sellers and brokers. When a user searching through the Tickets.com website requests tickets to a specific event, Tickets.com either sells the tickets directly or it provides the user with hyperlinks to those websites where the tickets are available. Ticketmaster is the world's largest ticket broker, so it was obviously a primary target site for the Tickets.com spider. But Ticketmaster resisted the efforts of this spider to copy data from its website. It also objected to Tickets.com practice of deep linking. Accordingly, Ticketmaster alleged that Tickets.com's actions gave rise to claims of copyright infringement, misappropriation, and trespass to chattels. While some of these claims were legally tenuous, the strongest part of the Ticketmaster case was the allegation of trespass to chattels. Ticketmaster's First Amended Complaint (2000) accuses Tickets.com of "access and intermeddl[ing] with Ticketmaster's computers and computer systems for Tickets.com's own commercial benefit."

In this case, however, the court refused to grant Ticketmaster's request for injunctive relief. It opined that while the trespass to chattels claim had merit, there was no evidence that Ticketmaster had been harmed by Tickets.com's intrusive activities.

eBay v. Bidder's Edge

Bidder's Edge (BE) is an auction aggregator, providing its users the ability to search for auction items across multiple online auction sites. It maintains a data base of comprehensive auction information assembled by scanning online auction sites such as eBay and Yahoo. The BE site contained information on more than five million items that were being auctioned off at 100 auction sites. Approximately 70% of the auction items in the BE database were from eBay auctions. This company also relied on a spider that traversed the Web to categorize and index pages of auction websites tracked by BE.

Both companies had tried to enter a licensing agreement, but this proved to be impossible. BE began to spider the eBay site anyway even though that site used "robot exclusion headers" to inform searching robots that its site does not permit unauthorized robotic activity. BE, however, ignored this robot exclusion message and continued to search through eBay's site without permission. eBay officials told BE to cease its robotic operations; the company still refused, and eBay filed suit claiming that the auction aggregator was liable for trespass.

According to court documents, BE accessed the eBay site about 100,000 times each day in order to keep its system current, and "eBay alleges that BE activity constituted up to 1.53% of the number of requests received by eBay, and up to 1.10% of the total data transferred by eBay ... " (*eBay v. Bidder's Edge*, 2000). The eBay law suit requested preliminary injunctive relief preventing BE from accessing the eBay system.

In May 2000 the district court issued the preliminary injunction sought by eBay. As a result, BE was banned from using its software robots to scan eBay's site without permission. The court concluded that BE had engaged in "trespass to chattels," that is, an unauthorized interference with another's personal property that causes some harm. The court accepted eBay's argument that failure to grant the injunction would be a green light for other aggregators to follow suit: "If BE's activity is allowed to continue unchecked, it would encourage other auction aggregators in similar recursive searching of the eBay system such that eBay would suffer irreparable harm from reduced system performance, system unavailability, or data losses" (*eBay v. Bidder's Edge*, 2000).

Although the outcomes in these cases are different, they all appear to orchestrate the same theme: total control over the terms of access and the unfettered power to exclude are critical objectives for many organizations, even if that control yields adverse effects on the openness of the Net's information environment.

SOVEREIGNTY OF INTELLECTUAL PROPERTY RIGHTS

Before considering the moral issues at stake in these disputes over trespass, it is also worth reviewing the matter of property rights in more depth. To begin with, a distinction should be made between the logical website and the physical server on which that website resides. Not everyone agrees that the website itself is really a form of property. Some might argue that the eBay website should be regarded as a commons with complete open access to its auction listings. Commercial websites, however, cannot be simply reduced to common property. If this paradigm became predominant, investment incentives would surely be undermined. In addition, there is certainly an analogous relationship between real property and the virtual property of a website. This analogy is reinforced by our use of language that assigns an "address" to each website. At the center of one's bundle of property rights is the right to exclude, and therefore the owner of real property has the legal prerogative to exclude intruders from his land. According to O'Rourke (2001), "[b]y analogy, website owners should have the right to exclude others under a trespass cause of action ... ." This analysis would imply a right to establish unambiguous borders and to exclude the intrusive activities of spiders, shop bots, and maybe even spammers. We have maintained that from a normative perspective a website should be classified as a type of intellectual property, entitled to some degree of protection (Spinello, 2000). Unlike physical property, however, this is an admittedly imperfect entitlement, as evidenced by some of the asymmetries between this form of intangible property and physical property. For example, a spider's access to a website is plainly different from a situation where an individual encroaches upon another's land. If a website complies with the request for a web page, it can be interpreted as implied consent to let the visitor traverse the website even if that visitor is a spider. As O'Rourke (2001) points out, by allowing the visitor "in," the only "actionable trespass that could occur would be if the visitor goes beyond its authorized access once on the site." In the Ticketmaster case, the court was unconvinced by the claim of virtual trespass to the actual Ticketmaster website.

The trespass cases we have cited, however, have for the most part focused on the physical server rather than the logical website. In order to substantiate the allegation of trespass to chattels, the complainant must demonstrate "intermeddling" with his or her property. Intermeddling occurs when there is "physical contact with the chattel [that is] harmful to the possessor's materially valuable interest in the physical condition, quality, or value of the chattel" or deprives the chattel owner "use of the chattel for a substantial time" (Restatement, 1965). The claim is advanced that the owner of the server, such as eBay, while not dispossessed of property in any way is nonetheless deprived of the server's full use and capacity due to the non-permissive activity of the spider. In their lawsuits, Intel, Ticketmaster, and eBay alleged impairment of their property due to unwanted e-mail or officious spiders.

Legal scholars are rightly skeptical of these claims, and various analyses have underscored flaws in the legal reasoning behind the decisions in the eBay and Intel cases. The claim of harm is suspect. Should courts now regard an increased server load as "injury of some sort"? How could one really argue that Hamidi's periodic e-mail or BE's spider resulted in real impairment to the physical servers of Intel or eBay? According to one analysis, isn't the spider merely engaged in "the relatively passive, unobtrusive act of receiving and recording information already present in the communication milieu?" (O'Rourke, 2001). A second problem arises from eBay's claim that the use of information by this spider was "unauthorized." Does eBay have the unqualified right to determine how information it has effectively made public will be used by those who visit its website? As Elkin-Koren (2001) observes, "The novelty of the eBay rule is in granting site owners the legal right to determine the terms of access to publicly available information."

Our purpose here, however, is not to analyze the nuances of the legal reasoning behind these decisions or to quibble with the legal outcomes. Rather, we intend to disengage the ethical issues in these cases and dwell on the morally proper course of action for companies facing unwanted web activity such as spiders, shopbots, deep linkers, or potential spammers.

While the companies like Ticketmaster are too quick to seize upon the legal claim of "trespass" to prevent unwelcome activity, it would be ludicrous to argue that all unwelcome activity should be permissible. There are clearly harmful activities, such as computer viruses, that should never be permitted or legally sanctioned. Excessive spamming that materially debilitated a server's performance would also be problematic. Even if we were to dismiss the claims of injury in the cases cited here, it would appear that under certain conditions, a website owner could have a legitimate complaint of impairment and trespass; for example, Ticketmaster's concerns about the deleterious effects of robots on their systems could prove be quite valid and understandable.

The problem then is twofold. First, websites such as eBay and Ticketmaster are too presumptuous and hasty in advancing their claims of trespass, labeling almost any unwanted activity as "trespass to chattels." So far, the courts are sympathetic to their claims. However, while these companies seem to be on relatively firm legal ground (at least for the present time), what can be said about the moral propriety of their conduct? Should eBay, Ticketmaster, or Intel strive to be more open to spiders, automated query programs, and e-mailers propagating unpopular messages? On what moral basis could this claim be advanced? Second, we also lack a clear criterion for when the trespass cause of action should have validity; not all unwanted activity is benign or socially constructive. Is it possible that sound moral analysis can help companies to make proper distinctions about which unauthorized activities they should accept? We turn now to a formal discussion of moral theory with the hope that it will provide some assistance in resolving these two questions.

TRESPASS AND THE COMMON GOOD

There are several salient moral issues that clearly emerge in the trespass debate. One could envisage these disputes as classic cases of conflicting rights; for example, Hamidi's free speech rights versus Intel's property rights. But debates about which right takes priority often lead to an intellectual and moral impasse. Indeed, reliance exclusively on a traditional rights-based approach may not be helpful for navigating these issues, since what gets lost is any sense of obligation to the Internet as a cooperative venture. Preoccupation with individual property rights often obscures the obligation one has to support the digital commons that enabled those rights to come into being in the first place. Intel, Ticketmaster, and eBay are vigorous defenders of their property rights, but none of these companies seem even remotely cognizant of any duty to support the common values or general welfare of the Internet. For example, in its public statements about the BE lawsuit, eBay consistently underscored the prerogative for companies "to proceed without fear of unwanted trespassers that will steal or profit from the fruits of their labor" (Wong, 2001). There is no apprehension that if some of these "unwanted trespassers" are providing a public service at little cost to eBay, then their "incursion" should at least be tolerated for the sake of a larger purpose. In short, what is lacking is a clear sense that for this common venture to succeed, for the Internet to achieve its full social and commercial potential, certain qualities such as self-sacrifice and a commitment to openness are indispensable.

The need for cooperation and the need to make sacrifices or adjustments for the sake of a higher good is recognized more explicitly in the Eastern cultural tradition where the welfare of the common project or the community is more often given priority over individual rights. The Japanese tradition crystallizes this obligation in the concept of *kyosei,* which emphasizes harmony and the social whole. The notion of *kyosei*, proposed as a unifying ethical concept by Japanese business leaders such as Mr. Kaku, the Chairman of Canon, Inc., is represented by two Kanji characters: *kyo* (working together) and *sei* (life) (Goodpaster, 1996). *Kyosei* incorporates the values of social well-being, justice, and community, with an emphasis on the need for "social cohesion," which sometimes requires "tempering the assertion of narrower entitlements" (Goodpaster, 1996).

In this case, the social whole or common venture could be construed as the Internet (including the World Wide Web), where innovation and stability is advanced by a cooperative ethos and a contribution of diverse efforts. This affirmation of the common good or social whole that we tend to find in Eastern thought complements more rights-oriented Western theories that have been "inattentive to larger duties of loyalty to a whole community" (Goodpaster, 1996). Attentiveness to *kyosei* compels us to recognize that the Internet is a social whole with its own value structure and that the common good of the

Internet can be articulated in terms of information sharing and interconnectivity. For example, the more sites openly available and interconnected, the more valuable the whole Web becomes.

The import of *kyosei* seems clear enough: the starting point of moral reflection becomes an affirmation of the common good or social whole with a recognition that the individual participants ultimately benefit through that affirmation. The problem is that many website owners or e-commerce companies are so preoccupied with their property rights that they do not take into account the interests of the larger community or the Net's common good, despite the fact that they derive enormous benefits from this social whole. But the integrity and advancement of the whole cannot exist without the contributions and sacrifices of its participants. Sometimes those sacrifices may come about through the assumption of externalities, such as allowing for unwanted linkages or permitting the entry of visiting robots.

The Western philosophical tradition is certainly not oblivious to the notion of the common good, though it sometimes gets confused with social welfare. The common good as traditionally understood is quite different from the utilitarian conception of aggregate social welfare or total utility. Quite simply, the common good refers to the shared values of a collective or a community.

There is ample discussion of this notion in the works of Aristotle and Aquinas. According to Aristotle (1941), laws and moral norms "make pronouncements on every sphere of life, and their aim is to secure the common good of all [either directly or indirectly]." Central to Aristotelian ethics is *phronesis* (prudence or practical wisdom). Those who have acquired this virtue are able to make deductions from general moral principles with a sensitive discernment of the particular factors in a given situation. But, in Aristotle's view, one could not be endowed with *phronesis* if one were egocentric and did not have a sense of measure regarding the public matters (or common values) of the City.

For Aquinas, the ultimate common good is the "common end of the whole of human life," that is, our fulfillment as human beings which is accomplished with the help of *prudentia,* that virtue that brings rational order into human affairs. But Aquinas also argued that this general common good takes on a more limited and practical reference to communities such as the state, a church, an organization, and so forth (Finnis, 1998). The political common good of the state, for example, consists of values such as justice and peace. One can also identify a limited common good for a household or a family, with its own form of prudence, i.e., domestic practical reasonableness. And, by extension, one can deduce that there is a common good associated with a community that comes into being as a social and economic venture such as the Internet, since it too is a cooperative action for some purpose. That common good is also realized through its own special version of *prudentia* that becomes manifest when we look at the Internet's end or telos. But what is the purpose (or telos) of the Internet and what type of prudence, i.e., good judgment attentive to the community's common values, is required of its participants? At the simplest level, the Internet exists for the sake of sharing and disseminating information. All those who use the Internet do so in order to disseminate or access information. Moreover, as McFarland (2004) points out, the purpose of information itself is to be shared and communicated. Thus, the common good of the Internet can be understood once we appreciate the social nature of information: the more widely information is shared and disseminated, the more value and worth it assumes. At a secondary level, the social nature of information implies that information also assumes greater value when it is recombined, linked, or aggregated with other forms of information. The Internet has many mechanisms that make this possible — hyperlinks, data aggregator programs, search engines, and so on. Thus, the more information that is accessible, hyperlinked, comparable, searchable, and indexed, the more valuable the whole Net becomes. Furthermore, open resources that allow for recombination stimulate innovation. As Nelson and Winter (1982) write:

"[I]nnovation in the economic system — and indeed the creation of any sort of novelty in art, science, or practical life — consists to a substantial extent of a recombination of conceptual and physical materials ... "

Two decisive moral considerations seem to emerge in this analysis. First, it can be persuasively argued that an exclusive focus on one's narrow entitlements (i.e., the right to exclude) should not thwart the furtherance of the Net's common good without adequate justification, such as the presence of some non-negligible impairment of resources or property rights. Second, morality is about justice and justice requires respect for the good of the commons (the city, family, or the Internet), not just the good of the individual. The just person has a "moral bond with the community whose fate is at stake" (Sandel, 1984). In this case, distributive justice considerations are also relevant. The tight restrictions on the use of information manifested by eBay and Ticketmaster results in an unfair distribution of the benefits and burdens among Internet users; these companies receive ample benefits from the Internet's open architecture but refuse to make even the smallest sacrifices to preserve this open environment, where information is easily accessible, in order to further the Net's natural purpose. It is unjust and egocentric to forego contributions or sacrifices that sustain the larger whole and foster the common good when one receives benefits from that whole unless there is a morally convincing reason for doing so. Lessig (2001) makes a similar point about cable networks using the Internet, but the principle he advocates could be applied to other major commercial enterprises operating in cyberspace and taking advantage of that technology's broad reach to the general public. If those companies "want to piggyback on the Internet's success [they] should piggyback with the values of the Internet kept in mind."

In summary, then, we conclude that in order to promote justice and avoid harmful impediments to the Internet's true purpose, Internet users have a prima facie obligation to support and foster the common good of the Internet in proportion to their use of its resources and the tangible benefits derived therefrom. Therefore, e-commerce sites such as eBay and Ticketmaster, which have thriving businesses thanks to the Internet's open protocols and global reach, obviously owe more to the Internet than ordinary Web users. Moreover, we can discern whether or not that moral duty is fulfilled by scrutinizing a company's patterns of cooperative behavior. Welcoming hyperlinks and aggregators, making one's website open and accessible in appropriate ways are all positive patterns of cooperation. On the other hand, obstructive activities that block e-mail or spiders build arbitrary borders and fences and represent negative patterns of cooperation that undermine the common venture of the Web. We recognize, of course, that while the Internet is a publicly accessible medium, it also has closed areas. Some organizations have password-protected websites and do not share information with unauthorized users. These websites cater to a small audience and do not take advantage of the Net's full potential to disseminate their information to a wider audience. Hence any theory about obligations to the common good must make a provision for organizations that operate with these restrictions. However, most companies, such as those engaged in e-commerce along with the ones in our case studies, host and share information quite freely. Our position is that these companies that benefit from the Web's openness and free flow of information should contribute to that openness and not enclose publicly available information when it doesn't suit their narrow competitive interests.

RIGHTS VS. DUTIES

This recognition of the social whole's primacy does not imply that individual property rights are irrelevant or that Internet users have a carte blanche prerogative to do whatever they like on a particular website. Nor does it imply that websites like eBay should be forced to liquidate their intellectual property rights for the sake of spiders and crawlers. The prima facie duty to support the common good is constrained by the reasonable exercise of intellectual property rights. As we have implied, one can envision situations where a robot or spam does cause harm, and in these situations we cannot expect companies to allow these intrusions, even if they appear to be in the public interest. In the long run, harmful activities that prevent companies from extracting value from their work will be counterproductive for the furtherance of the Net's common good. But how do we determine when activities such as the use of a shopping bot or hyperlinking are really harmful and counterproductive? We contend that overall the metaphor of trespass is not helpful. Rather, trespass should be reinterpreted as "nuisance to website" (Burk, 2000) or *appreciable injury* to website, i.e., non-negligible injury that is the direct result of heavy spamming, excessive spidering, hacking activities, or some other intrusion.

The moral challenge is to determine when extrinsic, unauthorized activities such as linking, incoming e-mail messages (spam), the use of robots, etc., constitute imprudent free riding or cause appreciable harm to a site. When does an external activity that enhances some degree of interconnectivity become a serious nuisance and source of injury and thereby warrant the intervention of the courts? How do we distinguish fair-minded actions that further the common good from free riding?

There is no formula or simple set of rules that can dictate when one must sacrifice the assertion of property rights, that is, the right to exclude others, for the sake of the common good. Rather, in Aristotle's (1941) terms, companies must learn to act "according to right reason" (*kata ton orthon logon*) by striking a prudential balance between asserting their proprietary rights (when necessary) and tolerating unwelcome activity that benefits the common good of the Web, when that activity does not yield sufficient harm. We contend therefore that the ideal answer to this problem of trespass does not lie in reinterpreting old statutes (such as trespass to chattels) or in other defensive actions pursued in the legal forum. Rather, the key to resolving this problem equitably is the responsible use of moral judgment (or *prudentia*) that constantly seeks a harmony between individual rights and an affirmative duty to support the collective good. The good citizen of cyberspace is law-abiding, but also has a habit of sound independent moral judgment and does not turn to the law frivolously.

While there is no substitute for moral judgment and prudence and no facile formulae to resolve these matters of alleged trespass, it is still possible to offer some guidance, that is, an overview of the relevant criteria to be considered when making these moral judgments. These general questions can assist the prudent manager in identifying unwanted activity that causes appreciable or durable harm:

- **Materiality:** what is the magnitude of the non-permissive, allegedly disruptive activity? For example, what proportion of computer resources is a spider or bot consuming? How materially harmful is the activity?
- **Reputational damage:** do the unauthorized activities cause any intangible harm? For example, while a data aggregator's spider may not cause tangible harm, information extracted from a website could be misrepresented, and this could adversely impact an organization's reputation.
- **Proportionality:** to what extent do the social or public benefits resulting from the unwanted activities outweigh the private harm or inconvenience to the website?
- **Commercialism:** if the "unwanted" activity is a form of speech, is that speech commercial or non-commercial? In general, *ceteris paribus*, there should be more latitude for forms of non-commercial speech that further the public interest.
- **Market effects:** do the activities have negative, material market effects such as direct loss of revenues or higher costs that directly inhibit the company's value-creating process? How substantial are those effects?
- **Probability of imitation:** is it likely that others will copy or follow the intrusive activity, creating a dangerous or uncontrollable precedent, resulting in substantial future harm if the initial activity is not abruptly terminated?

These and other relevant factors should be carefully weighed together and decisions made on a case-by-case basis. By following these general criteria and their good common sense, companies can formulate an appropriate moral judgment about unauthorized activities.

For example, in the Hamidi situation a strong case can be presented that Hamidi's speech, though unwelcome by Intel, should not be considered as a nuisance or source of injury for several reasons: five or six messages dispersed over two years is not enough to be disruptive; there is benefit to society from hearing this speech that is non-commercial in nature; the benefits of promoting free speech of some public interest appear to outweigh any inconvenience to Intel. Had Mr. Hamidi been e-mailing Intel employees on a daily basis or had the messages been of a commercial nature, one might conclude differently.

APPLICATION TO THE eBAY CASE

Unlike the Hamidi case, the dispute between eBay and Bidder's Edge (BE) has certain complexities that make it an ideal case study for applying the approach proposed in this chapter. As we have discussed, those at eBay saw this confrontation purely in terms of "property rights," that is, the violation of those rights by an intrusive spider and their subsequent defense of those rights through legal action. Critics of eBay, however, have argued that the company "seems to want it both ways by combining the high traffic of an open public website with the exclusivity of a private site" (Kehoe, 2000). It is difficult to see how BE's singular activity is preventing eBay from realizing the "fruits of its labor." Thus, on a purely intuitive level, it is easy to appreciate why there is so much sympathy for the plight of BE.

If we apply the criteria above in an effort to come to a more nuanced moral judgment, I submit that it is hard not to arrive at the same conclusion. Since eBay is an open (vs. closed) website, it should be held to the highest standard for information sharing. Arguably, the magnitude of the intrusive activity does not cause real harm to the eBay site or to its servers. Recall eBay's argument that BE was infringing upon its property rights by consuming bandwidth and capacity against its wishes. This argument is unpersuasive, however, since the BE spider was consuming only 1.5% of eBay's resources. While this is not negligible, eBay would have to make a case in good faith that this consumption level represented an onerous load on its system and therefore caused impairment to that system. Further, there are significant public benefits that can potentially result from BE's work as an aggregator. Consumers benefit from having metasites, like this one that displays comparative information about auction sites. It reduces their search costs and increases their choices. According to Baker (2000), companies like BE help to realize the Internet's capacity for "conducting faster and more efficient searches of information accessible to all." Since eBay is the dominant auction site and 70% of BE's listings were from eBay auctions, it is apparent that eBay would be unlikely to suffer any appreciable revenue losses at the hands of BE's aggregated information. In fact, Bidder's Edge might even benefit eBay by referring traffic to the sellers on its site.

Finally, what is the likelihood that other aggregators would mimic Bidder's Edge? The court was particularly worried that if injunctive relief were withheld, other companies would begin crawling the BE site, thereby causing serious impairment. But is this hypothetical scenario a realistic possibility? If so, there might be good reasons to thwart the BE spider in order to prevent this snowball effect. It seems unlikely, however, that there will be a great rush to enter the auction data aggregation business. To be sure, there may be other spiders that will crawl the eBay site without an injunction, but the fundamentals of Internet economics suggest that spiders will not overwhelm the eBay website. Aggregators make money through advertising, and advertising revenue will only support a small number of these auction metasites. According to O'Rourke (2000), "Chances are high that the number of indexing sites that could attract enough money to remain in business is less than the number that would materially adversely affect system performance." In all likelihood, then, any predictions of substantial future harm are unlikely to be realized in this particular situation.

Thus, when all of these factors are weighed together — the small resources consumed by the BE spider, negligible (and possibly positive) market effects, the public interest in having access to aggregated meta data, and the low probability that BE's business model would be mimicked by others — the only reasonable and measured conclusion is that eBay has an obligation to allow this activity for the sake of the Net's common good.

ECONOMIC EFFICIENCY AND POLICY CONSIDERATIONS

This solution to trespass that we have proposed can be characterized as ethical self-regulation, which also has the advantage of promoting social and economic efficiency. When organizations like eBay fall back on the legal system to solve the problem of unwanted spiders, the direct costs are obvious (for example, legal fees, administering the court system, etc.). But there are also less obvious indirect costs, since legal activities usually breed distrust and an adversarial attitude that can infect the cooperative ethos of the Net. On the other hand, if companies like Ticketmaster more freely allowed spiders and web crawlers, unless there is real demonstrable harm, fewer of society's resources would be consumed in trying to deter such activities. When companies resolve problems through normative decision making, there are no transaction costs, and hence there is an enhancement of natural economic efficiency. A frequent resorting to traditional legal mechanisms without adequate cause fails to advance the goal of maximizing total surplus, since, as Stone (1975) observes, "at some point the costs of enforcing the law are going to transcend the benefits."

Even if there is some degree of harm such as a burden on a company's servers, the preferred course of action for a legitimate trespass claim is not to seek immediate injunctive relief or other remedies through the courts. Following the Coase theorem, when there are social costs or externalities in the marketplace whereby one company's actions cause harm to another company, the optimal solution is for both parties to negotiate a mutually agreeable arrangement. As we have written elsewhere: "The Coase theorem argues that in the absence of transaction costs (the costs of coordinating and bringing together the affected parties, negotiating contracts, etc.) the preferred solution to externalities when rights are properly assigned is to allow the relevant parties to negotiate a private arrangement" (Spinello, 2002).

Coase assumed that the privatization of these settlements regarding negative externality disputes depended on the proper assignment of property rights. Saba (2002) argues that this is one reason why policymakers should clarify the scope of website property rights: "If legal rules, such as Internet trespass, are sculpted to grant property rights in websites, the cyberspace market can reach efficiency, assuming low transaction costs." He also asserts the need for legislation preventing the "pirating of existing online databases." In his view, this could make it easier for companies to work out their own solutions to "trespass" in the manner proposed by Coase. However, as Burk (2000) points out, unclear property entitlements might actually facilitate the bargaining process, whereas "bright line rules appropriate to low transaction cost situations may simply lock the parties into their respective ownership positions, unable to reach a beneficial exchange." He cites the theoretical work of Merrill (1985) and others to substantiate this claim. Thus, in this context, where property entitlements are murky, private resolutions that optimize social welfare might be a more realistic possibility.

But even if theories about unclear property rules are flawed, the main thesis of this chapter remains intact. If both parties negotiate in good faith and take their moral responsibilities seriously enough, it should be possible to solve trespass disputes without costly legal intervention or the need for new regulations.

CONCLUSIONS

Trespass disputes are becoming commonplace in cyberspace as companies like eBay and Ticketmaster seek to restrict any unauthorized use of their data. Many companies are responding by asserting their property rights to deter these alleged trespassers. We have argued here, however, that the rhetoric of "rights" will not clarify the issues at stake in these contentious trespass disputes. What is missing is a corresponding concern for the common good of the Internet. We must regard the Internet as the organization's analogue, that is, as a mutually beneficial scheme of cooperation requiring the contribution and reasonable sacrifices of the many participants who enjoy those benefits. The more benefits one receives, the greater the obligation to make some sacrifices for the good of this common venture. The moral obligation to the common good is expressed in the notion of *kyosei* in the Japanese tradition. Philosophers like Aristotle and Aquinas have also underscored this obligation in their discourses on morality. One discerns the common good or common values of the Internet by focusing on its purpose, "the free flow of information." Companies have no right to undermine this value, that is, to thwart the free flow of information for an insufficient reason.

In keeping with these traditions we argue that there is a prima facie moral obligation to foster the common good of the Internet. This obligation, of course, must be constrained by intellectual property rights in a website (however incomplete those rights are), since no organization should be forced to welcome devious or burdensome activities that cause harm or impair valuable property. Rather than rush to court at the first sign of a spider, however, companies should engage in a conscientious process of moral judgment in order to achieve this precarious balance. In Aristotelian terms, they must act with prudence or "according to right reason."

The formidable challenge is to differentiate between egregious free riding that does not generate socially beneficial results or imposes too high a burden on website property rights and non-harmful, legitimate activities that enhance the free flow of information. We have proffered certain criteria to help in this process. While these criteria obviously cannot function as an exact formula providing answers with scientific certainty, they can offer general parameters with broad applicability. The Internet will have a better chance to fulfill its full promise and potential as an "innovation commons" (Lessig, 2001) once businesses get beyond their preoccupation with individual property rights and their myopia about the common good and begin to recognize the need for sustained levels of cooperation in building the future of cyberspace.

REFERENCES

Aristotle (1941). *Nicomachean ethics* (R. McKeon, ed.). New York: Random House.

Baker, D. (2000). Bid for fair practice: Online auctioneer gains business from link site but doesn't want e-shoppers using the back door. *A.B.A. Journal,* April, 22.

Burk, D. (2000). The trouble with trespass. *Journal of Small and Emerging Business Law,* 4, 27.

eBay, *Inc. v. Bidder's Edge, Inc.* (2000). 100 F. Supp. 2d 1058 [N.D. Cal.].

Elkin-Koren, N. (2001). Let the crawlers crawl: On virtual gatekeepers and the right to exclude indexing. *Dayton Law Review,* 26, 179.

Finnis, J. (1998). *Aquinas.* Oxford, UK: Oxford University Press.

Goodpaster, K. (1996). Bridging east and west in management ethics: Kyosei and the moral point of view. *Journal of Human Values,* 2, 529.

Intel Corp. v. Hamidi (1999). No. 98A505067 [Cal Super Ct].

Kehoe, L. (2000). Fair use policy for web content needed: Court ruling impacts on automated crawlers. *National Post*, May 31.

Lessig, L. (2001). *The future of ideas.* New York: Random House.

McFarland, M. (2004). Intellectual property, information, and the common good. In R.A. Spinello & H. Tavani (Eds.), *Readings in cyberethics (2nd ed.)*, pp. 294-304. Sudbury, MA: Jones and Bartlett.

Merrill, T. (1985). Trespass, nuisance, and the costs of determining property rights. *Journal of Legal Studies*, 14, 13.

Nelson, R. & Winter, S. (1982). *An evolutionary theory of economic change.* Cambridge, MA: Harvard University Press.

O'Rourke, M. (2000). Shaping competition on the Internet: Who owns product and pricing information? *Vanderbilt Law Review,* 53, 1965.

O'Rourke, M. (2001). Property rights and competition on the Internet: In search of an appropriate analogy. *Berkeley Technology Law Journal*, 16, 561.

Restatement (Second) of Torts (1965), 217.

Rosenfeld, J. (2002). Spiders and crawlers and bots, oh my: The economic efficiency and public policy of online contracts that restrict data collection. *Stanford Technology Law Review,* 28, 112.

Saba, J. (2002). Internet property rights: E-trespass. *St. Mary's Law Journal,* 33, 367.

Sandel, M. (1984). *Liberalism and its critics.* New York: New York University Press.

Spinello, R. (2000). An ethical evaluation of website linking. *Computers & Society,* December, 25-32.

Spinello, R. (2002). *Regulating cyberspace: The policies and technologies of control.* Westport, CT: Quorum Books.

Stone, C. (1975). *Where the law ends: The social control of corporate behavior.* New York: Harper & Row.

Thrifty-Tel v. Beznik (1996). 46 Cal. App. 4th 1559.

Ticketmaster's First Amended Complaint (2000). *Tickemaster Corp. v. Tickets.com, Inc.,* CV99-7654-HLH U.S. Dist.

Wong, M. (2001). eBay, Bidder's Edge end lawsuit. Retrieved online at: http://the.honoluluadvertiser.com/2001/Mar/03/business18.html (quoting eBay spokesperson Kevin Pursglove).

Chapter IX

New Threats to Intellectual Freedom:
The Loss of the Information Commons through Law and Technology in the US

Elizabeth Buchanan
University of Wisconsin-Milwaukee, USA

James Campbell
Modular Media, USA

ABSTRACT

This chapter explores the growing threats to intellectual freedom through the loss of the information commons in the U.S. as a direct result of advances and changes in technology and laws. In particular, the Digital Millennium Copyright Act and the Sonny Bono Copyright Extension Act are considered, as is the 2003 Federal Communications Commission ruling on media consolidation. When these laws are combined with current technological developments, intellectual freedom faces serious threats. As a foundation in a democratic society, consumers should take heed of this growing erosion of rights and access to information.

INTRODUCTION

In the United States' recent war in Iraq, while soldiers guarded oil wells and the records stored in Iraq's Oil Ministry building, looters, unimpeded by occupying forces, pillaged the National Museum in Baghdad, and an important part of the precious shared heritage of both Western and Islamic civilizations disappeared right before the world's eyes. Some of that heritage will probably be recovered. But some of it will go to the highest bidders on the black market, or fall into the hands of private "owners" and be lost to the public for years, decades, lifetimes.

When news slowly trickled in through the media to American shores of the looting, many American citizens, along with the rest of the world, were horrified at the loss and at its implications for our shared heritage and understanding of civilization and culture. It was a great tragedy with grave consequences that will affect this generation and many generations to come.

Back in the U.S., there is another tragedy occurring daily, one that threatens our shared memory and understanding of ourselves as a society, that threatens our future creativity as a culture, that challenges traditional ethical ideals of a common good, and that threatens the intellectual freedom that is the foundation of America's progress over the past three centuries.

The tragedy is, in Harlan Onsrud's (1998) words, "The Tragedy of the Information Commons." Onsrud's extension of the "The Tragedy of the Commons,"(Hardin, 1968) brings to recognition a serious loss: the tragedy, in a remarkable parallel to the enclosure of the physical commons in England during the 1700s and early 1800s, is that the information commons in America is being "enclosed" or even destroyed by a combination of law and technology that is privatizing what has been public and what may become public, and locking up and restricting access to ideas and information that have heretofore been shared resources. Notably, the notion of the information or intellectual commons, as Drahos (1996, p. 54, emphasis added) calls it, is "that part of the objective world of knowledge *which is not subject to any of the following*: property rights or some other conventional bar…; technological bars…, or a physical bar…." It took over 4,000 acts of Parliament to enclose the physical commons in England (Bollier, 1999). A half-dozen American laws and new digital technology — two of the three types of bars referred to by Drahos — are doing the job as well or better in the information society of 21st century America.

The implications for the theory and exercise of intellectual freedom are enormous, as we shall explore. The assumption underlying a democratically organized society is that citizens will exercise intellectual freedom through unfettered access to the information and ideas they need to make sound judgments about governance and the common good—being fully informed and free is necessary for effective decision making. That is one reason that the First Amendment to the U.S. Constitution guarantees freedom of speech and of the press. And, beyond participation in governance, access to information and new ideas is the engine that enables a society to prosper and grow. Thus, in Article I, Section 8, of the U.S. Constitution, the Founders charged the Congress to "Promote the Progress of Science and Useful Arts, by securing for limited Times to Authors and Inventors the exclusive Right to their respective Writings and Discoveries." The Founders' reasoning was straightforward: enable authors and inventors to benefit from their works and they will have incentive to produce more "Writings and Discoveries." The understanding was that after "limited Times," the use of those works would become available for general use by the body politic, which use would inspire more writing and invention, and subsequently, more progress. Intellectual freedom is therefore a very practical and necessary component of a democratic society, as well as an integral part of "Life, Liberty, and the pursuit of Happiness."

If we adopt the definition of intellectual freedom as the American Library Association (2003) articulates it:

Intellectual Freedom is the right of every individual to both seek and receive information from all points of view without restriction. It provides for free access to all expressions of ideas through which any and all sides of a question, cause or movement may be explored. Intellectual freedom encompasses the freedom to hold, receive and disseminate ideas.

We can easily see how this very important principle of information provision and stewardship is being threatened by the enclosure or destruction of the information commons, by the erosion of traditional rights under copyright law, and by the consolidation of ownership in the scholarly and mass media.

WHAT'S HAPPENING TO INTELLECTUAL FREEDOM?

As the above definition suggests, the exercise of intellectual freedom is seriously impaired without the ability to "receive information from all points of view without restriction." It is precisely this ability that is endangered by the enclosure or "killing" of the existing information commons; by limitations upon what will be added to the commons, and when it can be added; and by the restriction of traditional rights to the limited use of protected information even before it becomes part of the commons as a whole.

At stake are the ability of public libraries to offer universal access to information; consumers to have competitive access to diverse sources of content, including non-commercial content; citizens to have free or cheap access to the government information that their tax dollars have financed; and students to perform research and collaborate online with each other. At stake are the ability of musicians and other artists to pioneer new forms of online creativity; creators in all media to freely quote and use a robust public domain of prior works; computer users to benefit from the innovations of competitive markets; and individuals to control how intimate personal information will be used (Bollier, 1999).

These are some of the basic issues that are now being shaped by a variety of new technology designs, market practices, court rulings, and intellectual property laws. A wide array of stakeholders — common citizens and the communal history to which they contribute and in which they participate — stand to lose considerably.

CHANGING NATURE OF INFORMATION COMMONS IN THE DIGITAL AGE
Definition of the Information Commons

The term "information commons" emerges from the tradition of the physical commons, a tradition handed down through hundreds of years of English history. In physical space, the commons was a resource, usually land, that was not owned by anyone privately but was cared for and used by the community as a whole. Any improvement in drainage in a common field, for example, benefited all who used the field for grazing livestock. Any discussions about how the field would be best used and maintained was a common discussion engaged in by all stakeholders. Even though wealthy landowners were able to pressure Parliament to reduce the amount of land held in common and to get it transferred to private hands in the 1700s and early 1800s, the principle of the commons never died completely, either in England or in the U.S. To this day, walkers have the right to cross privately owned fields in England as long as they "close the gate behind them," and many a small town in New England and elsewhere still has a town common today.

In the past, discussions of commonly held rights of access to information have usually referred to the "public domain." Bollier (1999) argues that this term is too narrow and too filled with specific legal baggage to be helpful, and argues forcefully for use of the broader term "information commons."

We propose the following as a simple working definition of the information commons: "A body of knowledge and information that is available to anyone to use without the need to ask for or receive prior permission from another, providing any conditions placed on its use are respected."

In addition to the material that is part of the information commons itself, there are also laws and traditions that make access to current, "protected" information and ideas available in a more limited way. Together, the information commons and the materials available through "fair use" provisions of copyright law (see below) have provided the basis for access to ideas that is the foundation of intellectual freedom.

U.S. Copyright and Intellectual Freedom

In the United States, copyright law deals with protecting the "tangible expression" of ideas, and patent law deals with protecting physical processes and inventions. This discussion focuses, for the most part, on the tangible expression of ideas and only occasionally on subjects that fall under patent protection. It is interesting to note, however, that the duration of patent protection extends for a period of 20 years. This conforms to most common-sense meanings of the term "limited," the term specifically used in the Constitution. Copyright protection, however, now extends to the author's life plus 70 years or, in the case of "works made for hire," 125 years from creation or 95 years from publication, whichever is shorter. This extended period contrasts rather sharply with Congress' original grant of copyright for a period of 14 years.

Many do not find this period of time (which was extended to its present length in 1997) to qualify as "limited" in any sense that the Founders intended. However, in *Eldred v. Ashcroft* (2003), the Supreme Court ruled in a 7-2 vote that even though the new extensions to copyright enacted by Congress might not conform to some definitions of the term "limited," the Constitution clearly granted Congress the right to decide what was "limited." In his notable dissent in *Eldred*, Justice Breyer refers to the extension as "virtually perpetual" and the "extended term" will fall not to authors, but to "their heirs, estates, or corporate successors."

A major dilemma with this decision, and the law that it was interpreting (the Sonny Bono Copyright Extension Act), is that protecting a work for 70 years after the author's death is certainly not going to inspire that author to produce any additional works during those 70 years, and thus will not have the effect of fostering "Progress of Science and Useful Arts." In the eyes of Onsrud (1998), Bollier (1999), and many others, including associations such as the American Library Association and the Association of American Archivists, it will have just the opposite effect since there will be severe limits on the use of materials produced in the past as a part of catalyst for new output. Too, Justice Breyer acknowledged that this progress of "Science" — "by which the Framers meant learning or knowledge," would in fact be *inhibited, not promoted* (*Eldred v. Ashcroft*, 2003). As John Perry Barlow (2001), songwriter for the Grateful Dead, has pointed out, there is no such thing as a completely new song. Anything that anyone writes today draws on a thousand songs that went before. Now, however, many songs and other works that would have become part of the information commons (which, in this context, also becomes the "inspiration commons"), and therefore freely available to become a component of or stimulus for something new, are now "enclosed" for another 20 years. No copyrighted material produced in the U.S. since 1923 will enter the information commons until at least 2017. Or, put more directly, consider that "For the first time in our history, no new works will enter the public domain for a full 20 years!" (Karjala, 2003).

While copyright protection is in effect, U.S. copyright law (17 U.S.C § 107) grants copyright owners four exclusive rights:

- To reproduce the work;
- To distribute the work;
- To prepare derivative works; and
- To display and/or perform the work publicly.

Against these rights, the law grants some limitations on the exclusive rights of copyright holders that are usually referred to as "fair use." Fair use does not infringe on copyright. Acceptable fair uses include, for example, quoting small sections of a work in a review or critical discussion, making an individual copy of sections of a work for research or educational use, and so on. There is also one other extremely important aspect of the legal use of copyrighted materials; i.e., a copyright owner may not control the use of a copy of his or her work once that copy has been sold to another. This is known as the "first sale" doctrine, established by the Court in 1908 (210 U.S. C § 339), and it is what makes libraries, video rental stores, and even personal lending or gift-giving possible.

These two concepts, fair use and first sale, have balanced user rights and owner rights in the U.S. system of copyright for decades, or more precisely, balanced private and public rights. They have also been the bedrock upon which intellectual freedom has been built — the freedom to hold, receive, and disseminate ideas. Without fair use and first sale, individuals — especially those without significant financial resources — would have access to much less information, particularly current information, than they historically have had. This limitation on access contributes to the ongoing battles surrounding the information rich and poor and has the potential to expand this division even further. And, of grave consequence, without unfettered access to information for all, intellectual freedom is an empty ideal — for all.

And, it is precisely these two concepts, fair use and first sale — and with them intellectual freedom — that are now under siege in the U.S. through a combination of law and technology made possible by the onset of the digital age.

Digital Changes Everything

Information, whatever its original form — be it book, audio or video tape, printed list, illustration, photograph, map, fine art print or anything else that can be captured in a digital representation — is simply a string of 0s and 1s in the digital domain. And once in digital form, any digital item can be copied perfectly, without degradation. In fact, video experiments have demonstrated that digitally encoded video can be copied 99 times without degradation. In other words, the 99th copy looks precisely like the original; printed materials, statistical information, maps, illustrations, photographs, all copy perfectly. The implications are staggering. The entire economic model of the production of items embodying the "tangible expression" of ideas is turned on its head.

In an analog world, there is an original cost of production for an item and then an incremental cost to produce each additional unit of the item. For example, it costs a certain amount to produce a new car model, which includes the costs of research, design, original machining, etc. But it also costs a certain amount to produce each additional car. Even though there are no additional research or design costs in an assembly line model of production, there are incremental material costs in steel, plastic, rubber, etc., as well as labor costs to assemble each new car. In the digital world, the original cost of production of an item, say a film, is still there, but once the film is transferred to digital form, the incremental cost to produce a copy is essentially zero.

Paul Hawken (1983) noted that there were almost exactly the same amounts of chrome, steel, plastic, etc., in the Chevrolet Chevette of the 1980s and the Honda Accord of the 1980s. Yet one went on to become the best selling car in the country for many years (the Accord) and the other died because of lack of consumer demand. The difference, he maintained, was the intelligence that went into the arrangement of the materials. In the digital realm, intelligence has become the entire product — all of the value is in the content. There are few material costs involved at all. The copy on one person's hard drive can go to another person's hard drive through wires that already exist, and absolutely no incremental cost is involved. In other words, what economists call "rivalous goods" become "non-rivalous goods." If one person has a physical copy of a book and lends it to another, the first person no longer has use of the book. If one person has an electronic copy of the same book and sends it to another, they both have use of it. "Rivalous goods" become "non-rivalous goods" in the digital domain, and the economic world is turned upside down.

Or so copyright owners claim.

TECHNOLOGY AND LAW: BARS TO THE COMMONS AND TO INTELLECTUAL FREEDOM?

Copyright owners are not too disturbed if the purchaser of a single music CD, for example, loans it to another. In fact, under the first sale doctrine, the purchaser has every right to do so. However, if the purchaser digitizes the CD and then offers to make it available to anyone who wishes to download it from his or her hard drive, the copyright owners are very concerned, indeed, as many recent cases in the news reveal; the Recording Industry Association of America (RIAA) has issued over 1500 subpoenas for alleged copyright infringement as of April 2004.

Present copyright law prohibits this type of distribution. The problem is that it is almost impossible for copyright owners to enforce copyright in the digital domain if many citizens choose to ignore the law. Owners may sue for relief if they can identify an individual who they believe has violated their copyright. But what do they do if millions of people choose to distribute copyrighted materials? According to the RIAA, millions of citizens have indeed made that choice, and it is impossible to track them all down and sue them using current legal remedies.

Lawrence Lessig, in his seminal book *CODE and Other Laws of Cyberspace* (1999), points to four regulators of behavior: law, architecture, the market, and social custom. They apply to society in general, and to the digital realm — the Internet — in particular. Here we focus on law and architecture.

Since copyright owners have found traditional copyright law itself insufficient to maintain controls over the distribution of materials to which they hold copyrights, those owners, particularly record companies and movie studios, have turned to technology. But attempts to control distribution through technology have been less than successful for one simple reason: there is no such thing in the digital realm as an "ultimate technology." Every attempt at copy control unleashes a counter measure, and copyright owners find themselves in an ever-escalating spiral of technical one-upsmanship. In the past, it was a combination of law and architecture — as well as social norms — that protected copyrighted works. "Architecture," in this context, means the design of things that makes them controllable. A physical book, for example, is very difficult to duplicate, even in an age of copy machines. Given the time and expense of copying a 300-page novel, a would-be copyright violator will probably decide it is just as easy to buy another copy of the book (a market decision that results from the architecture). Given the degradation inherent in analog copying technology, attempts to copy the latest *Star Wars* movie on a consumer level and pass it around will probably fizzle as the third or fourth generation of the copy turns out to be unviewable. There certainly have been significant instances of analog "piracy," as the movie and record companies refer to unauthorized copying. Usually, however, this type of "piracy" occurs on a large scale — often in countries other than the U.S., requires a large investment in equipment, and is fairly easy for law enforcement or movie company sleuths to track down, if not to stop.

Today, however, while copyright law has not loosened, technical architecture has grown more restrictive. Digital changes everything. And once again, a combination of law and architecture is necessary to provide effective regulation. But in today's digital environment, this combination of law and architecture does not maintain the historical balance between the rights of owners and the rights of users. To the contrary, the combination today results in overregulation and tips the balance dramatically in favor of copyright owners at the expense of users, of the private interests over the public. This diminution of traditional, legal access to copyrighted material poses an enormous threat to intellectual freedom and the information commons.

DMCA and the Abridgement of Historical Rights of Purchasers and Users

Since the combination of traditional copyright law and architecture (the technical schemes copyright holders adopted to protect works) did not, in the eyes of corporate copyright holders, solve the problem of unauthorized distribution, the RIAA and the Motion Picture Association of America (MPAA) and their members lobbied Congress heavily for a law that would make architecture more effective[1]: The Digital Millennium Copyright Act (DMCA).

The DMCA consists of a multitude of sections, but the one that is of particular import for this discussion is Section 1201. This section makes it a criminal offense to circumvent — or to supply knowledge of how to circumvent — any copy protection scheme that a copyright holder chooses to apply to copyrighted material. There are no exceptions to this dictum for fair use, and there are no restrictions on what kinds of technical protections a copyright holder may put on a copyrighted work.

The DMCA[2] has had a whole string of comical unintended consequences, including adversely impacting cities in the U.S. that bid on technical association conventions. But from the standpoint of intellectual freedom and the free access to information, this law is a disaster. This single law may well have the same impact on closing off the information commons today as thousands of Parliamentary laws did in closing off the physical commons 300 years ago. In a single act, the DMCA essentially negates the first sale doctrine and fair use, not through the process of revising those provisions of the copyright law, but simply by handing complete control of technology to copyright holders — private parties with no accountability to voters or to the common good. Commercial interests, those who could afford to pay to be heard, have won this battle over what Karjala (2003) sees as our "cultural development." And ultimately, the Congress and then the U.S. Supreme Court put the narrow interests of a few over the greater interests of the people. "What was deemed good for Disney was deemed good for America" (Vaidhyanathan, 2003). The implications and consequences reach much further than America's boundaries, as the global information commons suffers dramatically as well. Moreover, the sheer quantity of information that originates in the States will now be enclosed in the United States and be available only to those who can afford it, having repercussions on global knowledge sharing and communication.

Additional issues surrounding the DMCA's consequences are farther reaching than seen at first glance. A copyright holder may unilaterally choose, for example, to use technical means to limit use of a legally purchased digital file to a single computer, whether the file contains music, movie, map, or prose is irrelevant—it is all digital. What this means is that when a consumer first opens a file on his or her computer, the digital file "binds" to that computer and will not play on any other nor allow itself to be copied. May a user give her copy of a work she has legally purchased to another to use, donate it her local library, or even sell it? Under the first sale doctrine, she is perfectly free to do so. She is even free to do so under the DMCA. But the file won't work on a friend's computer or on the library's computers. And neither she nor anyone else can undo the copy protection, no matter how simple or rudimentary it may be. In doing so, she commits not a civil violation—as former violations of copyright in the analog world were and still remain—but a criminal violation punishable by fine and imprisonment.

Can she make a copy of the file for her own protection in case something happens to the original? No. Can she employ a traditional fair use such as bringing part of the file to her classroom for educational purposes if she is a teacher or a student? No, not without bringing her home computer to school with her as well.

In short, what she *may* do with a work she purchased legally is still controlled by traditional copyright law. What she actually *can* do with her legally purchased work is controlled totally by the copyright owner—backed by the threat of criminal penalty in law. This changing relationship between technology and law should give us pause—is technology driving law? Law driving technology? Is big business driving both? Where are ethics in this discussion?

Our example above is purposely extremely simplistic and black-and-white. But it is perfectly permissible under the DMCA and, in fact, these kinds of total control technologies have been applied to copyrighted works in digital form, from songs to books to software. If copyright holders choose to impose more lenient restrictions on their works, that is a matter of their choice, not of a purchaser's or user's rights, or what is best for the commons, or what is best for the principles of intellectual freedom. We believe Warwick (2001, p.264) is absolutely correct when she notes "copyright in the United States is an economic regime that pays homage to ethics only when it wishes to invoke a higher ground than economic damages for reasons to obey copyright law."

Architecture Controls Access: Law Validates Architecture

The DMCA in and of itself constitutes a serious threat to intellectual freedom by limiting access to information that has traditionally been available under fair use and first sale provisions of the law. But the DMCA is not the only "validator" of changes in architecture that is affecting access to information, and thus intellectual freedom. Two other major areas of law are affecting access in combination with changes in architecture: contract law and laws regarding the concentration of media ownership.

As DMCA changes the balance between the rights of owners and of users, so does contract law. "Click through" licenses, for example, often contain provisions that override traditional fair use and/or first sale doctrines even if the works in questions are not protected by technological copy protection tools. "Click-through" licenses get their name from the fact that they are presented before a user can access a digital file. The terms of the license are presented and users must click agreement to proceed. The courts have thus far viewed click-through licenses as generally enforceable, providing that the user had adequate opportunity to read the license before using the product. In practice, few people read the "fine print" and therefore accept many limitations on their usage of the product that they would be much less likely to accept in the analog world. This is especially common in software licenses, but is also true for e-books and other products. Courts are very hesitant to invalidate the provisions of a contract, no matter what those provisions may be, and if a license says, for example, that the purchaser of the license may not make a copy for any reason, then fair use is trumped. If the license says that the purchaser may not transfer the license to any third party, then the first sale doctrine is trumped.

Some licenses go beyond these provisions and represent even more egregious threats to intellectual freedom. (Note that software is generally protected by copyright although in some specific cases, unique processes may also be protected by patent.) Some software vendors, for example, have included provisions in their "click-through" licenses that prohibit a user from publishing a review of the software's performance without the express permission of the vendor. This is not a prohibition of quoting or showing screens from the software. This is a prohibition against even commenting on or reviewing the software. Although these prohibitions have not been tested as yet in court, because they are part of a mutually agreed to license, history indicates that there is a good chance they would be upheld.

A particularly troubling instance of licensing in the digital realm arises in the case of professional journals. More and more publishers of professional journals are choosing to publish only in digital form. In addition, there has been an ongoing consolidation in the business, and the result is increased control of professional publishing in the hands of ever fewer owners. The results have been devastating for libraries in particular (Albanese, 2001):

The latest statistics from the Association of Research Libraries (ARL) paint a rather grim picture. From 1986 to 2000, serial unit costs have risen a staggering 226 percent. Monograph unit costs rose 66 percent. In contrast, the Consumer Price Index, the standard measure of consumer inflation, increased just 49 percent over the same period of time. Serials cancellation exercises have become routine. The scholarly monograph, once the hallmark of academic achievement in the humanities and social sciences, has withered. (p. 50)

In one mid-sized academic library alone, at the University of Maine, the number of available journal titles has dropped by 1,100, or almost 20%, in three years because of price increases that outstripped budget increases (Onsrud, 2003). This is a common occurrence in academic libraries across the nation. At first glance, it seems like publishers are cutting their own throats by raising prices and thereby losing customers. But in the digital world, incremental production costs are essentially zero. In a digital situation in which a producer has a monopoly, maximizing profit is no longer a function of balancing supply and demand with costs of production. Maximization is a function of maximizing overall income while minimizing administrative overhead, since that is the only incremental cost. Fewer subscribers who are paying more is the proper formula in that case. And if publishers also control reproduction — and most do — then there is an additional income stream that is maximized if fewer people have initial access to the product, since they will have to pay per use. With a paper subscription, even if the subscription lapses, the library still offers access to the publications it bought while subscribing. With an electronic subscription, users at a particular library only have access as long as the subscription is in effect. If the subscription lapses, there is no access to the editions published while the subscription was in effect.

This reduction in access to scholarly journals is a serious problem for scholars, particularly scientists, and for non-scholars alike. As e-books become more ubiquitous in library settings, the same problem will apply to popular literature. It is a serious problem for intellectual freedom, and the problem arises not because of changes in copyright law but because of changes in architecture validated by contract law.

Media Concentration and Ownership

Moreover, in concert with contracts, access and expression are under assault by the consolidation of ownership in the publishers of scholarly journals. But, there has been an even more pronounced consolidation of ownership in the mass media: 80% of music is distributed by five companies, and 70% of the major radio markets are controlled by four companies. In 1996, in the U.S., no single entity owned more than six radio stations. Today, Clear Channel owns more than 1,200 stations after the FCC relaxed ownership rules in 1996. Of the 91 "major" televisions networks (including cable), 80% are owned by six companies. In 1947, 80% of newspapers were independently owned. Today, less than 20% are independently owned. In 1992, 70% of prime-time network programming was independently produced. Today, after the FCC rescinded rules separating content and transmission ownership, 75% of prime-time programming is owned by the networks (Lessig, 2003).

In the most recent dramatic change in media ownership rules in June 2003, the Federal Communications Commission voted along partisan lines to allow even more consolidation of media. Dissenter Jonathan Adelstein (2003) said gloomily, "I'm afraid a dark storm cloud is now looming over the future of the American media. This is the most sweeping and destructive rollback of consumer protection rules in the history of American broadcasting." Other vocal critics include Robert McChesney and John Nichols (Moyers, 2003a), who see such consolidation as a significant threat to the foundations of democracy in general:

And what we've had happen to our media system in the United States in the past 50 years especially, is it's increasingly become the province of private commercial interests to use — to suit their own naked self-interest to advance their commercial concerns. And the political concerns and the social concerns of free press as a hallmark of democracy have been lost in the shuffle.

Ultimately, with the proposed changes, there will be no rules against the same company owning newspapers, radio stations, and television stations in the same market. In effect, a single owner could determine what people in a geographic area read, hear, and see. With this consolidation comes loss of diversity, fairness, and competition, as small media outlets will undoubtedly be swallowed up by their large corporate counterparts. A prime example of the disastrous effects this has on local news and communities comes from the consolidation of radio under Clear Channel, quoted from the PBS report (Moyers, 2003b):

In January of last year, a train derailed in Minot, North Dakota. Two hundred and ten thousand gallons of ammonia and a toxic cloud spilled out of it.

Authorities wanted to get the word out to Minot residents: stay indoors and avoid the area near the derailment. So they tried to get in touch with six local commercial radio stations.

All six of those commercial stations — out of a total of seven in Minot — are owned by one huge radio and advertising conglomerate: Clear Channel Communications. It's been buying up radio stations across the country and replacing their live local programs with shows recorded in far-off studios that only sound local.

Minot authorities say when they called with the warning about the toxic cloud, there was no one on the air who could've made the announcement. Clear Channel says someone was there who could have activated an emergency broadcast. But Minot police say nobody answered the phones. Clear Channel owns more than twelve hundred radio stations nationwide; they have an audience of over one hundred ten million listeners a week. Critics of the company say that its way of doing business is symptomatic of what's wrong with the American media today — that it's grown too big for the public's good.

This example demonstrates that we as members of communities are losing this battle — for our airwaves, our right to access information, and our right to be informed in order to make decisions. We believe that the media has an ethical obligation to its constituents. We believe a democratic society must be grounded in a plethora of perspectives and viewpoints. We believe money should not be able to buy access. We believe law and architecture must be balanced with rights and responsibilities. And we believe in the principles of intellectual freedom for all.

And, it is very difficult to see how the principle of "free access to all expressions of ideas through which any and all sides of a question, cause or movement may be explored" will be promoted by these changes in architecture made possible by law. It seems much more likely that intellectual freedom and the commons will suffer, and suffer greatly.

CONCLUSIONS

There are many forces that affect access to "free access to all expressions of ideas," the *sine qua non* of intellectual freedom. The forces discussed in this chapter impinge specifically on the enclosure of the information commons and on the reduction of traditional avenues of access to current information through fair use and first sale protections under copyright. Both are being undermined by the confluence of architecture and law in the digital age and by a dramatic reduction in the diversity of information sources due to media ownership consolidation in the U.S..

There are other forces, which this chapter does not touch upon, that also affect access to information. Policies regarding distribution of the information that government controls, market forces and their effect on access to information, and the social mores and values that act as regulators — or permissors — of social behavior are all crucially important parts of the discussion that others will undoubtedly take up.

There are also efforts to reverse, mitigate, or bypass the restrictive effects of architecture and law on intellectual freedom. These efforts fall generally into one of two categories: remedies in law, and the creation of alternative routes into the information commons — the strengthening of what Bollier (1999) refers to as the "gift economy." Chronicling these efforts will also have to fall to others, but it is important for this discussion to know they exist. These efforts to create alternatives to the restrictive controls on information at work in the digital domain take on a special importance since it seems unlikely that remedies in law will be successful in the present political and ideological environment in Washington, DC.

In summary, free access to information is essential to the exercise of intellectual freedom. Access to information is under assault in this digital age by law, architecture, and technology, and the restrictions on access made possible by this confluence exceed anything Americans have known to date in their history. Digital distribution of works tips the traditional balance of the rights of users and owners under copyright law far toward the owners. The balance has swung away from the public, the public interest, and the commons.

Digital changes everything. With respect to access to information, the change is not for the better.

ENDNOTES

[1]   Some suggest that the rationale behind the DMCA was to bring U.S. laws into greater conformance with WIPO treaties.
[2]   A fine example of hubris brought low is the case of the music industry group called the Secure Digital Music Initiative, or SDMI, that got so

cocky about how good their copy protection technology was that they issued an open challenge to anyone to break its system. A Princeton professor and some of his students took up the challenge as an academic exercise and broke the scheme in no time at all.

What happened next is the chilling part. As Professor Edward Felton prepared to go to an academic conference to discuss the technological process of meeting the SDMI challenge with other academic researchers, the SDMI, even though it issued the challenge, threatened to sue the researchers and their university under the DMCA. Professor Felton, after consulting with the university's attorneys, withdrew from the conference. Another example: only one criminal prosecution has been brought at the time of this writing (Spring 2003) under the DMCA. The indicted party is a Russian company called Elcomsoft that designed software to make it possible to actually use an electronic book protected by Adobe's e-book format as you would a regular book. Adobe had the government arrest one of the Russian programmers when he attended a professional conference in Las Vegas.

Adobe got a bit red-faced when what it had done came out, and programmers all over the country and the world began pelting Adobe with email and promising never to write another line of code that would work with an Adobe program. Adobe tried to drop the charges, but the government continued the prosecution.

The jury in the case brought in a "not guilty" verdict even though everyone agreed, including Elcomsoft, that its software broke the Adobe copy protection. Some speculated the jurors were bringing in a verdict on the law more than on the defendant, and no one has been prosecuted successfully in a criminal proceeding since. However, private companies effectively use the threat of suit and prosecution as a big stick against competitors. And, yes, at least two professional computer organizations moved their annual conferences to Europe from the U.S. after the Russian programmer, Dmitry Sklyarov, was arrested.

REFERENCES

Adelstein, J. (2003). Commissioner Adelstein. Retrieved online December 8, 2003, from the PBS Online Newshour at: http://www.pbs.org/newshour/media/conglomeration/adelstein_statement.html.

Albanese, A. (2002). Revolution or evolution. *Library Journal, 126*(18), 48-50.

American Library Association, Office of Intellectual Freedom. (2003). Intellectual freedom and censorship Q and A. Retrieved online November 14, 2003, at: http://www.ala.org/Content/NavigationMenu/Our_Association/ Offices/Intellectual_Freedom3/Basics/Intellectual_Freedom_and _Censorship_QandA.htm.

Barlow, J.P. (2001). Presentation at the Camden Conference on Technology.

Bollier, D. (1999). Why we must talk about the information commons. Retrieved online May 15, 2003, at: http://www.newamerica.net/ Download_Docs/pdfs/Doc_File_103_1.pdf.

Drahos, P. (1996). *A philosophy of intellectual property*. Aldershot, UK: Dartmouth Publishing.

Eldred v. Ashcroft (2003). 123 U.S. 769.

Hardin, G. (1968). The tragedy of the commons. *Science, 162*, 1243-1248.

Hawken, P. (1983). *The next economy*. New York: Holt, Rinehart, Winston.

Karjala, D. (2003). Help protect your right to the great works in the public domain. Opposing copyright extension forum. Retrieved online May 2003 at: http://www.law.asu.edu/HomePages.Karjala/OpposingCopyright Extension/.

Lessig, L. (1999). *CODE and other laws of cyberspace*. New York: Basic Books.

Lessig, L. (2003). Presentation at the Computers, Freedom, Privacy Conference. New York. April 4.

Moyers, B. (2003a). Bill Moyers talks with John Nichols & Robert McChesney. Retrieved online December 8, 2003, at: http://www.pbs.org/now/tran-script/transcript_nicholsmcchesney.html.

Moyers, B. (2003b). Tollbooths on the digital highway. Retrieved online November 15, 2003, at: http://www.pbs.org/now/transcript/transcript 214_full.html.

Onsrud, H. (1998). The tragedy of the information commons. *Policy Issues in Modern Cartography*, 141-158.

Onsrud, H. (2003). Presentation at Wells Commons. University of Maine, Orono, ME, May 8.

Vaidhyanathan (2003). After the copyright smackdown, what next? *Salon*.com. Retrieved online May 2003 at: http://www.salon.com/tech/feature/2003/ 01/17/copyright/print.html.

Warwick, S. (2001). Is copyright ethical? In R. Spinello & H. Tavani (Eds.), *Reading in cyberethics,* (pp. 263-279). Boston, MA: Jones and Bartlett.

Chapter X

Would Be Pirates:
Webcasters, Intellectual Property, and Ethics

Melanie J. Mortensen
Montreal, Canada

ABSTRACT

The debate in Canada that occurred prior to the amendment of the Copyright Act *regarding the regulation of television retransmission on the Internet emblematizes significant ethical issues arising from shifts in communications technologies. The alleged piracy of Internet retransmitters demonstrates the broader consequences of the regulation of communications technologies and intellectual property at a variety of levels. Future treatments of new media innovations should be spared the retransmitters' fate, whereby the innovators were called "pirates" and the law was amended to make them appear so in response to industry pressure. Instead, appropriate criteria should be determined with ethical foundations to administer decisions regarding the responsible governance of communications technologies. Legal, political, and social observations complete the analysis in this chapter, whereby such considerations are raised to advocate a principled approach to the regulation of new media and innovations in communications technologies.*

Often there are no persons or organizations with clear authority to make the decisions that matter. In fact, there may be no clearly defined social channels in which important moral issues can be addressed at all. Typically, what happens in such cases is that, as time passes, a mixture of corporate plans, market choices, interest group activities, lawsuits, and government legislation takes shape to produce jerry-built policies. But given the number of points at which technologies generate significant social stress and conflict, this familiar pattern is increasingly unsatisfactory.

- Langdon Winner (1995, p. 65)

INTRODUCTION

At a convention of the Canadian Association of Broadcasters (CAB) on October 29, 2001, then Canadian Minister of Heritage Sheila Copps announced, "We cannot allow a loophole to permit pirates to steal your product" (Scoffield, 2001). These would-be "pirates" to whom she referred were Internet retransmitters of television signals, or "webcasters." Copps further indicated that Canadian copyright law would be modified by the year's end to exclude the medium of the Internet from the Canadian retransmission compulsory licensing scheme that exempts traditional cable retransmitters from copyright breach. Her announcement was significant. The reference to Internet retransmitters as "pirates" simplified and made seem morally reprehensible precisely the kind of innovation that the Canadian government had previously seemed eager to support. Since then, the Canadian government has indeed closed the "loophole," exempting Internet retransmitters from taking advantage of the retransmitters' compulsory license provided by Section 31 of the Canadian *Copyright Act*.

Webcasting, or Internet retransmission, has appeared on the Internet in a variety of forms. In Canada, certain webcasting companies emerged, retransmitting television signals in such a manner as to make them available for viewers via their Internet connections. The activities of the webcasters may be said to demonstrate one of the outgrowths of convergence in communications technologies. Here, "old" media can be streamed via digitization. This is commonly accepted as one of the effects of the digital revolution, which has changed both the carriage and the content of communications (Handa, Janda, Johnston, & Morgan, 2000, para. 10.8). Television retransmission on the Internet may therefore seem to be simply another attempt to profit from the new technologies by bringing the old media to market in new ways. However, the debate in Canada regarding television retransmission on the Internet is in fact emblematic of significant issues that arise from the present shifts in communications technologies.

The attention garnered by the Canadian Internet broadcasters JumpTV.com (JumpTV) and, earlier, iCraveTV, is paradigmatic of the debate over the nature of intellectual property, specifically copyright in this regard, how it forms value, and the significance of how choices are made with respect to its scope in the information economy (deBeer, 2000, pp. 522-524). At the same time, the issue has broader theoretical implications. The growing significance of intellectual property gives rise to new international norms that affect the balance of state sovereignty and the influence of international trade agreements, particularly with respect to international sanctions that flow from the breach of the increasingly stringent international protections for intellectual property that have accompanied the growth of the information industry. Thus, the debate regarding Internet retransmission of television signals reveals the considerable influence of major content providers and broadcasters in addition to Canada's trade commitments.

The webcasting debate in Canada is all the more interesting due to domestic constraints that have traditionally been placed on television broadcasting and telecommunications. The would-be piracy of Internet retransmitters demonstrates the broader consequences of the regulation of communications technologies and intellectual property at a variety of levels. Not only do we see outgrowths in the relatively new technology of the Internet due to our reliance upon old media, but we may also note the responses of industry and the government to reflect upon the nature and the ethical significance of intellectual property and democracy during this information revolution.

ETHICS AND THE GOVERNANCE OF COMMUNICATIONS AND INTELLECTUAL PROPERTY

Communications technology may not seem at first to be as ethically troubling as the types of considerations that form, for example, debates regarding patent law and biotechnology. Nevertheless, ethical considerations should be fundamental to policy and legislative treatments of communications technology and its governance by communications and intellectual property laws. Some see the value of ethics in relation to these topics in such particular applications as thinking about privacy concerns on the Internet. However, considerations of privacy, security, and other current branches of interest represent only the immediate concerns with respect to ethics. Rather than focusing on such singular concerns, a more thorough and broad-based system of ethics should form the foundation for theoretical approaches to communications law.

The regulation of webcasting may therefore be subject to ethical considerations. These ethical considerations, furthermore, create a foundation for my later points regarding the broader consequences of the shifting debates about how best to govern communication technologies such as webcasting. This brief treatment of the ethical considerations first surveys the philosophical foundations for the necessity of an ethical view of this issue. Then, it treats the types of new social paradigms that make up the new business economy and make webcasting seem a natural extension of the developments of convergence. Finally, the particularities of this communications technology and its social significance will be explored in order to demonstrate why webcasting serves as a particularly apt example of the ontological shifts that are presently demanded by the information industry.

Ethical Foundations

In order to adequately link ethical considerations to such a specific manifestation as webcasting, it is necessary to provide a methodological structure that links the two fields in such a way as to serve as a foundation for my later assertions with respect to the larger consequences of my observations about webcasting, specifically, and the treatment of communications and intellectual property law, generally. Various treatments of the philosophy and ethics of technology already exist. The main ethical principles that are relevant in connection with such technology may be differentiated according to the various viewpoints that observers take with respect to the utility, efficacy, and safety of a particular technology. The roots of the philosophy of technology are usually situated in the classic ontological notion of technology: "technology refers [in Aristotelian thought] to a device or method created by man (and thus external to him) as a secondary means of achieving his primary ends (i.e., having only instrumental value)" (Vig, 1988, p. 11). Other more recent analyses of the ontological dimension of technology refine the classic, instrumentalist approach with more or less contextualized views of how technology relates to the essential nature of people (Vig, p. 11). The epistemological notion of technology is also significant, whereby technology can refer simply to the tools and machines of society, or be defined with a far greater scope to include the organization of systems and institutions that serve society, or even the quality of social life that results from the accumulation of technological activity (Vig, p. 10).

Thus, perspectives in the philosophy of technology vary. Norman Vig (1988) argues that a "soft determinist" approach provides the most effective foundation for the philosophy of technology (p. 18). According to this view, technologies are viewed as "conditioning" or "encouraging"—rather than fully determining—certain political and social structural changes that may or may not be appropriate to a given society's value system (Vig, 1988, p. 18). Vig indicates that it is necessary to exercise foresight and control at the design stage as well as in the implementation of technology to prevent problems (p. 19). The analysis herein of the ethical consideration of decision-making regarding webcasting, as it is situated in the information industry, is based on this "soft determinist" approach. This approach provides a theoretical and practical assessment of technologies that is properly contextual, and allows for qualitative appraisals of specific technologies. Also, the soft determinist approach allows for an analysis of technology while taking account of the social context, but in a manner that does not depend upon the particular social context as the basis for analysis.

The consideration of ethics should be integral to policy decisions about communications technologies and their governance. The regard to ethics in the realm of communications technologies may seem unnecessary since there is less apparent risk than with other technologies. New kinds of interference, or intervention, in communities and the direct or indirect effects that communications technologies have on individuals' lives necessitates more care with respect to the governance and policy of such technologies and their influence upon the global power structure (Jonas, 1986):

[Ethics] must be there because men act, and ethics is for the ordering of actions and for regulating the power to act. It must be there all the more, then, the greater the powers of acting that are to be regulated; and as it must fit their size, the ordering principle must also fit their kind. Thus, novel powers to act require novel ethical rules and perhaps even a new ethics. (p. 23)

The great social and political influence that communications technologies possess requires a system of applied ethics that would have foundations and premises that could be applied in a variety of contexts, premised on the notion of community consent in order to make effective decisions regarding ethical governance and the implementation of communications technologies.

The array of possibilities whereby communications technologies may become significantly integrated into individuals' and communities' lives requires a singular ethics that is based on sound philosophical premises. The concepts of values, trust, and risk draw the focus to the concepts that are significant in the classic philosophical treatment of ethics, but are especially relevant to the consideration of large ethical questions that arise in light of the rapid scientific developments of the last few decades and the hype surrounding the "genetic revolution" and the "information revolution."

The nature of the networks that make up the information industry make the concept of the "system" appealing as a basis for the engagement of ethics. The changes that have come about in communications technologies have given rise to convergence. The networks that make up this converging environment and make the communications technologies increasingly flow together provide the current for the stream of information that seems to be a kind of "force," the necessity for which is becoming as important, arguably, as the provision of energy resources in the maintenance of certain standards of living. Therefore, the increasingly essential nature of communications technologies calls for careful decision-making with respect to applicable policy and legislation. The system ethics that would apply in such a circumstance would therefore be used to inform policies and decisions at the network level.

New Paradigms

Various social consequences flow from the new paradigm that emerges from the phenomenon of convergence. Part of the effect of convergence involves the commercialization of innovations with respect to technology. Webcasting perfectly demonstrates this aspect of the phenomenon since it shows how the new digitized communications and computer realms can carry media and entertainment content to consumers in the marketplace in ways that become increasingly intriguing as the wireless trend picks up steam. The more that this occurs, the more possible it is that people may be constantly accompanied by their multimedia devices for information, communication, and entertainment purposes. In turn, this offers more potential markets for hardware and software manufacturers, as well as the carriers and content providers.

Some argue that the increasing connectivity that results from new communications technologies will have greater repercussions and even affect individuals' phenomenological experience of the world. Critical theorist Mark Poster

(1989) predicts: "Electronic systems of communication are changing the fabric of advanced society. A great social upheaval is taking place, which promises to transfigure the structure of human interactions" (p. 124). Such paradigmatic changes are echoed in the sentiments of Marshall McLuhan, who with Bruce Powers made the prescient argument in a 1989 posthumous publication that anticipated the effect of convergence in business, carriage, and content: "The next step in diversity will not be simply distributive, it will be interactive — a condition in which the user merges with the data base or the system" (p. 129).

Such early theorizing has already begun to be represented not only by the more obvious example of specialized Internet advertising that is suited to the apparent interests of the user, but also by the development of new computer-based technologies that use "fuzzy logic" or "soft logic" to allow software-optimized products to respond to user behavior patterns. The economic and social consequences of convergent media such as webcasting, and the legislative battles that take place to control how intellectual property regimes effectively govern them, reflect how we view the world. It is for this reason that an ethical perspective may be necessary to effectively balance all of the factors involved in decision-making with respect to policy directions and regulatory action.

Webcasting is a clear manifestation of the phenomenon of convergence. The phenomenon of convergence is significant not only because it represents broad shifts in the move toward the coming together of communications, computers, and electronic formats, generally, but also because its consequences are so significant economically and socially. The economic effects of convergence include the consequences of policy shifts toward exploiting the changing environment from material-based industry to information-based marketplaces. Concomitant with such a shift has been what may be called the price of obsolescence (Estabrooks, 1995, p. 245). Shifts in the emphasis of carrier technology will likely have deleterious consequences on industry participants that do not conform to the convergence phenomenon. Not only does the Canadian Association of Broadcasters refer to this concern in its *Response to the Consultation Paper on Digital Copyright Issues* (2001), so too do webcasters such as JumpTV refer to this effect in reference to their own competitiveness and innovation. Indeed, such innovation typified the initiative that the New Media Report exemption had initially intended to foster. Thus, the *JumpTV Response to the Consultation Paper on the Application of the Copyright Act's Compulsory Retransmission License* (2001) declared, "JumpTV sees no good reason for preventing Internet-based retransmitters from carrying signals in a manner fully sanctioned by law simply because other parties, whether broadcasters or others, have failed to enter the Internet market in a more timely manner."

Webcasting as Internet Communications Service

Multimedia technologies and the general trend toward convergence have created a new environment that has an enormous market demand for such services as webcasting. Users have grown accustomed to new developments of technological convergence that make webcasting possible and enable other multimedia Internet-based services such as digitized music swapping, wireless developments, increased communication capabilities, telephony, and data management. New media players will inevitably emerge to try to take advantage of these demands, as Michael Geist (2000) suggests: "Rather than turning to legislative change ... perhaps it is time for traditional broadcasters to embrace the new medium by establishing their own online broadcasting services" (p. 239). Nonetheless, it is necessary to understand how fundamental such evolution is to our society and how the eventual streaming and convergence are inevitable, if slow. It is therefore troubling to see so many legal battles being fought as a result of the inconsistencies that arise in intellectual property when faced with technological convergence:

Traditional broadcasters and content creators may be well advised to alter their strategy in the face of new technologies, as their battle may be a losing one. First, attempting to stop companies such as iCraveTV or Napster is much like playing the "whack a mole" game. For every iCraveTV that is stopped, two or three new versions will quickly appear. It becomes a never-ending fight resulting in wasted energy and legal bills. (Geist, 2000, p. 238)

What this represents is traditional players attempting to maintain control over the Internet while the information industry's "cost of obsolescence" (Estabrooks, 1995, p. 245) threatens their existence.

Less than a decade ago, there was evident enthusiasm for the Internet's potential to present a space for divergent and alternative thinking and for revolutionary democratic potential. It was then observed that "the communications revolution has fundamentally transformed the strategies and potential of pro-democracy activism, and has placed powerful constraints on the ability of authoritarian forces to suppress anti-regime organisation and mobilization", even though "when we view state-society relations in the broader context of patterns of global hegemony, technology's impact is more ambiguous—even ominous" (Jones, 1994, p. 161). Now, though, with such conflicts that have so far involved webcasting, media-swapping sites, and trademark/domain name disputes, we see that courts, legislators, and international organizations more frequently make decisions and design regulations so that, on the one hand, the Internet increasingly resembles the commercial marketplace of the "real" world and, on the other, the real world of nation states more rapidly resembles the borderless realm of "cyberspace," with national sovereignty eroded by trade obligations while globalization shifts the focus from political clout to corporate might. While multimedia convergence may seem ethically unproblematic, the scope and effect of the societal dependence and economic significance of converging technologies demand critical vigilance with respect to the nature of the governance of communications technologies.

GOVERNING INTERNET RETRANSMISSION

The approach of the Canadian government and the Canadian Radio-television and Telecommunications Commission (CRTC) has in fact made the webcasting innovations an attractive possibility due to Canada's policy and legislative environment with respect to new media undertakings. While the announcements made regarding the "piracy" of Internet retransmission fore-shadowed the recent amendments to Canadian copyright law that excluded Internet retransmitters from the compulsory licensing scheme for retransmitters of television signals, the earlier perspective was more balanced. Initially, the federal government's "Consultation Paper on the Application of the Copyright Act's Compulsory Retransmission License to the Internet" (Consultation Paper, 2001) reflected a balanced approach to weighing the issues at the start of the public consultation phase:

In the view of the departments, an Internet exclusion would be justified if the compulsory licensing of Internet-based retransmission within Canada were not appropriate under any terms and conditions. However, as has been noted, it has also been argued that a wholesale Internet exclusion could inappropriately limit the ability of existing participants and new entrants to the Canadian broadcasting distribution sector to adopt the most effective technologies available at a time of rapid technological change. ... In fact, it is possible that in the future the preferred means for broadcasting distribution will be over secure, virtual paths rather than over dedicated paths on proprietary networks.

Nevertheless, the federal government appeared to shift positions with surprising speed after the September 17, 2001, deadline for submission to the public consultation — which received over 700 responses — to then affirm the stance of the broadcasters and go so far as to refer to JumpTV as "pirates" less than six weeks later. The legislative battle that followed, while ostensibly over the nature of Section 31 and the availability of the compulsory license to Internet retransmitters, reveals the absence, at present, of harmonious and principled policy standards to guide the governance of new media and communications technologies.

While a detailed discussion of the technology that is involved in Internet retransmission is beyond the scope of this chapter, it may be briefly summarized as follows: television retransmission involves streaming digitized television signals to make them available from an Internet site for viewing. The television signals are relatively easy to come by. In the case of iCraveTV, as has been frequently publicized, the company simply transformed them from their source — an antenna on top of its Toronto headquarters (Geist, 2000):

iCraveTV provided users with the capability to watch seventeen channels directly on their personal computers. Included were all major Canadian broadcasters (CBC, CTV, Global, and City-TV) and a number of United States broadcasters (NBC, ABC, PBS, and WB). The broadcasts were picked up through antennae located atop a north Toronto building. The signal was tuned into a retransmission signal, digitized, and then streamed onto the Internet. The end user accessed the iCraveTV signal by using a personal computer, a piece of software called the RealPlayer, and a fast connection to the Internet. (p. 225)

Different versions of similar convergence technologies are currently under development by many new media and "old media" participants (Dillon, 2001). The example of iCraveTV demonstrates the many different elements of convergence that presently exemplify the field of communications (Handa, 2002; Handa et al., 2000).

Regulatory Exceptions with Respect to Retransmission

In Canada, Internet retransmission activities involve two controversial exemptions. The first is the decision of the CRTC to refrain from regulating new media undertakings for a period of five years, as announced by the Telecom Public Notice CRTC 99-14/Broadcasting Public Notice CRTC 1999-94

("New Media Report", 1999) and the Public Notice CRTC 1999-197 ("New Media Exemption", 1999). The second is the retransmission compulsory license set forth at Section 31 of the *Copyright Act*. A recent amendment to the *Copyright Act* has followed the spirited debate regarding Internet retransmission; this amendment effectively excludes Internet retransmitters from taking advantage of the compulsory licensing scheme.

The CRTC released its New Media Report in May 1999. The intention of the New Media Report had been to examine the following issues: the ways and extent to which new media would likely affect Canadian broadcasting and telecommunications undertakings; whether new media constituted broadcasting or telecommunications services; the extent to which the CRTC should regulate the new media to the extent that they constituted broadcasting or telecommunications services; and whether the new media raises other broad policy issues of national interest (Geist, 2000). The CRTC decided that certain Internet content would fall under the definitions of Canada's *Broadcasting Act* and constitute "programs" and "broadcasting." Therefore, as Michael Geist (2000) explains, an exemption order was made with respect to all new media undertakings that are providing broadcasting services over the Internet, in whole or in part, in Canada: "As it realized that it did not contribute to achieving the objectives of the Act, the CRTC recognized that any attempt to regulate new media broadcasting might put Canadian industry at a competitive disadvantage in the global marketplace" (p. 231).

Thus, this decision to refrain from regulating the new media for five years was ostensibly made in order to stimulate innovation. This is clearly indicated in the New Media Report (1999):

On balance ... the Commission is confident, based on the record of this proceeding, that the industry is moving in a direction that will result in a strong Canadian new media industry and a strong Canadian presence on the Internet. Most noteworthy was the expression of excitement and energy that was communicated by those who discussed their work in new media. The Commission does not intend to impede this creative energy through unnecessary regulatory measures but rather to encourage the continued leadership and innovation of the Canadian new media sector. (para.88)

Nevertheless, it is possible that the CRTC was not prepared for the rapidity with which participants were willing to take advantage of the exemption, as Michael Geist (2000) suggests:

In the wake of the CRTC decision, the stage was set for Canadian media companies to blossom under a regulatory framework that placed their development at the top of the policy priority list. Into this framework leapt Bill Craig, an "old media" executive, who in the fall of 1999 launched iCraveTV, an online "webcaster." He began to provide Internet users with the opportunity to watch television in real-time directly on their personal computers. ... Craig created a firestorm of protest from broadcasters and content creators across North America. Those parties, who only months earlier had vehemently opposed Internet regulation, now watched in horror as an unregulated Internet hatched new business models that caught many of them by surprise. The reaction in both the United States and Canada was swift — legal actions demanded an immediate cessation of all unauthorized webcasts on both sides of the border, and injured parties filed massive damage claims sought for alleged infringements. (p. 224)

Indeed, in his 2000 article, Geist indicated that a strong argument could be made, based mainly on the New Media Report, that such undertakings as iCraveTV should legitimately be viewed as exempt from broadcasting regulation at this time.

Nevertheless, the role of the New Media Report in determining the fate of Internet retransmission was soon overshadowed by the relevance of copyright law with the application by JumpTV for a retransmission license under the compulsory licensing regime provided in the Canadian *Copyright Act*. Section 31 of the Canadian *Copyright Act* provides a compulsory licensing regime for the retransmission of television signals that would otherwise infringe copyright. Prior to the amendment, Section 31 of the *Copyright Act* provided as follows:

1. In this section:
    *   "retransmitter" does not include a person who uses Hertzian waves to retransmit a signal but does not perform a function comparable to that of a cable retransmission system;
    *   "signal" means a signal that carries a literary, dramatic, musical or artistic work and is transmitted for free reception by the public by a terrestrial radio or terrestrial television station.
2. It is not an infringement of copyright to communicate to the public by telecommunication any literary, dramatic, musical or artistic work if
    (a) the communication is a retransmission of a local or distant signal;
    (b) the retransmission is lawful under the *Broadcasting Act*;

(c)   the signal is retransmitted simultaneously and in its entirety, except as otherwise required or permitted by or under the laws of Canada; and

(d)   in the case of the retransmission of a distant signal, the retransmitter has paid any royalties, and complied with any terms and conditions, fixed under this Act.

This section had been the main defense relied upon by Internet retransmitters to justify the legitimacy of their actions. Therefore, the amendment of this section, as we shall see, was able to have a significant effect on retransmitters.

Amending Copyright Law to Exclude Internet Retransmitters

The Canadian *Copyright Act* was subsequently amended to exclude Internet retransmitters from the purview of the compulsory licensing regime. As discussed above, following significant pressure by cable television organizations and major content producers within Canada and from the United States, as well as a public consultation process on the topic of Internet retransmission, the federal government's Bill C-11, *An Act to Amend the Copyright Act*, received royal assent on December 12th, 2002. The amendment of Section 31 of the *Copyright Act* presented a sector-specific exclusion from the compulsory licensing regime by excluding new media retransmitters from the definition of "retransmitter". Thus, the new Section 31 reads:

1.   In this section,
   - "new media retransmitter" means a person whose retransmission is lawful under the *Broadcasting Act* only by reason of the Exemption Order for New Media Broadcasting Undertakings issued by the Canadian Radio-television and Telecommunications Commission as Appendix A to Public Notice CRTC 1999-197, as amended from time to time;
   - "retransmitter" means a person who performs a function comparable to that of a cable retransmission system, but does not include a new media retransmitter;
   - "signal" means a signal that carries a literary, dramatic, musical or artistic work and is transmitted for free reception by the public by a terrestrial radio or terrestrial television station.

2.   It is not an infringement of copyright for a retransmitter to communicate to the public by telecommunication any literary, dramatic, musical or artistic work if

    (a) the communication is a retransmission of a local or distant signal;

    (b) the retransmission is lawful under the *Broadcasting Act*;

    (c) the signal is retransmitted simultaneously and without alteration, except as otherwise required or permitted by or under the laws of Canada;

    (d) in the case of the retransmission of a distant signal, the retransmitter has paid any royalties; and

    (e) the retransmitter complies with the applicable conditions, if any, referred to in paragraph (3)(b).

3.   The Governor in Council may make regulations

    (a) defining "local signal" and "distant signal" for the purposes of subsection (2); and

    (b) prescribing conditions for the purposes of paragraph (2)(e), and specifying whether any such condition applies to all retransmitters or only to a class of retransmitter.

As such, the amended section is largely identical, but effectively excludes Internet retransmitters from the compulsory licensing scheme set forth in this section of the *Copyright Act*.

After the *Copyright Act* amendment, the CRTC issued its Broadcasting Public Notice 2003-2 ("Internet Retransmission Notice", 2003). The Internet Retransmission Notice revisited the CRTC's New Media Decision in light of the amendment, indicating the position of the CRTC regarding the Internet retransmission of television signals:

The Commission does not consider it necessary or appropriate to require the licensing of Internet retransmitters. Rather, Internet retransmission undertakings should remain exempt from these and from other requirements under Part II of the Broadcasting Act. *In addition, since the recent amendments to the* Copyright Act *address the main concern identified in this proceeding, the Commission sees no need to amend the New Media Exemption Order at this time (para. 79).*

The CRTC thereby circumvented the implications of the amendment by relying upon the separate regime of the intellectual property legislation.

BROADER IMPLICATIONS OF THE INTERNET RETRANSMISSION DEBATE

As explained above, the ethical basis for assessing technology is used to guide this consideration of the various implications of the governance of Internet retransmission. The discussion of the governance of Internet retransmission shall be divided into the legal, political, and social repercussions. The first involves more immediate legal questions with respect to the nature of copyright law and its application to the products of technological convergence. The second involves the political realm and questions about the balance of national sovereignty, the rising international influence of intellectual property policymakers, and the rise of competition law as a governing force. The third involves the social realm of individual actors, as well as the nature of democracy, public consultation, and legislative process.

Legal: Intellectual Property Regimes, Competition, and Control over Communications

The recent focus with respect to Internet retransmission has been on the copyright protection of content and the right to its retransmission. The comparatively technologically neutral nature of copyright law draws attention to the troubling sector-specific split in the present governance of communications in Canada. Indeed, the convergent media (such as webcasting) troubles the traditional split between the Canadian *Telecommunications Act* and the *Broadcasting Act*, which is difficult to sustain as convergence increasingly blurs the division between carriage and content (Handa et al., 2000). The move toward convergence in the technological realm will likely be accompanied by increasing confluence in legal regulation as well. Thus, in addition to the influence of the international trade obligations discussed below, there will likely be a move toward more technologically neutral language in the regulation of communications technologies; this would include attention to the broad protections afforded by copyright law and the control over reviewable practices by competition law.

When he was the outgoing president of the Canadian Association of Broadcasters (CAB), Michael McCabe singled out webcasters in his discussion of how the broadcasting industry was shifting its structure and focusing on copyright law in the CAB submission to the House of Commons committee on the review of the broadcasting system (Hyatt, 2001):

We'll have a significant focus on copyright and there are two areas of copyright that we will be wanting to talk about. One of them is JumpTV, the successor to iCraveTV, and the battle to change Section 31 of the Copyright Act *so that Internet companies cannot use the compulsory licenses that cable operates under to deliver conventional television services. That's what iCraveTV was doing — without our permission they were taking our services, CTV, Global etc., and putting them on the air and selling advertising. And that's what JumpTV wants to do.*
So this is a battle at the copyright board, to get the government to do what other countries like the U.S. have done and say that any services like JumpTV, if they want to deliver CTV and Global to audiences around the world they should negotiate with CTV or Global. Not just go to the copyright board and get them to give you a tariff of a few percent of revenue (Hyatt, 2001).

This demonstrates the significance of Internet retransmitters with respect to the future direction of copyright law in Canada and general future trends in broadcasting. With the shift in the economy toward technological participation and competition, Canada is still in a transitional position with respect to the CRTC regulatory power over telecommunications and broadcasting and the Competition Bureau's jurisdiction over the open market (Corley, 1997; Stanbury, 1996). Nevertheless, in November 1999, this situation was clarified when the Competition Bureau issued information regarding the *CRTC/Competition Bureau Interface* to provide guidance with respect to the intersections of authority between the CRTC and the Competition Bureau (1999):

1.   Where the Commission has unconditionally exempted or has forborne from regulation in whole and unconditionally, until such time as it exercises its authority to review, rescind or vary its exemption or forbearance orders and decisions, the *Competition Act* would apply.
2.   Where the Commission has forborne only in part or has exempted or forborne conditionally, the Bureau considers that the *Competition Act* would apply to the activities exempted or conditionally forborne from regulation.
3.   To the maximum extent possible, the Commission identifies in its orders and decisions the powers and the duties which the Commission will no longer exercise.

Both the CRTC and the Competition Bureau retained authority over merger review and marketing practices. The CRTC retained exclusive authority over issues related to interconnection and access. The Competition Bureau retained exclusive authority over activities traditionally falling under its jurisdiction, such as price fixing, bid rigging, and price maintenance (*CRTC/Competition Bureau Interface, 1999*). The interface was seen as particularly beneficial due to the "complementary roles of the two organizations and the fact that the [CRTC] is now moving beyond opening markets to competition and is exercising its powers to forbear from regulation in the area of telecommunications" (*CRTC/Competition Bureau Interface*). As the webcasting debate demonstrates, however, there is still a great deal of protection afforded to broadcasters by the federal government, even where there has been such forbearance from regulation as provided by the New Media Report.

Thus, Canada seems to exhibit contradictory stances regarding the way that the legal regimes intersect to govern areas where there has been technological convergence. While some may consider the reliance by JumpTV on the compulsory retransmission license under Canada's copyright law to be taking advantage of a "loophole," this situation demonstrates fundamental, but not surprising, problems that exist in our regulatory scheme as the new business economy and its reliance upon the protection of intellectual property law grow increasingly important for global competition (Flate, 2000):

Technology will play a major role in preserving territoriality, as it is evident that the law alone cannot solve the problems of the digital domain. Technology is progressing at an astonishing rate and it is virtually impossible for the law to keep up. This will in turn leave copyright holders in "search of their own solutions" as Internet technology continues to outpace intellectual property law. The law must adjust to the rapidly advancing technology and attempt to keep up with this new technological age. However, technology will not slow down to allow the law to "catch up" and cutting edge technology requires cutting edge lawmaking. (p. 188)

Such debates over and reforms of intellectual property should not arise whenever a new technology-based conflict emerges. To allow such a situation to continue would be to be overly protectionist of the traditional industry corporations.

In his recent commentary on the latest copyright reform discussions and the broad range of submissions to the public consultation, Geist (2001) indicates that the scope of copyright law is significant for more than just the industry figures:

It is the industry players that stand virtually alone in arguing for ever-increasing standards of copyright control ... In a battle that pits scientists, educators, librarians, historians and everyday users against a small group of large content creating companies, one might think that Canadian leaders would recognize the need for balance and fairness.

It seems likely that there will be an increase in concern about the nature of intellectual property control over such areas as communication technologies, which may even take the form of constitutional arguments (Fewer, 1997):

Given that freedom of expression rights attach to both access to and communication of information, it seems self-evident that any revision to the Copyright Act — or judicial interpretation of the existing Act in conformity with the Sub-Committee's recommendations — should attract considerable constitutional scrutiny. (p. 238)

This is particularly evident as Canada's control over its intellectual property law is increasingly influenced by trade agreements.

Political: International Order and National Sovereignty

The vehemence of the debate about retransmission rights as Canada approached its most recent copyright reform exemplifies the kinds of pressures faced by Canada, with greater demand for international cooperation and harmonization with respect to intellectual property law. The present reform of Canadian copyright law is taking place in order to comply with international trade agreements. Nevertheless, with such areas as retransmission rights, Canada retains a certain amount of freedom to decide on its own degree of protection, provided it does not fall below the minimum standards, such as the national-treatment principle; by that standard, the nationals of other signatories must be afforded treatment no less favorable than that accorded to a nation's own nationals with regard to the protection and enforcement of intellectual property rights, as provided by Article 1703(1) of the *North American Free Trade Agreement* (NAFTA) (Handa, 1997). Even so, the kinds of stringent controls over protection of intellectual property and the resolution of related disputes demonstrate a certain loss of control at the national level that seems problematic from an ethical perspective, since it inevitably shifts power from the electorate and the elected bodies of Canada to the requirements of its trade agreements (Estabrooks, 1995; Schiller, 1986).

Copyright © 2005, Idea Group Inc. Copying or distributing in print or electronic forms without written permission of Idea Group Inc. is prohibited.

A constellation of international commitments imposes obligations on Canada with respect to the regulation of intellectual property (Handa, 1997). These commitments include the following agreements: the *Berne Convention for the Protection of Literary and Artistic Works* (Berne Convention), *Universal Copyright Convention* (UCC), *General Agreement on Tariffs and Trade* (GATT), *Agreement on the Trade-Related Aspects of Intellectual Property* (TRIPs), *Canada-United States Free Trade Agreement* (FTA), and NAFTA. While Canada has not officially ratified the most recent revisions of the Berne Convention, it is nonetheless obliged to comply with the early international copyright regime standards in accordance with the commitments of NAFTA (Handa, 1997). As a result of NAFTA, the effect of Canada's 1962 ratification of the UCC is now largely insignificant, since it had lower minimum standards than the Berne Convention. With the American ratification of the Berne Convention, Canada is, in fact, held to the Berne Convention standards by the operation of NAFTA (Handa, 1997).

The dispute resolution mechanisms that accompany such trade commitments are extremely important since they demonstrate how important competition law is becoming in the new international arena. There has been a great deal of speculation as to how competition law would function internationally (Gates, 2000), and whether multilateral trade agreements impose competition law principles upon their signatories. The OECD's 1999 *Annual Report on Competition Policy Developments in Canada* (OECD, 1999) indicates that the Competition Bureau, which implements the Canadian *Competition Act*, has been active in a World Trade Organization (WTO) working group "examining the interaction between trade and competition policy":

Rather than continue with the ad hoc approach to competition policy reflected in recent WTO agreements, the Bureau has been active in examining the viability of establishing a sound multilateral framework at the WTO which will advance competition policy internationally. Roundtable discussions with domestic stakeholders on the internationalization of competition policy were conducted by the Economics and International Affairs Branch of the Bureau. (p. 15)

It has been suggested that a cooperative transnational framework for negotiating core competition law principles should be developed, or a broad set of minimum requirements that may be established for the regulation of international competition law problems (Gates, 2000; Shelton, 1998). Like intellectual property protection, therefore, it seems that the area of competition law will grow increasingly significant with respect to the governance of corporate action, but it remains to be seen whether such internationalization would disproportionately favor highly developed capitalist systems in the global marketplace.

Social: Democracy and the Legislative Process

The federal government's reaction after the public consultation with respect to Internet retransmission is demonstrative of an attitude toward intellectual property that is at once instructive and illustrative of the more profound implications of the new business economy. While stressing the importance of the public consultation process, Copps's remarks demonstrate the influence of the industry stakeholders — in this case the broadcasters — and suggest the likelihood of further harmonization with the international, but mainly American, treatment of Internet retransmission. The government's choices about how to implement policy with respect to communications and intellectual property reveal several factors about the new business economy, as well as such broad notions as democracy and its apparent counterpart, the legislative process. The public consultation on copyright reform with respect to retransmission demonstrates certain issues with respect to the governance of technology. Individual participation in the democratic process seems to be limited to choosing which group would likely make the best policy choices with respect to the well-being of the state.

In this way, then, some may argue that the government is compelled by globalization and the new business economy to actively, aggressively participate in championing the new technologies and new media in order to be sufficiently competitive members of the global marketplace. Indeed, the policy statements of the CRTC and the Competition Bureau reflect this attitude. The new openness to liberalization in Canadian regulatory policy of telecommunications and broadcasting is representative of the shift in regulatory policy toward competition in recognition of the growth of convergence that has been explored in the CRTC's report, *Competition and Culture on Canada's Information Highway: Managing the Realities of Transition* (1995), and the policy statements included in the recommendations of the Information Highway Advisory Council (IHAC) in *Connection, Community, Content: The Challenge of the Information Highway* (1995) and *Preparing Canada for a Digital World* (2003). Such statements are not simply empty rhetoric. In the U.S. and Japan, for instance, such policy-based articulations of the individual nations represent how each respective government views the relevance of the necessary future concentration on the information industry in order to continue to be viable, competitive, and successful in the new business economy (Estabrooks, 1995; Handa, 2001).

Two other aspects of the nature of democratic participation in the governance of intellectual property and communications technology should also be raised. The first aspect is that general discussions about democracy and globalization have been growing more prominent, usually in protest of international trade organizations and their growing dominance, since technological developments contribute to the shift in governing power structures from political state-based governments to global corporations and international alliances (Estabrooks, 1995; O'Brien, 2000; Schiller, 1986). These kinds of concerns are also representative, typically, of calls for the democratization of communications technologies and the promotion of "alternative communication"(Ramirez, 1986):

The establishment of a system of communication in which people matter entails the struggle of all sectors of society to obtain control of communication processes which can lead to collective understanding of human situations. Such an understanding, based on reality, action and reflection, is the basis for an alternative economic, political and communicative order. (pp. 108-109)

Such perspectives should be taken into consideration as they represent the interests of individuals within political systems — whether in developing or developed nations — whose lives may be profoundly affected by the decision-making of elites with respect to communications technologies.

The second aspect regarding the nature of democratic participation involves the focus on the effects of capitalism and the tendency of technology and communications observers to presuppose a market made up exclusively of uncomplicated, industrialized states filled with ready and willing consumers. Too often this simplified vision excludes considerations of the equally important alternate applications of these types of technologies in developing nations, or, alternatively, to thoughts of the price of obsolescence and of development for individuals who would voice their resistance to such societal reliance upon new and ever-improving communications technologies. The corporate choice of which technologies are developed, and for what purpose, is of vital interest. To this end, Cees Hamelink (1986) warns that:

The myth of the information revolution, interpreted historically, is meant to cater to the interests of those who initiate and manage the "information revolution": the most powerful sectors of society, its central administrative elites, the military establishment and global industrial corporations. But the myth does not hold promises for those in today's society are the losers. In the information society they will simply be computer-controlled losers. (p. 13)

Nevertheless, it is important to remember that such pessimism is not the only critical avenue to understanding communications technologies and the laws and organizations that govern them: "Systems must be analyzed in light of a theory that can account for new forms of power and that can provide a new normative foundation for policy development (Deetz, 1990, p. 44). A balance of perspectives is required. The commentary by Geist in late 2001 on this issue refers to the necessity of such balance:

Comments in late October [2001] from Heritage Minister Sheila Copps cast significant doubt on the government's receptiveness to a truly inclusive and open consultation process. Only one week after the copyright reform comment period ended, Ms. Copps — along with Industry Minister Brian Tobin — announced Ottawa's position on the highly contentious Internet retransmission issue. Dispensing with the measured tones of the government's policy discussion papers, Ms. Copps derided Internet retransmitters — who want the right to retransmit radio and TV broadcasts over the Internet in exchange for a royalty — as pirates and announced that the government would move to change the law before year-end.
In doing so, she dealt a severe blow to the consultations, leading many to wonder whether there is a meaningful desire for public debate among elected officials. The process, which began with the question of whether the right people would speak out, may now turn into a new question: While the right people may be talking, are the right people listening?

In order to make ethical decisions about communications technologies, it is necessary to ensure that not only immediate industry concerns be considered, but also the larger implications, which include the political and social ramifications. These range from the effects of such preferential protection upon smaller innovative businesses to the larger issues of democratic accountability in the face of greater international pressures with respect to policies of intellectual property.

Putting the Ethics to Practice: Law as Medium

The consideration of the ethics of communications technologies and their governance might appear unnecessary due to the seeming lack of risk to the health and welfare of individuals, the public, and the environment. However, risk assessment in ethics is not limited to strictly health-related effects. The notion of risk is a description for an element of the assessment of consequences in the broader scheme of ethical assessment. What is more relevant with respect to the consideration of infrastructure-level technologies that affect so many aspects of individuals' lives, and have even further effects at a global political level, is the basis for the authority to create policy, make decisions, and enforce standards with respect to the system of communications technologies. Is there a loss of freedom at a fundamental level to make choices regarding how techno-dependent our society is becoming, and to make choices regarding the development, ownership, and administration of these communications technologies? Indeed, what risk there is to human life may be considered as part of the consequences in the larger ethical assessment since, as discussed above, the nature of certain applications of communications technologies could have injurious results. For the system ethics proposed here, however, such a consideration of risk would be only a part of the primary rationale for imposing ethical standards, and would constitute an element in the assessment of the ethics of particular circumstances, but should not be considered the only reason why ethics needs to be considered, as sometimes seems to be the case in other disciplines or popular opinion.

Risk assessment is usually considered to be an important aspect of modern applications of the philosophy of technology and assessments of the impact of technology on society and people. Indeed, some consider the nature of the risk to justify imposing ethical standards. This is certainly a valid consideration in creating ethical standards for decision making about technologies, but it can also lead to troubling questions and quandaries. When risk is used as the basis for ethical assessment, it may lead to a hierarchy of ethical orders. In other words, the greater the possible harm, the more important the ethical standard. The likelihood of harm occurring is also important. Thus, in such areas as environmental ethics and, increasingly, in bioethical assessments of biotechnology, the "precautionary principle" is gaining momentum as a useful standard. According to the precautionary principle, the burden of proof is shifted from the party that wishes to impose the risk to prove that there is little risk, rather than the ethicist needing to prove the nature of the risk before the technology will be discontinued, barred, or enjoined. Nevertheless, the emphasis on the nature of the risk in such areas of applied ethics as bioethics and environmental ethics has led to a perception that particular kinds of risks require ethical assessment, while seemingly harmless technologies such as communications technologies would therefore seem to be exempt from ethical considerations.

There are several ways to address the problem of the centrality of risk in justifications for ethics in order to allow communications technologies to be as validly applicable in ethical considerations and the theories of the philosophy of technology. One option would be to demonstrate that the scope of "risk" extends to a much larger range of injuries. Thus, the loss of freedom to choose regarding a community's reliance upon a particular kind of communications technology may be considered an injury, and even more so if a system failure occurs that led to economic losses for the members of the community (Maner, 2001). Another option would be to argue that risk should not be included in ethical assessment since it could lead to a cost-benefit analysis that would ultimately lead to indifference regarding the development or implementation of technologies with little risk of harm. The approach that will be adopted here is that the notion of risk should properly be considered as part — albeit an important part — of the "consequences" in the overall ethical assessment according to the traditional breakdown of the elements of ethical assessment.

Nevertheless, despite my reduction of the notion of "risk" to a more minor position with respect to assessments in ethics, risks do exist in the system of communications technologies. As discussed above in relation to the existing theoretical approach to security issues and communications technologies, there is a great deal of integration and dependency upon communications technologies, generally, and computer networks, specifically, in certain technologically advanced realms of industry, e.g., the administration of medicine, transport, resources, or the military. This dependency suggests that system errors may have devastating consequences. Similarly, there is a great risk of economic harm flowing from system failures as a result of the increasing reliance upon the system by financial and securities institutions and commercial enterprises. Furthermore, there are hazards involved even in the production of the communications technologies (Siegel & Markoff, 1991). Such considerations with respect to the dependency of the societal infrastructure do not often arise in discussions of communications technologies, which tend to focus instead on the possible impacts upon the consumer or user of the Internet and other convergent media. When the entire system of communications technologies is regarded as a whole, however, the impact and consequences of societal reliance upon the system becomes more apparent and ultimately makes the risk and scope of harm seem more ominous.

At the most basic level, the law would seem to draw upon the same basis as ethics, since moral reasons are often cited to justify the creation or existence of the laws. When it comes to the kinds of laws that typically govern communications technologies, however, the notion that there is a fundamental "morality" that inspires the law seems untenable. Neither ethical nor unethical, the legislation in Canada that governs intellectual property and communications technologies is mainly protectionist in nature. While justifications may be made for the nature of intellectual property as inherently ethical, or the way that telecommunications and broadcasting legislation could seem to embody custodial features in its stated purposes, the goals of the laws are not necessarily to seek ethical assessments of situations; rather, they are meant to address and regulate potentially contentious areas of interests and claims with respect to the provision of the services, content, and carriage of the communications technologies.

Within the scope of the regulation that is imposed by existing legislation over communications technologies, it may be possible to include or impose ethical standards for policy making and decision making if the principles are rationally connected to the nature of the technologies, as we will see in the next section. The example of various applied ethical fields is instructive since, in some cases, ethical considerations have been included in domestic legislation. Thus, there are guidelines and standards in Canadian regulations and statutes that govern certain medical, biotechnological, and environmental developments or procedures. Furthermore, international organizations also create policies, guidelines, and standards by which ethics may be placed in a central position regarding the assessment of actions or proposed action. Indeed, the areas of bioethics and environmental ethics are extremely important for the creation of standards to be used in these policies.

In addition to the seemingly systematic introduction of ethical considerations in policies and review boards, ethics should be introduced in an interactive and consultative manner. The attitude of this system ethics proposal is not anti-technological. Observing the trends of industry and technology with respect to communications demonstrates that, while there is a trend of convergence that is manifested in various ways, the communications system is not being developed as systematically as it could be in order to meet its goals. The interaction of ethical assessment and system development would enable the goals of the system to be more accurately defined, particularly where the implementation is in previously unexposed cultural or societal contexts. In order to effectively provide creative interaction and consultation, it would be necessary for appropriate input to be sought from ethicists and the affected communities to help ensure that the purpose of the system is indeed consonant with the requirements of the participants. The consultative role could even extend to the system design, which could be critiqued for its underlying ideology and hierarchy, while possibilities for better profit and administrative schemes could be suggested that would more judiciously benefit all of the participants.

Finally, while the monitoring and enforcement of ethical standards would likely be difficult to implement, it is extremely important to emphasize the necessity for this consideration at present, since the system has not yet been fully developed and integrated. Above, I discussed the danger of the loss of control over democratic participation due to increasing control by trade commitments. It may thus seem illogical to look to the same kinds of international bodies to oversee the enforcement of ethical principles. Nevertheless, the legitimacy for international oversight would derive from the nature of consent of the participants, the standards for which could be determined by policy that has its foundations in the types of ethical considerations proposed herein. By setting up a system ethics with a set of standards that would help guide the global implementation of communications technologies, it would be easier to ensure that there is community consent and that there is fairness in the way that the technologies are being integrated.

CONCLUSIONS

Webcasting, some may say, simply represents the bringing together of old media and new media. Nonetheless, the struggle over Internet retransmission in Canada, the legislative solution, and CRTC's response reveal a fundamentally problematic response to a new — though foreseeable — development of communications technology. The legal, political, and social issues that may be canvassed with respect to this technology demonstrate the manner by which ethical foundations that can provide clear guidance in future treatments of communications technologies in policy and legislation, no matter which legislation is forborne, invoked, or amended. Thus, emerging issues with respect to communications and the information industry reflect new junctures from which to examine the governance of intellectual property and communications technologies, the close scrutiny of which is required since significant courses of action are presently open to policy-makers and legislators. This topic is all the more significant as it involves the convergence of two of the most important communications formats in our present society: the old dominant media, television, and the newcomer, the Internet.

The debate over Internet retransmission, broadcasting, and copyright law in Canada tells us something about the society we have been in the choices of our technology governance, and perhaps something about the society we are becoming. The issue is not simply about what constitutes piracy, but who gets to decide how and when to draw that line and, furthermore, whether this tells us something different about how we conceive of intellectual property in a time and space that is adapting to, adopting, and accommodating the Internet and innovations in media and communications technologies. These may ultimately be considered as ethical problems. To avoid problems arising from regulation, as we have seen in the example of Canadian Internet retransmission, ethical principles that are based upon the essential nature of communications technologies should provide new policy and standards that would be taken into account no matter which legislative regime is brought to bear. The Canadian government's amendments of its copyright law in response to industry pressure to exclude media innovations such as webcasting, to call the innovators "pirates," and change the law to make it so, should be avoided in future treatments of new media innovations. Instead, appropriate criteria should be determined with ethical foundations to administer decisions regarding the responsible governance of communications technologies.

The criteria that are proposed herein to allow ethical assessment to be considered for the governance of communications technologies are, broadly, legal, political, and social. The systemic integration of communications technologies requires that we transcend the sole notion of risk as the appropriate justification for ethical assessment. Thus, the legal realm for ethical assessment would involve the analysis of the nature of intellectual property regimes, as well as the role of competition and the nature of control in the governance of communications technologies. The political realm allows for assessments of international relations and order, as well as national sovereignty, which are particularly important given the international reach of many communications technologies. Finally, the social realm includes the nature of democratic participation and the legislative process in decision-making with respect to communications technologies and their integration in the various communities. Together, these considerations provide a system ethics approach that may provide a more harmonized decision-making process in view of problems that we have seen arise with the introduction of new communications technologies. Such an approach may allow for a more effective response to the kinds of regulatory issues we have seen posed by webcasting.

REFERENCES

Legislation

Bill C-11, *An Act to Amend the Copyright Act*, 1ˢᵗ Sess., 37ᵗʰ Parl., 2002 (assented to 12 December 2002, S.C. 2002, c. 26).

Broadcasting Act, S.C. 1991, c. 11.

Competition Act, R.S.C. 1985, c. C-34.

Copyright Act, R.S.C. 1985, c. C-42.

Canada-United States Free Trade Agreement Implementation Act, S.C. 1988, c.65.

Telecommunications Act, S.C. 1993, c. 38.

Government and Organizational Sources

Canadian Association of Broadcasters, Comments of the Canadian Association of Broadcasters in Response to the Consultation Paper on Digital Copyright Issues (17 September 2001), online: Strategis <http://strategis.ic.gc.ca/epic/internet/incrp-prda.nsf/vwGeneratedInterE/rp00257e.html > (date accessed: 7 May 2003).

Canadian Heritage, Copyright Policy Branch & Industry Canada, Intellectual Property Policy Directorate, "Consultation Paper on the Application of the Copyright Act's Compulsory Retransmission License to the Internet" (22 June 2001), online: Strategis <http://strategis.ic.gc.ca/epic/internet/incrp-prda.nsf/vwGeneratedInterE/rp00008e.html> (date accessed: 7 May 2003).

Copyright Board. Interim Tariffs for the Retransmission of Distant Radio and Television Signals during 2001. Interim Decision of the Board (8 December 2000).

CRTC, *Competition and Culture on Canada's Information Highway: Managing the Realities of Transition* (16 September 1995), online: CRTC <http://www.crtc.gc.ca/ENG/HIGHWAY/HWY9505.HTM> (date accessed: 7 May 2003).

CRTC, Broadcasting Public Notice CRTC 2003-02: Internet Retransmission (17 January 2003).

CRTC, Public Notice CRTC 1999-197: New Media Exemption (17 December 1999).

CRTC, Telecom Public Notice CRTC 99-14/Broadcasting Public Notice CRTC 1999-94: New Media Report (17 May 1999).

Industry Canada, Competition Bureau, *CRTC/Competition Bureau Interface* (19 November 1999), online: Strategis <http://strategis.ic.gc.ca/SSG/ct01544e.html> (date accessed: 7 May 2003).

Information Highway Advisory Council, *Connection, Community, Content: The Challenge of the Information Highway* (Ottawa: Supply and Services Canada, 1995).

Information Highway Advisory Council, *Preparing Canada for a Digital World* (Ottawa: Supply and Services Canada, 1997), online: Strategis <http://e-com.ic.gc.ca/english/strat/doc/september1997.pdf> (date accessed: 7 May 2003).

International Instruments

Agreement on Trade-Related Aspects of Intellectual Property Rights, Annex 1C to G.A.T.T. 1994: Final Act and Agreement.

Berne Convention for the Protection of Literary and Artistic Works, 9 September 1886, Can T.S. 1948 No. 22, 828 U.N.T.S. 221, rev. by *Paris Act relating to the Berne Convention*, 24 July 1971, 1161 U.N.T.S. 3.

Canada-United States Free Trade Agreement, 22 December 1987, Can. T.S. 1989 No. 3, 27 I.L.M. 281.

General Agreement on Tariffs and Trade, 30 October 1947, 55 U.N.T.S. 194, Can. T.S. 1947 No. 27.

North American Free Trade Agreement Between the Government of Canada, the Government of the United Mexican States and the Government of the United States of America, 17 December 1992, 32 I.L.M. 289.

OECD, *Canada—Annual Report on Competition Policy Developments in Canada* (1 April 1999 to 31 March 2000), online: OECD <http://www.oecd.org/daf/clp/Annual_reports/1999-00/canada.pdf> (date accessed: 7 May 2003).

Universal Copyright Convention, 6 September 1952, 216 U.N.T.S. 132, U.K.T.S. 1957 No. 66, Can. T.S. 1962 No. 13, rev. in Paris 24 July 1971, 943 U.N.T.S. 1978.

Secondary Sources

Corley, R.F.D. (1997). The Competition Act and the Information Economy. In J.B. Musgrove (ed.), *Competition law for the 21st century: Papers of the Canadian Bar Association competition law section, 1997 Annual Conference,* pp. 143-162. Aylmer, QC: Juris Publishing.

deBeer, J.F. (2000). Canadian copyright law in cyberspace: An examination of the Copyright Act in the context of the Internet. *Saskatchewan Law Review*, 63, 503.

Deetz, S. (1990). Representation of interests and the new communication technologies: Issues in democracy and policy. In M.J. Medhurst, A. Gonzalez & T.R. Peterson (eds.), *Communication & the culture of technology*, pp. 43-62. Pullman, WA: Washington State University Press.

Estabrooks, M. (1995). *Electronic technology, corporate strategy, and world transformation*. Westport, CT: Quorum Books.

Fan, B.M. (2000). When channel surfers flip to the Web: Copyright liability for Internet broadcasting. *Federal Communications Law Journal, 52,* 619-646.

Fewer, D. (1997). Constitutionalizing copyright: Freedom of expression and the limits of copyright in Canada. *University of Toronto Faculty of Law Review*, 55, 175-240.

Flate, L.A. (2000). New technology clauses aren't broad enough: Why a new standard of interpretation must be adopted for Internet distribution. *Hastings Communications and Entertainment Law Journal*, 23, 171-194.

Gates, A. (2000). Convergence and competition: Technological change, industry concentration and competition policy in the telecommunications sector. *University of Toronto Faculty of Law Review*, 58, 83-119.

Geist, M. (2000). iCraveTV and the new rules of Internet broadcasting. *University of Arkansas at Little Rock Law Review*, 23, 223-242.

Hamelink, C.J. (1986). Is there life after the information revolution? In M. Traber (ed.), *The myth of the information revolution: Social and ethical implications of communication technology,* pp. 7-20. London: SAGE Publications.

Handa, S. (1997). A review of Canada's international copyright obligations. *McGill Law Journal,* 42, 961-990.

Handa, S. (2001). Retransmission of television broadcasts on the Internet. *Southwestern Journal of Law and Trade in the Americas,* 8, 39-81.

Handa, S. (2002). *Copyright law in Canada*. Toronto, ON: Butterworths.

Handa, S., Janda, R., Johnston, D., & Morgan, C. (2000). *Communications law in Canada*. Toronto, ON: Butterworths.

Jonas, H. (1986). *Imperative of responsibility: In search of an ethics for the technological age*. Chicago, IL: University of Chicago Press.

Jones, A. (1994). Wired world: Communications technology, governance and the democratic uprising. In E.A. Comor (ed.), *The global political economy of communication: Hegemony, telecommunication and the information economy,* pp. 145-164. New York: St. Martin's Press.

Maner, W. (2001). Unique problems in information technology. In D.M. Hester & P.J. Ford (eds.), *Computers and ethics in the cyberage,* pp. 39-50. Upper Saddle River, NJ: Prentice Hall.

McLuhan, M. & Powers, B.R. (1989). *The global village: Transformations in world life and media in the 21st century.* New York: Oxford University Press.

Poster, M. (1989). *Critical theory and poststructuralism: In search of a context.* Ithaca, NY: Cornell University Press.

Siegel, L. & Markoff, J. (1991). The high cost of high tech: The dark side of the chip. In J. Zerzan & A. Carnes (eds.), *Questioning technology: Tool, toy or tyrant*, pp. 54-74. Philadelphia, PA: New Society Publishers.

Stanbury, W.T. (1996). Competition policy and the regulation of telecommunications in Canada. In W.T. Stanbury (ed.), *Perspectives on the new economics and regulation of telecommunications,* pp. 103-116. Montreal: Institute for Research in Public Policy.

Vig, N.J. (1988). Technology, philosophy, and the state: An overview. In M.E. Kraft & N.J. Vig (eds.), *Technology and politics,* pp. 8-18. Durham, NC: Duke University Press.

Winner, L. (1995). Citizen virtues in a technological order. In A. Feenberg & A. Hannay (eds.), *Technology and the politics of knowledge,* pp. 65-84. Bloomington, IN: Indiana University Press.

Online Sources

Dillon, M. (2001). Convergence: Controversy and caution. (20 August 2001), online: Playback <http://www.playbackmag.com/articles/magazine/20010820/converge.html?print=yes> (date accessed: 7 May 2003).

Geist, M. (2001). Copyright debate turns one-sided. online: globetechnology.com <http://www.news/globetechnology.com> (last modified: 6 December 2001).

Hyatt, L. (2001). McCabe's last curtain call. (October 2001), online: Broadcaster Magazine.com <http://www.broadcastermagazine.com> (date accessed: 7 May 2003).

JumpTV.com Canada Inc. (2001). Response to the consultation paper on the application of the Copyright Act's compulsory retransmission licence to the Internet issued on June 22, 2001 by the Departments of Canadian Heritage and Industry (13 September 2001), online: Strategis <http://strategis.ic.gc.ca/epic/internet/incrp-prda.nsf/vwGeneratedInterE/rp00270e.html> (date accessed: 7 May 2003).

Scoffield, H. (2001). Broadcasters promised relief. *Globe and Mail* (30 October 2001), online: Friends of Canadian Broadcasting <http://www.friendscb.org/articles/GlobeandMail/globe011030.htm> (date accessed: 7 May 2003).

Shelton, J.R. (1998). Competition policy: What chance for international rules? (Wilton Park Conference 545, 25 November 1998), online: OECD <http://www.oecd.org/daf/clp/Speeches/JS-WILTO.htm> (date accessed: 7 May 2003).

About the Authors

Richard A. Spinello is an associate research professor in the Carroll School of Management at Boston College (USA), where he teaches courses on information technology ethics, social issues in management, and corporate strategy. Prior to joining the faculty of Boston College, he worked as a programmer and marketing manager in the software industry. He has written and edited five books on information technology ethics, including *CyberEthics: Morality and Law in Cyberspace* (now in its second edition), and *Regulating Cyberspace: The Policies and Technologies of Control.* Dr. Spinello has also written numerous articles and scholarly papers on ethics and management that have appeared in journals such as *Business Ethics Quarterly* and *Ethics and Information Technology.*

Herman T. Tavani is professor and chair of the Philosophy Department and director of the Liberal Studies Program at Rivier College, Nashua, New Hampshire (USA). He is co-executive director of the International Society for Ethics and Information Technology (INSEIT) and secretary/treasurer of the ACM Special Interest Group on Computers and Society (SIGCAS). The author of numerous publications in computer ethics, his recent books include *Ethics and Technology: Ethical Issues in an Age of Information and Communication Technology* and *Readings in CyberEthics* (second edition, co-edited with Richard Spinello). Tavani is editor of the *INSEIT Newsletter*, bibliography editor of *Computers and Society Magazine*, and book review editor of the journal, *Ethics and Information Technology.*

*   *   *

Ann Bartow has been an assistant professor of Law at the University of South Carolina School of Law (USA) since August 2000. She currently teaches courses in intellectual property law, cyberspace law, and constitutional law. Her research interests include copyright law, trademark law, patent law, privacy law, and the First Amendment.

Elizabeth Buchanan is assistant professor and co-director of the Center for Information Policy Research at the School of Information Studies, University of Wisconsin-Milwaukee (USA). Her research areas include information ethics, research ethics, and distance education. She lives in Cedarburg, Wisconsin, with her husband, son, and four cats.

Dan Burk holds the Oppenheimer, Wolff & Donnelly Professorship in Law at the University of Minnesota (USA), where he teaches courses in patent, copyright, and biotechnology law. An internationally prominent authority on issues of high technology, he has taught intellectual property and cyberlaw courses at institutions across North America and the European Union. He is the author of numerous papers on the legal and societal impact of new technologies, and has served as a policy advisor to a variety of private, governmental, and intergovernmental organizations. Professor Burk holds a BS in Microbiology from Brigham Young University (1985), an MS in Molecular Biology and Biochemistry (1987) from Northwestern University, a JD from Arizona State University (1990), and a JSM from Stanford University (1994).

James Campbell works as a communication planning and production specialist with both non-profit and for-profit enterprises. He has produced radio and video programming for both broadcast and non-broadcast audiences; and has won numerous national and international industry awards for writing, editing, and producing. He has taught courses in linguistics, contemporary fiction, writing, business design and development, communication planning, radio, and video production on an adjunct basis at a number of academic institutions. He has also designed communication plans, training packages, and corporate meeting content for many Fortune 500 companies including AT&T, American Express, Dun & Bradstreet, and IBM.

Kai Kimppa works as an assistant professor of Information Systems at University of Turku (Finland). He has graduated with a Master of Social Sciences, Philosophy, from the University of Turku. He currently teaches

Information Technology ethics. His research interests lie in major ethical theories and their derivations in regard to the justification (and lack of) IPR's in software and other digitally distributable media. He also has experience from the industry as he has worked for Nokia Mobile Phones as a design engineer.

Melanie J. Mortensen is an associate with the Montreal law firm Greenspoon Perreault (Canada), completed degrees in both common and civil law from McGill University's National Program in Law (2002), and, at the time of publication of this book, is studying toward her Master of Laws at McGill University. The present focus of her research is on policy, technology, and Internet law, generally, and legal issues in connection with digital games, specifically. Mortensen wishes to express her gratitude and appreciation to Professors Sunny Handa, Richard Gold, and Margaret Somerville of McGill University for their inspiration, supervision, and guidance, and also to her colleagues at Greenspoon Perreault for their encouragement and support.

Thomas M. Powers received his PhD in Philosophy from the University of Texas at Austin (1994) and has taught philosophy at the College of William & Mary, and philosophy and computer engineering at Santa Clara University. His primary research interests are in Kant's ethical theory, computer ethics, and the philosophy of technology. Currently he is National Science Foundation Post-doctoral Research Fellow in the School of Engineering and Applied Science at the University of Virginia, USA.

Michael J. Scanlan is an associate professor at Oregon State University (USA). He received his PhD in Philosophy from SUNY-Buffalo (1981). His research and publication is mainly in the history and philosophy of logic. As a result of teaching computer ethics, he also has an interest in aspects of the ethics of information technology. His chapter in this book had its genesis in brief skeptical remarks in a previous paper about the possibility of a nonconsequentialist theory of information ownership ("Informational privacy and moral values", *Ethics and Information Technology* 3 (2001) 3-12).

Index

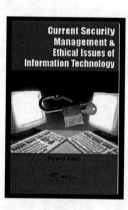